T0359999

Professor John Croucher is one of Australia's most prominent academics and has been recognised with multiple awards for outstanding teaching. His extensive consulting background to both business and government led to receiving his university's inaugural Community Outreach Award.

John is a scholarly researcher with an international reputation and over 30 books, 120 scholarly papers and more than 1000 other articles published in newspapers and magazines. He is also well known for his weekly newspaper column *Number Crunch* that was read by up to two million people across Australia.

In 2005 John completed a second PhD in Modern History to complement his previous doctorate in Mathematics and Statistics. After an honorary PhD in 2011, he gained his fourth PhD in 2015, also in Modern History, from the University of Technology, Sydney.

John was the winner of the *Prime Minister's Award for the University Teacher of the Year 2013–14* as the best teacher in any discipline in Australia. In 2015 he was made a Member of the Order of Australia (AM) for his outstanding services to mathematics, statistics and education.

Woodslane Press Pty Ltd
10 Apollo Street
Warriewood, NSW 2102
Email: info@woodslane.com.au
Tel: 02 8445 2300 Website: www.woodslane.com.au

First published in Australia in 2020 by Woodslane Press
© 2020 Woodslane Press, text © 2020 John Croucher

A catalogue record for this
book is available from the
National Library of Australia

Printed in Australia by McPhersons Printing Group
Book design by: Jenny Cowan

Front Cover image: Gold Washing Fitz Roy Bar Ophir Diggings 1851 –
by George French Angus, courtesy of the State Library of New South Wales
Back Cover image: Bank of New South Wales Maitland Branch £5, courtesy of
Wikimedia Commons

A CONCISE HISTORY OF NEW SOUTH WALES

John S. Croucher AM

BA (Hons) (Macq) MSc PhD (Minn) PhD (Macq)
PhD (Hon) (DWU) PhD (UTS) FRSA FAustMS

Other books by John Croucher

Exam Scams
Great Frauds and Everyday Scams
Number Crunch
The Secret Language
Eighteen Days on the Toilet (Woodslane Press)
657 Gorillas on the Run (Woodslane Press)
Love by Numbers (Woodslane Press)
The Kid from Norfolk Island (Woodslane Press)
Mistress of Science: the story of the remarkable Janet Taylor
Women of Science: 100 inspirational lives

*Dedicated to the magnificent people
of New South Wales who helped shape
our wonderful state's history*

*The author and publishers would like to acknowledge
the traditional custodians of all lands within the State
boundaries of New South Wales and pay their respects
to their elders past, present and emerging.*

Contents

Forword		viii
Preface		xii
1.	*Indigenous History*	1
2.	*The Arrival of British Convicts*	25
3.	*Further Non-indigenous Colonisation and Settlement*	35
4.	*Cities, Towns and Localities*	51
5.	*Agricultural and Pastoral Industry*	105
6.	*Politics*	121
7.	*Education*	133
8.	*Infrastructure and Transport*	151
9.	*Manufacturing and Industrial Development*	175
10.	*Health*	183
11.	*Entertainment*	199
12.	*Science*	225
13.	*Crime, Punishment and Law Enforcement*	233
14.	*Finance*	255
15.	*Community Organisations*	269
16.	*Organised Religion*	285
17.	*Sport*	297
18.	*Art, Literature, Music and Architecture*	321
Bibliography		337
Chapter Reference Notes		347
Index		371

Foreword

When presented with the request to write the Foreword to Professor John Croucher's *A Concise History of New South Wales*, my mind immediately went to that other 'concise' work—the *Concise Oxford English Dictionary*—a volume of nearly 2,000 pages. We perhaps should be thankful that the editors of the English-speaking world's most prestigious dictionary considered that a concise version was a good idea, given that the full dictionary is over 21,000 pages. As defined in the shorter tome, 'concise' means 'Expressed in few words; brief and comprehensive in statement; not diffuse'. If the number of pages is anything to go by, it would appear that conciseness is a relative term and perhaps better captured in the expression 'a lack of extra or unnecessary information', so defined in the *Oxford Learner's Dictionary*. And so it is with Professor Croucher's *Concise History of New South Wales*, although I would add 'highly readable and fast moving' to the description of this work.

Descended from two British convicts on the paternal line of his family, the author has long had an interest in the early days of the colony and its development thereafter. He is a person of eclectic and wide-ranging interests and accomplishments—across mathematics, statistics, sport, history and education. He holds a PhD in three different disciplines and an honorary doctorate conferred by the Divine Word University in Papua New Guinea for 'services to mankind'. Already a noted author of over 30 books, Professor Croucher has neatly captured the detail of the history of Australia's oldest and most populous state without losing the substance of the narrative.

Professor Croucher commences his work with the history of Australia's Indigenous people, 'the oldest surviving geographically stable human culture on earth', a source of Indigenous pride and increasing national appreciation and wonderment. He follows with an examination of Australia's convict and early colonial history, including the roles played in the colony by Bennelong and Barangaroo, husband and wife, who acted as intermediaries between the local community and the new arrivals. Professor Croucher continues with a 'page turner's art', as he allows the story of the growth and development of a diverse community to unfold. There is no apology or embarrassment in Professor Croucher's story telling. He states facts without embellishment, unless it is to make a point, as he does when referring to the 'bitter irony' that when Indigenous pastoral workers were awarded equal pay, 'many were sacked and forced off the land that had been their home'.

Perhaps befitting a colony whose foundation was based on the transportation of convicts, there is a chapter dedicated to 'Crime, Punishment and Law Enforcement', including the stories of some of New South Wales' more colourful identities. Tilly Devine, who ran brothels in the 1930s, taking advantage of the law that banned men, not women, from living off the 'immoral earnings' of prostitution, and Darcy Dugan, whose serious criminal history is often overshadowed by his reputation in popular lore as a skilled prison escape artist, both feature.

Professor Croucher recounts the waves of migration that followed the penal settlement and describes the physical aspects of the cities and towns, the development of transport, manufacturing and industry in response to the growing population. He covers the social and intellectual development of the colony and State in areas of entertainment, sport, the arts, as well as education, science and religion. There are cameos of some of the many women and men who contributed to the early life of New South Wales. The Macarthurs feature prominently, Elizabeth Macarthur's contribution to the wool industry being of particular note. One finds the story of Marie Louise Mack, a poet in the *Bulletin*, who became a frontline journalist in the First World War. The men and women of politics also feature, telling the tale of the slow entry of women into formal political life, stalled for over two decades after women's enfranchisement, due principally to the absence of enabling legislation. Thus, it was not until 1925 that Millicent Preston Stanley was elected to the

NSW Legislative Assembly, the first woman to be elected to our State's parliament.

Early philanthropists are acknowledged. These include Dr William Bland (1789-1868), also recognised for having founded the Australian Medical Association; Lady Mary Windeyer (1836–1912), an active promoter of economic independence for women; and Dr Lucy Edith Gullett (1876–1949), who, with Dr Harriet Biffen, established the Rachel Foster Hospital for Women and Children. The Country Women's Association (NSW), The Benevolent Society and The Smith Family, each moving towards their centenary celebrations, are included in the many community organisations which have provided bedrock support to the different sectors of the community they were founded to serve. And there is much, much more.

Professor Croucher's *Concise History of New South Wales* provides a wonderful introduction for anyone who is interested in the rich tapestry of our State. If it answers some of your questions and sparks your curiosity to learn more, then Professor Croucher has achieved his aim—and it is far less daunting and much more accessible reading than the *Concise Oxford English Dictionary.*

The author is to be congratulated.

Her Excellency the Honourable Margaret Beazley AC QC
Governor of New South Wales
July 2020

Preface

My interest in Australian history really began when some years ago my father traced his ancestors as a retirement hobby. To his, and my, astonishment, he found that we were descended from not one but two convicts who were transported from England to NSW.

The first of these was William Williams (a common enough name) who was conveyed on the 'fever ship', the *Hillsborough*, for the crime of assault and robbery. Of the 299 convicts who started the 212-day voyage from Portsmouth in December 1798, 95 died from yellow fever and dysentery before reaching their Sydney destination. Governor John Hunter wrote to the Secretary of the Colonies:

> *The Hillsborough has just arrived with a cargo of the most miserable and wretched convicts I ever beheld. Were you, my dear Sir, in the situation in which I stand, I am convinced all the feelings of humanity, every sensation which can occasion a pang for the distresses of a fellow creature, would be seen to operate in you with full force.*

William was lucky in several respects. He not only survived the journey, but had been initially sentenced to death. Although he could not read or write, after serving his sentence he became a wealthy landowner.

William's daughter Ellen married another convict, Samuel Callaway, who was serving seven years for stealing copper from a roof. Arriving on the *Hindostan* in 1821, he was only 19 and had been the assistant harbour master in Bristol, as well as being unusual in that he could both read and write. As a result, Samuel was employed by the police department and after release he and Ellen settled down in Windsor, west of Sydney, where he built several houses.

This book was inspired by my desire to provide a concise historical account of the early days of the colony and how it has progressed. Naturally there is some overlap between the chapters, but the end result is an account of how NSW has changed from those early days to where it stands now.

Of course, no such work would be complete without acknowledging and exploring the exceptional role played by the Indigenous population. There are copious references made to the valuable contributions they made, and continue to make, in shaping not just NSW but our great nation as Australia's First Peoples.

The research involved spanned several years and numerous sources were called upon to create the final product. In some cases, there were discrepancies in the historical aspects of certain places, people and events, but all efforts were made to relate the one that seemed correct. There are around 500 references and notes provided at the end of the volume, and special thanks must go to the outstanding Macquarie University researcher Stephanie Hon who worked untiringly to piece together an unformatted volume into a completed book, a difficult task she performed with enormous diligence.

Much appreciation also goes to the historian Dr Annette Salt, who undertook much of the tremendous amount of research required to obtain relevant information, and was also able to provide a valuable list of references. This was a wide-ranging and daunting challenge that she approached with relish. Her own knowledge of Australian history was a tremendous help in obtaining vital information.

I am profoundly grateful to Her Excellency the Honourable Margaret Beazley AC QC for writing the Foreword to this book. Her Excellency is a true woman of New South Wales—born, educated and having worked her whole professional life in the state and now holding the Vice-Regal office as its 39th Governor.

Special thanks also goes to Andrew Swaffer at the publishers *Woodslane Press* for believing in this volume.

John S. Croucher
Sydney, June 2020

1. *Indigenous History*

INTRODUCTION

Pre-contact Indigenous history is very much open to investigation and enquiry. Bridges have to be constructed between evidence, such as archaeological finds, including middens, scarred trees, quarries, camp sites, ceremonial sites and rock art, and the observations of non-Indigenous people and Indigenous stories handed down for generations. In discussing the latter, respect must be shown for the intellectual property rights of Indigenous stories, especially when the writer of this account is not Indigenous.

Writing an Indigenous history of New South Wales is also made difficult as that state is a political consequence of the British occupation of Australia. It obviously had no relevance to the two distinct Indigenous groups: mainland Aboriginal Peoples and Torres Strait Islander Peoples. Within these two groups there is a wide variety with different clans and nations having diverse languages and cultural practices. The boundaries of the areas that different clans called 'country' bear no relationship to the delineated area of New South Wales, itself changing over the period of European occupation as it initially included Queensland, Victoria and Tasmania. To identify Indigenous people specifically of New South Wales therefore has its problems. However, in New South Wales, while people had clan names, they also referred to themselves generally as *Koori* or *Murri*.

The Indigenous peoples of NSW (and of Australia generally) are representatives of perhaps the oldest surviving geographically stable human culture on earth. It is estimated that Indigenous occupation of Australia has lasted approximately 65,000 years and that there were between 250 and 500 'nations' or language groups. In New South Wales, Mungo National Park has yielded evidence from two skeletons, usually referred to as 'Mungo Lady' and 'Mungo Man', probably buried ritualistically. In 2003, these were estimated to be about 40,000 years old, with other estimates being up to 43,000 years.

Although the following observations are divided into sections for the sake of discussion, this in many ways distorts the Aboriginal world view, which is holistic. The spiritual affects the social; the social affects the environmental; and the environmental is inextricably linked to the spiritual as when sacred sites overlap ecological sanctuaries. Note that the terms 'Aboriginal' and 'Indigenous' have been used interchangeably in this book.

COUNTRY AND AGRICULTURE

Aboriginal peoples' attitude towards land is quite different from that of Europeans, as they do not 'own' land but are tribal-based custodians of it. As an Australian based ethnographer of Aboriginal peoples, Deborah Bird Rose, explains, 'Country, to use the philosopher's term, is a nourishing terrain. Country is a place that gives and receives life. Not just imagined or represented, it is lived in and lived with.'

While not being conservationists in the modern sense, the control and care of land was an active pursuit intended to ensure that resources were not depleted. To this end, Aboriginal people did not try to tame the country, but worked with it. They knew the local conditions: which plants could be successfully encouraged, and which would attract what animals. They understood the migratory patterns of birds and many other animals They dammed and directed rivers, carving out cut channels through waterways and swamps. At Brewarrina on the Darling River in north-west NSW, for example, extensive and complex fish pens were created to use the currents of the Barwon River and trap fish and eels.

This care of the land was observed by knowledgeable and eminent Europeans. Both James Cook and Joseph Banks were astonished to find what looked like plantations and lawns, while Elizabeth Macarthur (1766–1850), the wife of John Macarthur (1767–1834), was pleasantly surprised to see what looked like an English park. The naval surgeon and author, Peter Cunningham, depicted the areas around Parramatta and Liverpool as being so lightly timbered that one could drive a gig through them unimpeded. Many early commentators were astonished at the 'parks' that they found timbered, covered with grass and no undergrowth. Despite this, the explorer and politician William Charles Wentworth (1790–1872) in his 1820 book, *A Statistical, Historical, and Political Description of the Colony of New South Wales*, declared 'they are entirely unacquainted with the arts of agriculture': a view that became endemic in colonial society despite strong evidence to the contrary.

What they did not realise, or did not wish to acknowledge, was that this was the result of Aboriginal land management. And one of its chief tools and allies was fire, mostly used to burn bush and undergrowth to encourage the growth of grasses for cropping, to attract animals for food and to prevent more volatile and unpredictable natural fires. This involved regular burning with low intensity fire which did not deplete the soil of nutrients but was sufficient to clear lands, encourage grass and allow for seeds which required heat to germinate. Areas of good soil were burned while forested areas were left standing, thus creating a rotating mosaic pattern of land clearing. Senior people, usually men, determined the burning path.

Aboriginal people were also agriculturalists, though perhaps not in the European sense. Land was not fenced nor soil ploughed. Rather than ploughing, they tilled across slopes, so avoiding the possibility of erosion. As people such as the explorers Thomas Mitchell and Charles Sturt observed, Aboriginal people collected grasses and piled them into haystacks awaiting threshing and grinding of the seed which was then baked. Such seeds were also traded with other groups, thus spreading the propagation of crops.

This selective harvesting and the use of fire assisted biodiversity. When Europeans commented on the abundance and regularity of the Aboriginal's food supply, they were really commenting on the Aboriginal peoples' skilful husbanding of resources. This care of land had a spiritual aspect, as land is full of rocks and trees which were regarded as containing spirits. As such, land was not to be assessed merely by economic potential. Within their clan lands, people were responsible for their own country, caring for it, singing of it and telling stories about it. They were not entitled to any role in other people's country unless so authorised.

All of this care and responsibility required detailed knowledge of seasons, movements of animals, availability of water, nature of soils, winds, sky, sea, vegetation and landforms. This represented a scientific knowledge of land management and, as Aboriginal peoples had occupied these lands for so long, this should not be surprising. All the elements related to country were interdependent and all were alive with their own laws and culture. According to Fred Biggs, a *Ngeamba* man from the Menindee in New

South Wales, 'Sky country in particular was linked to the earth through seasons and weather'.

CULTURE AND SOCIAL ORGANISATION

Kinship was a very broad concept, but basically indicated how people were related to one another. Relationships went beyond the family in a European sense, or immediate kin, to the broad community in which Aboriginal people belonged, to a clan of variable size, even up to around 50 members. Each clan had a totem, usually an animal. But individuals could also have totems based on other factors such as their place of birth.

Totems were seen as linking people to the universe and all that was in it, with people of a particular totem being responsible for the care of it and its habitat. The concept of land was interwoven with culture and knowing one's totem was part of ecological management: one knew the creature, but also the plants and habitat that nurtured it. The *Yuin* people of the south coast of NSW, for example, considered that the killer whales herded injured whales to the shore as food for the local people. They believed that they would be reincarnated as killer whales and would in no way harm these creatures. It was this combination of the practical and the spiritual that was common in Aboriginal culture.

Kinship and totemic affiliations also determined other social rituals, such as marriage. Marital relationships were arranged to avoid people marrying someone of their own broad family. These betrothals would often be organised at clan ceremonies, quite often with the woman's mother being the chief organiser. The people of south-east NSW, for example, banned a man from having any dealings with his mother-in-law, except through a third party.

The husbanding of land was inextricably bound to spiritual beliefs, with the 'Dreaming' or 'Dreamtime' being a concept not unlike all creation stories. Supernatural creation spirits shaped all aspects of life and the paths on which they travelled across the land, giving it its form as 'songlines' or 'storylines'. Songlines were very practical as they contained information concerning the land through which one travelled; for example, where there were waterholes. Laws were handed down to the ancestors, who then passed them on. Dreaming explained creation and determined correct behaviour, much as all religions do. These Dreaming stories carried morals, warnings, laws and culture. They were enshrined in an oral tradition of storytelling, with only some people having the right to tell specific stories. All species were regarded as having their origins in the Dreaming and different creatures changed from animal to human and back again.

In New South Wales and the south-east of Australia generally, a creator being, *Nguril*, was responsible for initiating the form of the land. A song from the Lachlan River area celebrates this:

Look here! Nguril did this!
That is what Nguril did.
Look here! Nguril did this!
Plain after plain, with flowing creeks,
To the River's water.

Some sacred Dreaming stories were for men and some for women and these distinctions created degrees of exclusion and respect. Men, for example, might not be able to visit certain places or even look at the smoke from the fires of women in those areas. Gulaga in the Wallaga Lakes area of the south coast of NSW is a sacred female mountain for the *Yuin* people. But while there are places on this mountain that only women can attend, there are also places for everyone.

Burial practices varied, but simple burial or burial and cremation rituals were common, albeit with variations. The *Darkinjung* people, north of the Hawkesbury, for example, placed the knees near the head of the deceased. For the people around Port Jackson, personal items were buried with the body. While the *Yuin* people of the south coast buried some items with the body, they gave weapons to friends.

Sacred places were frequently indicated by the marking or painting of the trunks of trees. This was so in the construction of ceremonial grounds and cemeteries. Graveyards were established in places of beauty and trees, when saplings, were interlaced to create arbours.

These were by no means the only evidence of Aboriginal construction practices obvious to the early European explorers. While they could adapt their living conditions to their surroundings, such as living in rock shelters when fishing in coastal areas, they also resided for long periods in houses and villages. In one instance, the explorer Charles Sturt saw 70 domed huts on the Darling River, which he estimated could each hold fifteen people. On the Gwydir River in the 1830s, another explorer, Thomas Mitchell, reported a similar large village with substantial permanent huts. These were not isolated observations.

In addition to the construction of villages, grain stores, essential to balance times of plenty with leaner times, were erected by various means. Clay and straw compartments were built to store foods such as grains, fruit and nuts. This was also necessary preceding inter-clan ceremonial meetings to feed the great numbers attending.

Early European observers commented generally on the lack of Aboriginal clothing. However, they also noted that Aboriginal people did use cloaks made from bark and animal skins for protection from the elements. The cloaks were softened by scraping with shells and sewn together with sinew from kangaroo tails.

Aboriginal culture was based on oral, not written tradition. Ceremonies, dances, songs, stories and artworks were part of this and were a means of passing on and confirming valuable knowledge about matters as varied as land control and behaviour of children. Such knowledge might depend on gender or age and was not open to everyone.

Art was an important aspect of Indigenous life, as evidenced by the abundance of rock art and engraving remaining. It was not art as Europeans necessarily understood it, as its intention was not aesthetics or valued as 'property'. Consequently, it was often overlooked by European observers and commentators. Engravings often had religious importance and were related to initiation processes or had totemic significance. They could indicate lore, obligations and the rules of the local culture. Additionally, they were often maps of the landscape. They could combine all these functions, being practical and spiritual, as the paths to be discovered in these 'maps' were those believed to be followed by creator spirits during the Dreaming.

While Aboriginal people resided in their own parts of the country, they would often travel great distances for trade, ceremony and social exchange. These meetings between different tribes were amicable and mutually beneficial, as well as being important for cultural exchange and reinforcing kinship.

Trade also provided what author Bruce Pascoe has called 'a civilising glue'. It allowed for the sharing of resources, although it was much more than this. Different clans would invite other clans' members to enjoy, for example, the Bunya nuts in south-east Queensland or the

Bogong moths of the alps in NSW. In this way, cultural exchange, stories and gossip also occurred and technical innovation could be shared.

Where there was conflict and punishment, it was determined by the execution of Aboriginal law. This law was implemented by Elders who had undergone levels of initiation to prepare them for their role of interpreting the law. Respect from all other people came through the status achieved by the process of advanced initiation. The security of resources depended on this esteem, which created peace and stability. Punishment often meant facing a barrage of spears, while armed with only a shield.

TECHNOLOGY

Aboriginal technology was not unchanging. Just because their culture was so enduring does not mean that it was static. Aboriginal people adapted, for example, to using fish bones for needles and shells for fishhooks. Climate and landscape fluctuated; and the changing environment saw the development of new technologies. About 20,000 years ago, during the last Ice Age, Aboriginal people moved and adapted in order to survive. About 10,000 years ago, spears started to have barbs and the boomerang was developed. The woods used for boomerangs varied with the environment. On the NSW coast, for example, they were made from mangrove trees and used for duck hunting. About 5,000 years ago, tools started to have finer points and blades.

Most tools were lightweight and therefore portable. However, many implements were not carried, but left at different sites, making mobility easier by reducing the need to carry them. The ability to move readily to new areas in turn ensured a continuous food supply.

An Aboriginal tool kit included stone tools, for cutting and drilling, and grindstones to exploit seeds. Resins from trees were used as glue, while fibres were woven into a type of string to make bags and mats, also made from bark and leaves.

For the essential activity of fishing, both saltwater and freshwater, Aboriginal people used canoes, nets and spears. Fishing spears were multi-pronged and barbed, sometimes with stingray spines. Nets and traps were used to catch small birds and small animals. Spears, boomerangs and clubs were used to bring down kangaroos and emus. Wooden spears using stone or shell points were often assisted by spear-throwers, which in some areas were called 'woomeras'. Bush foods, such as honey, yams, edible tubers and nectar, were gathered or dug from the ground using digging sticks. To trap animals, such as ducks, emus and kangaroos, nets as long as 17 metres were used in conjunction with brush walls.

The Brewarrina fish traps provide a good example of Aboriginal knowledge and technology to trap fish and eels. Built on the Barwon River at Brewarrina in NSW, they utilised an existing long rock bar that traverses the riverbed.

At this point the river is fast-flowing and has a series of cataracts. Aboriginal people placed rocks closely together, sometimes following the rock bar, sometimes across it, capping it all with larger stones. The traps were teardrop shaped curves, to provide greater stability against the impact of the current. They are also known as *Baiame's Ngunnhu*. For the people of south-east Australia, *Baiame* was the creator spirit who came from the sky and shaped all living things, the landforms and the law. The *Yuin* people of the NSW south coast also built fish traps comprising huge boulders, which they manoeuvred into place using the currents of the river.

The stone tool collection in the Australian Museum offers further evidence, including large heavy pendulum shaped artefacts with marks consistent with a handle. These implements could have been used like picks, suggestive of use in a form of agriculture or cultivation.

SCIENCE

There are many indicators of the scientific knowledge of the Indigenous peoples of NSW. Knowing how to live with the land meant knowledge of how to use the products present on it. Potentially poisonous plants were prepared in different ways to make them edible or usable. Cycads, for example, were leached and baked to remove toxins, and Nardoo had to be sluiced, pounded, winnowed and baked to dispel thiaminase, an enzyme which prevents the absorption of Vitamin B. Understanding the medicinal properties of plants was important knowledge gained by the scientific methods of observation, prediction, experiment and evidence gathering. This knowledge was captured as culture.

Stone arrangements were used for a range of purposes, both spiritual and practical. The Brewarrina fish traps attest to the latter. The spiritual is seen in the ceremonial 'bora rings', which were constructed for initiation. They were often composed of two circles, the outer a public space and the inner the place of ritual. Some structures are, however, more complex. The so-called 'Aboriginal Stonehenge', constructed by the *Wathaurong* people, has three outlying stones which, it has been suggested, indicate the location on the horizon of the setting sun during equinoxes and solstices. Research by a group from CSIRO has tested this theory and found it very likely to be so. Further investigation by archaeologists and astronomers on NSW stone circles confirm that knowledge existed of the cardinal points—east-west and north-south—with some indication that even magnetic north may have been identified.

Cultural astronomy was important to Indigenous people for daily life and for ceremonies. As the Commonwealth Scientific and Industrial Research Organisation (CSIRO) astrophysicist Ray Norris pointed out, if you live in the outback of Australia and each night you see 'the magnificent Milky Way' in the sky:

then of course the night sky becomes important to you. It becomes an integral part of your understanding of the world.

The sky was part of the understanding of the land—and of spirituality. Stories were told of the various constellations and their origins and purposes. The Pleiades, to the *Kamilaroi* people of NSW, for example, were young women who were placed in the sky to avoid the unwanted attention of a number of young men. The story of the Emu in the Sky, seen as a dark patch in the Milky Way, belongs to many Indigenous people. The *Guring-gai* people of Sydney particularly observe it in April and May, but note its changing position throughout the year. Near the Elvina Track in Ku-ring-gai Chase, north of Sydney, the Emu is engraved into a rock and shows the same posture and bearing as the constellation. When the Emu in the Sky and the engraved emu are aligned, this is also the time when the emu lays its eggs. Culturally, therefore, the skies were used as calendars and as an indication for harvesting.

The constellations were also used as what archaeologist and anthropologist Bob Fuller calls 'star maps'. Unlike some other Indigenous Australians, the tribes of NSW did not usually travel at night and so did not navigate directly by the stars. They did, however, use their observational knowledge of the skies as analogies for routes by which they would travel on land. When people had to travel in and outside of their country, these star maps could be used to describe their intended journey.

Most discussion of the significance of natural phenomena involved stories, indicating close observation of land, sea and sky. The *Euahlayi* people of northern NSW observed eclipses and explained them as the Sun-woman chasing the Moon-man until she caught him. Their neighbours, the *Kamilaroi* people, watched for the waning of Orion to commence their initiation ceremonies. Aboriginal people had observed the Magellanic Clouds and developed a range of stories concerning their spiritual significance. For the *Kamilaroi* people, for example, it was a place where people went when they died. For the *Euahlayi* people, when two brolgas—a mother and daughter—died, they became the dust of the Magellanic clouds.

Such knowledge was passed on to children in stages. Aboriginal society, culture and world view were complex. Their practices showed an ability to adjust and learn throughout their history.

Despite the many observations of the early European explorers, Aboriginal peoples' systems of agriculture and law were, to a very large extent, not 'recognised', or were simply ignored by the European eyes that encountered them. This was in fact almost inevitable as British political culture had largely reached a point where the empire required of itself some legal justification for the occupation of new territory. An official perception of the lack of evidence of complex Indigenous culture and that culture's claim on the land was necessary for, and directly enabled the legal categorisation of Australia as 'terra nullius', with all its consequences in 18th century (and later) international law.

POST–COLONISATION

To a large extent, European eyes did not see, or 'recognise' the significance of what they saw: colonial preconceptions simply precluded the possibility of a complex native culture. For example, Lieutenant General Watkin Tench, a British marine officer on the First Fleet, while generally a sympathetic and compassionate observer, called Aboriginal rock engravings 'very poorly cut'. He described the people as dirty and commented on their 'natural hideousness', their 'rude' huts, their 'unskilfully executed' nets, hatchets and fishhooks. Artists depicted Aboriginal people as shadowy primitives compared to the burgeoning townscapes of the colony. They saw little which they could recognise of themselves in Aboriginal people—physically, politically, spiritually, militarily and culturally—and many colonists were unsympathetic or uninterested. Aboriginal physical bearing, society, lifestyle, and practices were pitied, despised or feared.

Yet, without their guidance, the much lauded 'explorers' would have fared even worse than they did. It was a couple of Aboriginal men who showed Gregory Blaxland how to cross that great barrier to settlement in NSW, the 'Blue Mountains' as the Europeans called them, by following the major ridges. Major Thomas Mitchell acknowledged that his task of surveying the area along the Murrumbidgee and Murray Rivers in 1835 would have been impossible without the assistance of his Aboriginal guides.

There are a number of significant stages in the relationship between Indigenous people and colonisers. Many early observers believed that they were witnessing the decline of Aboriginal people and culture, paying little attention to what they deemed to be a waning race, especially when the 1789 smallpox epidemic decimated great numbers of Aboriginal people in the Sydney area. Governor Lachlan Macquarie may have had some commitment to the continuing existence of native Australians when he established the Parramatta Native Institution at Parramatta in 1814. It aimed to educate, train and Christianise Aboriginal children in an attempt to assimilate them into colonial society. However, as it began with only twelve Aboriginals, it may have been more hopeful than optimistic.

Although many colonists preferred to ignore or to denigrate Indigenous Australians, various early encounters were amicable and mutually advantageous. Aboriginals, as long as transportation continued, were no competition for free convict labour. However, a number were employed for small tasks in towns where they would sell fish and other wares to colonists.

As mentioned, the new colony of NSW was quickly regarded legally as 'terra nullius', which meant that no native Aboriginal or group of Aboriginals 'owned' the land in a way recognised by the British. Settlement was encouraged by free grants of land to colonisers, both free and emancipated. There was also little to no understanding of Aboriginal husbanding of the land. As a result, Indigenous control of land was diminished by European land clearing and grazing.

Some British settlers recognised the Aboriginals as occupiers, although not owners, of their land, allowing them to remain on their runs and utilising their skills and knowledge. One such, William Archer (1818–1896), a squatter who occupied four stations, considered it unjust to drive Aboriginals from their territory, declaring in 1858 that 'They must exist somewhere; they cannot be driven from the face of the earth altogether.' Hence some Aboriginal people managed an accommodation with pastoralists: labour in return for land on which to dwell.

Aboriginal people were not passive victims of the incursion on their lands. As European settlement extended, contact and conflict increased. One example is of Pemulwuy, the 'Rainbow Warrior', and his son Tedbury. Together they carried out a guerrilla war for over a decade in opposition to the early British takeover of their country, the area near Parramatta. When colonists expanded to the inland side of the Blue Mountains, the *Wiradjuri* people resisted the intruders. In response, Governor Thomas Brisbane declared martial law in 1824 and soldiers indiscriminately killed Aboriginal men.

In revenge, a warrior, Windradyne, with other *Wiradjuri* men, attacked properties.

For a while, the stock route from Sydney to Adelaide that followed the Murrumbidgee, Darling and Murray Rivers, was notorious for violent clashes. The most infamous of these was the Myall Creek Massacre on 10th June 1838, in central NSW, in which 28 Indigenous women, children and old men were killed. There was no apparent reason for this slaughter as their tribe, the *Wirrayaraay* people of the *Gamilaraay* nation, were helpful to local landowners and had established friendly relationships with them. It was significant because, after one trial had declared the instigators innocent—largely on a technicality—seven of them were retried, found guilty and executed. This was the first time that white men in NSW were executed for the murder of Indigenous people.

Many Aboriginal people who survived introduced diseases and loss of land were faced with the policy of 'assimilation' of Indigenous people by white society. Bennelong, an Aboriginal man from Sydney Cove, for example, was encouraged by Governor Arthur Phillip to dress in European clothes and to learn English. Governor Phillip also took him to London. Bennelong's wife, Barangaroo, also played a role as intermediary with the early settlers. Both Bennelong and Barangaroo came to be recognised in the late 20th and early 21st centuries with landmarks in Sydney being named after them.

From the late 1830s, attempts were made to protect, civilise and Christianise the Aboriginal people by the establishment of Aboriginal protectorates (1838—1849) as a way of assimilating them. Missions were also established by the various denominational groups from about 1825 for over a century. By the 1880s, many Aboriginal people had been pushed onto Government reserves, thus removing Aboriginals largely from public view. On these reserves, life was regulated, and Aboriginals were segregated and officially 'protected'. Some were used for labour as a laundress, handyman, groom or nurse. Those who were not on reserves or mission stations clung to the edges of white settlement where their health was affected by sugar, tobacco and alcohol.

A policy of taking children from their parents commenced, leading to what is now known as the 'Stolen Generation'. This was also part of the general policy of assimilation: if Indigenous people could be made 'white', they needed to be taken from their families and placed in institutions to teach them to be useful in non-Indigenous society. In NSW, under the Aborigines Protection Act of 1909, children could be removed from their Aboriginal parents without parental consent or court order. The Aboriginal Welfare Board, created in 1940, had the same right.

At the beginning of the 20th century, Aboriginal people were entitled to a wage—but only at the rate of one-third of a non-Indigenous wage. It was a bitter irony that, in

1966, when award wages were granted to Indigenous pastoral workers, many were sacked and forced off the lands that were and had been their homes.

In 1962, Indigenous Australians were given the right to vote. In 1965, a number of students from the University of Sydney, including *Arrernte* man Charles Perkins, organised what they called 'The Freedom Ride'. This was a bus tour of NSW intended to draw attention to the social distinctions and discrimination based on Aboriginality. Two years later, in a referendum in 1967, citizenship status was granted to Indigenous people. This meant they were formally included in the Census, although they had been counted from the very first Commonwealth Census in 1911, except in remote areas, but their numbers were removed from final population figures for constitutional purposes.

In 1983, one of the most generous Aboriginal Land Rights Acts in Australia was passed in NSW. It created Land Councils, both central and local, and aimed to provide economic support for Aboriginal people by compensating for lost lands. In May 2000, over 300,000 people, Indigenous and non-Indigenous, walked over Sydney's Harbour Bridge in a large and collective demonstration in support of reconciliation. The process of reconciliation is still ongoing.

As the historian Paul Irish has pointed out, cross-cultural relationships were encouraged by Indigenous people as they sought to weave the newcomers into their cultural ethic. The mission-raised activist, shearer and political leader, William Cooper (1860–1941), was a *Yorta Yorta* man from the area overlapping southern NSW and north-eastern Victoria. In 1887 he presented a petition of eleven signatures to the Governor of NSW, Lord Carrington (1843–1928), calling for land rights. In 1937, with a document containing 1,800 signatures, he petitioned the British King, George VI, for Aboriginal franchise and parliamentary representation. The Australian Government did not see fit to pass the petition on to its intended royal recipient.

This same William Cooper had another distinctive moment in history. He was incensed by the attacks on 9th November 1938 by Nazi authorities and civilians in ransacking and destroying Jewish homes, shops and synagogues across Germany and Austria—the night that became known as 'Kristallnacht', in recognition of the glass broken that night. On 6th December, Cooper led a delegation of the Australian Aborigines League, walking 10 kilometres across Melbourne to deliver a formal petition to the German Consulate. It criticised the 'cruel persecution of the Jewish people by the Nazi government of Germany'. They were refused entry and the German Consul would not receive their protest. The National Museum of Australia considers this to be the only civilian protest of its kind in the world at the time.

2. *The Arrival of British Convicts*

Eighteenth century Britain had severely limited means for enforcing law and order. Yet there were increasing numbers of crimes being committed following the dislocation of many people affected by growing industrialisation (and later by the demobilisation of men after the end of the Napoleonic Wars in 1815). Severe penalties were the cheapest and preferred means of deterrent. Executions became popular entertainment and had the added advantage of providing no occasion for further crimes from the person. However, there was also an increasing public sentiment away from the brutality and barbarity of capital punishment for non-violent offences, and for some time deportation to the American colonies had been one important way of addressing this sentiment.

After the loss of those colonies, following the American War of Independence in the 1770s, the British Government needed somewhere else to send criminals. Prisons could not hold them and so hulks, disused and discarded ships, were moored in the Thames River to house them. However, these also proved inadequate to the task of accommodating increasing numbers. Dislocation drew rural dwellers to towns and cities. Vagabonds and beggars congregated, and crime became a way of life. They worked in groups, sometimes families and often in gangs, as fictionalised in Charles Dickens' *Oliver Twist* in the gang of young pickpockets run by Fagin.

New South Wales, recently surveyed by Captain Cook and referred to generally as 'Botany Bay', was a great distance from Great Britain but had the possibility of yielding new resources and could facilitate trade with China and the Pacific, all with little cost to the home government. Historians have argued about which of these motives was the driving force behind the British Government's decision to send convicted felons to New South Wales, but the decision was made and acted upon with considerable conviction and resources: from 1788 until 1840, New South Wales was the recipient of over 80,000 convicts.

The 'First Fleet', commanded by Captain Arthur Phillip, departed Spithead, England in May 1787 and arrived in Botany Bay on 26 January 1788. It comprised two Royal Navy vessels, three store ships and six convict transport vessels. Marines accompanied Phillip to act as guards for the convicts. There were 775 convicts (582 men, 193 women) who departed England of whom 43 died along the way, leaving 732 convicts to land at Sydney Cove. In all, about 1500 people landed.

Depending on the crime, a convict's sentence was for seven or fourteen years or for life, with about half receiving the lesser sentence. Many were recidivists and a great number of juveniles were professional criminals with their major crime being general larceny (theft). Objects stolen varied and were done so opportunistically. Although pickpockets favoured handkerchiefs, they stole whatever came their way. Items stolen were not normally for personal use but were quickly passed on to receivers. Animal theft was more common in rural areas, normally of horses and sheep, but any livestock was fair game. There were more serious offences such as highway robbery or stealing from premises such as post offices and private residences.

Although thieving was the most common, crimes were varied. Forgers or those who passed counterfeit money were usually given fourteen-year sentences, reflecting the problems that the British government had with its currency. Those convicted of rioting were mainly Irish, although English rioters from southern districts were tried following the agricultural disturbances of the early 1830s. There were also those transported for embezzlement, fraud and murder. The non-criminal skills that convicts brought with them were few, most men claiming that they were labourers and women that they were domestic servants. Some had education, usually listed as 'clerks', but there were those with particular talents, such as the architect Francis Greenway (1777–1837) and the artist Thomas Watling (1762–1814), both transported for forgery.

The transports on which the convicts arrived in the colony of NSW had a varied history and were of widely different quality. While the charters to which masters of ships were answerable seem reasonable, supervision of the practice on the transports was varied until the appointment in 1814 of Surgeon-Superintendents on each ship. This improved the lot of convicts who had been at the mercy of contractors who skimped on rations and clothing. Conditions also improved once payment of the contractors covered convicts landed as well as those embarked.

Even those aboard a ship such as the *Hillsborough*, a well supervised and provisioned ship, could endure terrible hardships. This ship departed Portsmouth in December 1798, fitted out to allow for more circulation of air in the prison areas. Its contractors were to be paid eighteen pounds for all who embarked and a further four pounds ten shillings and sixpence for all who landed safely. But the convicts suffered from an outbreak of typhoid—known as 'gaol fever'—a disease probably brought with the men from the hulks. Their 212-day journey to Sydney was made even worse by a report of an intended mutiny of the prisoners, leading the captain to reduce rations. Conditions on the voyage further deteriorated thanks to the harsh weather that saturated bedding and the captain's practice of keeping the men chained together when on deck. Of the 299 convicts who had set sail, 95 died on the voyage. Several more died once they had landed and almost all required hospitalisation.

Transported convicts were a motley crew, mainly coming from lower social orders and often referred to as the 'criminal classes'. They mostly came from the slums of the expanding industrial cities of Britain, including some originally from rural areas and attracted to the towns in the hope of increased opportunities. Within the colony, there were many complaints that convicts were drunk and idle, an understandable condition for those who were sent to what must have seemed like the ends of the earth, with little or no hope of returning to their homeland. Despair had many faces, with crime and immorality being frequently commented on. Secondary offenders were sent to such penal settlements as Norfolk Island, Newcastle, Moreton Bay and Port Phillip.

But if convicts were well-behaved, they could be assigned to private service. This was thought to prevent consorting and teach the benefits of honest labour, along with relieving the government of the cost of maintaining them. In Sydney, from 1818, those in government employment were housed in the Hyde Park Barracks, still extant today, where they received board and lodging. A bell would ring at sunrise to summon the men to breakfast, while a second bell indicated that they should go to their respective workplaces. This work allowed them to utilise their existing skills but also taught them new ones. Their work varied. They might transport goods, work in the shipyards or lumberyard, clear land, grow or harvest crops or work in the various workshop at the Barracks that produced tools, clothing and bread.

Controversially, convicts were permitted to work for gain in their spare time. Frequently convicts were given tasks to perform and, if these were completed early, they could use their spare time to their financial advantage. Even when this was questioned, private employers were primarily concerned with getting work done and would ignore irregularities to this end.

Convicts who became free by completing their period of servitude or were emancipated as a result of good behaviour, were given grants of land, often of 30 acres but with 20 acres extra for a wife and 10 extra for each child. While this provided an opportunity for some, turning urban criminals into industrious farmers was never going to be easy. Seed was inadequate and the soil and environmental conditions were foreign, compared to Britain. Many found themselves in debt, lost their land and turned to employment in the small developing industries.

But there were stories of success. One such is that of Samuel Terry (1776–1838), referred to as the 'Botany Bay Rothschild'. Convicted in England in 1800 of the theft of 400 pairs of stockings, and sentenced to seven years, he went on to become the richest man in NSW. One of the main ways forward in colonial society was by amassing wealth. Terry acquired property by allegedly tricking inebriated men who frequented his hotels to sign over their assets to him. Terry also acted as an unofficial private banker, not uncommon for men of means in that period. His ventures included milling, brewing and shipping.

To encourage reform and industry, a 'ticket of leave', first introduced by Governor Philip Gidley King in 1801, was granted to convicts whose behaviour warranted reward. This enabled them to work for themselves. At times, however, these passes were granted simply to relieve the government of the cost of maintenance. As a further incentive to keep convicts as far from Britain as possible, after 1816 the families of convicts were allowed to join them in the colony and the cost of this was borne by the government, a practice that was continued throughout the period of transportation.

The unusual convict rights in the settlement have led to the argument that this was not a 'penal settlement' but rather a 'colony of convicts'. The historian and social commentator, John Hirst, argued that they had the sort of legal rights undreamed of in their country of origin. For practical purposes, for example, they were allowed to give evidence in court and to bring actions in court themselves. The first such case was that of two First Fleet convicts, Henry Kable and Susannah Holmes, who had already had a child together before they arrived in NSW. The ship's captain, however, refused to allow Susannah to take the baby with her. This prompted the gaoler, moved by her plight, to take the baby to the offices of Lord Sydney until he granted permission for all three members of the family to go to the new colony. A parcel of goods, the money for which was raised by people impressed by the family devotion of the two convicts, had been sent on the transport on another vessel but was plundered on the journey. Both the convicts took successful action on arrival against the ship's captain who had to pay them compensation.

Female convicts, who comprised about 15% of those transported, provided a different challenge. Like their male counterparts, they were predominantly from urban areas—though not necessarily born in cities—and were from the lower classes of England, Ireland, Scotland and Wales. They arrived in the gaol that was New South Wales without useful skills, as the majority declared that they came from a background of domestic service. Their economic potential was considered limited and they were generally denigrated as prostitutes.

The solution was to concentrate convict women in one institution where they could be controlled, and their labour put to good use. It could also regulate assignment, marriage, employment, act as a hospital and as a gaol for secondary punishment. There had been an earlier attempt at such an institution, but from 1821 to 1848 the Parramatta Female Factory became the initial home for all women who arrived in the colony. Here they were classified according to behaviour. For the well behaved, the Factory acted as an asylum, protection and a place of employment, a marriage bureau and a labour bureau. Those who, in Governor Lachlan Macquarie's words, were of 'disorderly Vicious habits' were punished in the gaol where they mixed with women punished for secondary offences in the colony, while those who were pregnant went to the Factory's hospital which also acted at times as a general hospital for colonial women. So, in one institution all the perceived problems of dealing with female convicts were seen to be solved.

Here they produced linen and clothing for the colony. Once assigned, they moved into domestic service either for government officials or private employers. A few worked in other employment: midwives and nurses, field labourers and hutkeepers, cleaning and cooking for male convicts in government employment.

Despite bad press and preconceived opinions of them, ex-convict women, as many of them soon became, were generally law-abiding. Most remained in domestic service where they were employed as housekeepers, nursemaids, kitchen maids and cooks. But some became self-employed as laundresses and seamstresses, and some entered the hotel business, or became butchers and bakers, often in their husband's businesses and then controlling those businesses as widows.

The locally-born children of convicts were referred to as 'currency' lads and lasses. To the surprise of most observers, they were also generally law-abiding and hard-working—and they were not ashamed of their convict parentage.

This system of 'forced migration' ceased in NSW in 1840. To many convicts, being sent to a colony on the other side of the world would have been, it has been said, like being exiled to the moon today. However, for both men and women convicts, New South Wales provided the opportunity to gain both a social status and economic security that they could not have had if they had remained in their country of origin.

The importance of the convict system to the development of the colony of NSW and to the whole of Australia was immense. The British Government paid the fares for these men and women to a remote land and then paid for the upkeep of both convicts and their gaolers. The colonisation of the land was based on the convict system: agriculture, commerce, industry and export all used the free labour it provided. In the words of Australian historian Geoffrey Blainey, 'Australia's main economic activities were suckled by the convict system'.

3. *Further Non-Indigenous Colonisation and Settlement*

When people decide to migrate, whether forced or voluntary, they must handle a range of issues. The reason for their departure will condition their attitude to their new world. How do they understand their new environment and their relationship to it? When and how do they gain a sense of belonging and create a new home?

Colonists and migrants who arrived in NSW also brought baggage from their countries of origin. Their culture, language/dialect, religion, social customs and values travelled with them and disembarked in a foreign land. But the circumstances that they met influenced and moderated their background. Some embraced the new frontier, while others clung persistently to the idea of creating an outpost of the familiar. From this conflict, a new identity was forged.

If convicts were forced migrants then they, in a different

sense, were also many of the earliest settlers. A generation after the initial penal colony was established, the impact of industrialisation and demobilisation in Great Britain (the aftermath of the Napoleonic Wars in 1815) caused rural distress, urban poverty and widespread unemployment, particularly for demobbed soldiers and sailors. Many looked to the new colony as an escape route or ended following the path of the earlier convicts. The prospect of acquiring land in the colony was also an attraction for many moneyed European settlers, not just to increase their wealth but to afford them status: after 1816, migration restrictions were amended, with free settlers required to have investment capital, and more affluent free settlers started arriving in NSW. All newcomers now received land grants and assigned labour.

Some of these newer settlers were forced migrants in another way: they were 'remittance men', who were sent to the colony by their families because of some perceived misdemeanour and who survived on the money remitted by their families—as long as they remained in the colony. The Irish surgeon, D'Arcy Wentworth (1762–1827), a prime example, was tried but acquitted on three charges of highway robbery and narrowly avoided a fourth. The prosecutor then informed the judge: 'My Lord, Mr. Wentworth, the prisoner at the Bar, has taken a passage to go in a fleet to Botany Bay and has obtained an appointment in it as Assistant Surgeon and desires to be discharged immediately'. His family subsequently arranged for him to serve as surgeon in Sydney Cove.

In addition to this occupation, he was granted 3,600 acres of land, an amount to which he added and on which he grazed sheep and cattle.

By the time Governor Lachlan Macquarie left in 1821, after 11 years, the colony had ceased to be a place which simply acted as a deterrent to crime in Britain. It was not even a settlement of modest subsistence farmers, even appearing attractive to those looking for opportunities not available 'back home'. The story of Mary Reibey (née Haydock) provides but one example of this. In 1790, at the age of 13, she was convicted of horse-theft at Stafford and sent to the colony for a seven-year sentence. When she was arrested, she was dressed as a boy, using the name of 'James Burrow', but at her trial her identity was disclosed. At the age of 17 in 1794, she married Thomas Reibey (1769–1811) in Sydney, and the couple became entrepreneurs with interests in shipping, trade, land and various businesses. When Thomas died, Mary pursued and expanded these concerns, visited England, where she toured, and then returned to the colony. She passed away in Newtown, Sydney, in 1855 at the age of 78.

In 1826, 'limits of location' were decreed by Governor Ralph Darling and land grants could only be issued within these boundaries. In 1829, the boundaries were extended to encompass the Nineteen Counties surrounding Sydney. It was an attempt to exercise government control over the expanding settlement in the colony. But settlement extended beyond these limits as acquisitive and enterprising settlers moved the frontiers as 'squatters'. The explorers and settlers became memorialised as 'pioneers' as they pushed back these boundaries, although it involved further intrusion without consideration into the traditional lands of the original inhabitants.

The ending of the Napoleonic Wars not only left many demobbed participants unemployed, but also gave rise to former officers seeking outlets for their energy and expertise. After 1826, considerable land grants were permitted to such officers, who also had the advantage of free convict labour. 'Clans' arrived with officers such as the Dumaresq brothers (William and Henry), bringing their families with them and establishing large estates while acting as civil officials.

In 1835, to encourage migrants from Britain (especially skilled workers) Governor Richard Bourke introduced the 'bounty' system, under which employers could promise employment to potential migrants and receive a payment when they landed. The system failed on a number of fronts. Skilled workers did not need to migrate; those selected often proved unsuitable to local needs and a depression in the 1840s created short-term unemployment. The colony had received the criminals of the 'mother country' and now considered that it was receiving the dregs of British society as migrants. The general system was revived and in 1852 the NSW Act meant that employers had more say in the selection of migrants.

As settlement extended, so did the issues of containing its attendant problems. Although the depression of the 1840s created unemployment, rural labour was still needed. The philanthropist Caroline Chisholm took it upon herself to do something about helping the assisted migrants, especially young women, to find work. With her husband, Captain Archibald Chisholm of the East India Company, Caroline had arrived in NSW in 1838 and settled in Windsor. She was appalled at the conditions in which newly arrived women and families lived and the vagaries of fortune to which they were subject. She met every immigrant ship and ran a type of labour bureau in which families, along with single women, were placed in employment.

In 1841 she established the Female Immigrants' Home in an old immigration barracks in Sydney, with the permission of Governor Sir George Gipps. She also personally accompanied groups of young women to places of rural employment. Using bullock drays and riding her grey horse, 'Captain', she led single women and families into the unknown outback to places as far afield as Gundagai, Bathurst and Armidale. Between 1838 and 1846 she established an astonishing 11,000 people on the land. In 1849, she founded the Family Colonisation Loan Society on a visit to England to promote her cause.

As a Catholic, albeit a convert at marriage, she suffered from accusations of giving preferential treatment to Irish Catholic migrants. Her gravestone in Northampton,

England, claims for her the title 'The Emigrants' Friend'. In 1967, her image was used on the new Australian $5 note.

The goldrushes of the 1850s attracted an even greater migrant population to the colony. The prospector Edward Hargreaves (1816–1891) discovered gold at Ophir, near Bathurst, in 1851. The result was a change in the demographics of the colony as people poured into the diggings from Sydney and overseas. People with new skills and expertise arrived—and many stayed. They came from Europe, North America and China. Most of them moved to the newly independent colony of Victoria to which the population of NSW was also lured in the hope of fortune, but the diggings in NSW were also attractive.

Migration to Australia generally was more expensive than to Canada or the United States, because of the distance involved, so many needed a financial subsidy. For this reason, there was no flooding of the labour market in the colony. In 1856, building workers in Sydney (and Melbourne) achieved an eight-hour working day. This milestone was celebrated every year with a parade through the streets until eventually it was achieved for more workers. The mantra became 'eight hours work, eight hours play, eight hours sleep, eight bob a day'.

Apart from the Chinese, most early arrivals in NSW were English, Scottish or Irish, but there had been migration from other areas. The first Jewish migrant to arrive without any connection to convicts or emancipists was Walter Levi. He had arrived with his family and high hopes of becoming a landed settler. This did not transpire and instead he became a merchant and shipping agent. Between 1830 and 1840, 36 free Jewish adults arrived in NSW with their 25 children.

Others arrived following upheaval or dislocation in their countries. Germans had established themselves in NSW early in its settlement, many of them valued for their skills as winegrowers. Six such families arrived in April 1838 to be employed in the vineyards of the family of the late John Macarthur (1767–1834), a pioneer of the wool industry. More were assisted immigrants after 1847, when the Colonial Government included European migrants with special skills in their migration scheme. German Lutherans had migrated to South Australia due to religious persecution in Prussia and some then relocated to the Riverina agricultural region of south-western NSW.

Chain migration then led to further Germans migrating to NSW, with the 1891 census indicating that there were 9,565 living there. They settled in a range of NSW towns (for example Grafton, Tenterfield and Bega) and also in rural areas such as Young, Bingara and Cooma. Afghan cameleers, famous for their work transporting goods in inland Australia, made their base in Broken Hill in far west NSW. Here they built a mosque which still functions as a place of worship and a museum.

Maltese families settled in western Sydney and, as Malta was a British colony, they could migrate to other parts of the empire. Their experience in intensive farming in Malta proved useful in agriculture on the Cumberland Plain, a region lying to the west of Sydney CBD.

Chinese settlement in NSW was considerable, particularly drawn by the goldrushes. One such adventurer, Wong Ah Sat (1837–1916), arrived at the goldfields near Burraga, south-west of Oberon. He met and married in Goulburn, on 19 March 1864, Amelia Hackney, the daughter of prosperous and well-educated family from England, involved in the drapery trade—a marriage not welcomed by her brothers. They established a store, selling Chinese and European goods, mainly to Chinese miners. Later they moved to Bolong, an area near Crookwell, where they opened another store and purchased land on which they ran sheep. Their store is a testament to life in rural areas, providing goods as diverse as shotgun cartridges, violin strings imported from Germany and ornaments for funeral coffins. The marriage is also interesting against the background of growing anti-Chinese sentiment in NSW.

From 1861, when the NSW Government passed the *Chinese Immigration Regulation and Restriction Act*, and despite its repeal in 1867 after the goldrushes had petered out, racial intolerance to Chinese was apparent. Intriguingly, another Chinese migrant, Mei Quong Tart (1850–1903), helped to bridge the gap. Arriving in NSW at the age of nine, he and an uncle went to the goldfields at Braidwood. By age 18, Quong Tart was a wealthy man. He opened a silk and tea store and a chain of tea shops and, like Wong Ah Sat, he married a young English schoolteacher, Margaret Scarlett, on 30th August 1886. He extended his empire with exotic restaurants in King Street and the Queen Victoria Markets, where he was known as an excellent employer providing, for example, paid sick leave. He was also known for his community involvement, his anti-opium crusades, his speeches and his renditions of Scottish songs and poems.

During the First World War, some migrants from countries previously acceptable were now reclassified as 'enemy aliens'. In consequence, approximately 7,000 people were interned in camps in NSW at Berrima, Trial Bay and Liverpool. Following the war, immigration of people from Germany was banned for five years, and for Turkish people immigration was banned until 1930.

Once peace was declared on 11th November 1918, assisted migration was resumed. Ex-servicemen arrived from Britain, paid for by the British Government. Some were sponsored by community and church organisations. Others, such as Greeks and Italians, paid their own way. Sponsored migration ended with the onset of the Great Depression in 1929 and was not resumed until after the Second World War. In the 1930s, more Jewish migrants arrived, fleeing Hitler's expansionist moves in Europe.

During the Second World War, many migrants who had lived happily in NSW were once again reclassified as 'enemy aliens' and were either interned or subjected to police surveillance, including Germans and Italians. A large group of Jewish refugees, many of whom were escaping Nazi persecution in Germany, arrived in NSW in September 1940 on the *Dunera*. They were interned first at Hay and Orange in New South Wales, and later at Tatura in Victoria. They included artists, scientists and writers and, on their release, many remained here, contributing to the wellbeing of their new homeland. Italian migrants were also affected. The well-known LoSurdo family of fishermen had lived in Leichhardt for decades. Some of the family were naturalised—and had fought in the Australian forces during the First World War. Two of the many LoSurdos, Dominic and Andy, were not in this category. Andy was interned but released due to poor eyesight, while Dominic was interned successively at camps in Hay, Loveday and Wayville.

Concern about cheap Asian labour and geographical security lay behind laws to restrict migration of certain groups. There had been much opposition in NSW to the attempts of pastoralists in the 1830s to introduce labour from India, Melanesia and China. In 1881 legislation was reintroduced, like the previous 1861 law, to restrict Chinese migration in the *Influx of Chinese Restriction Act* and, in 1898, another restrictive law was passed, aimed at excluding all non-Europeans, even if British subjects. It included a dictation test.

With the formation of the Commonwealth of Australia in 1901, power with respect to immigration was vested in the Commonwealth parliament. The first Act of the 1901 federal government continued the concerns about Chinese migration in particular, through the *Immigration Restriction Act*. It became known as the 'White Australia' policy and, throughout its existence, its focus changed. A distinctly racist illustration was the deportation in 1928 of the visiting Afro-American jazz band, 'Sonny Clay and the Colored Idea'. They were especially hounded by the Sydney newspaper, *Truth*. It was not until 1954 that black musicians could once again enter the country.

After the Second World War, Arthur Caldwell (1896–1973), first federal minister for immigration, insisted Australia needed to 'populate or perish'. Called by Caldwell the 'New Australians', hopefully a welcoming and inclusive term, European migrants were sought out, and were expected to assimilate. Thousands of people displaced by the war came—most were those who could not or did not want to return to their countries of origin. So arrived Poles, Latvians, Ukrainians, Hungarians and Yugoslavs (as they were known then), part of the agreed 12,000 migration intake of refugees. The scheme operated for seven years and broadened its base to include, for example, Dutch, Spanish, Swiss and Scandinavians. Most displaced persons went to Sydney or Melbourne, where they were taken to migration hostels located in the country. The accommodation was quite primitive, con-sisting of Nissan huts, and the food was often unfamiliar. Things improved a little when Sydney's Villawood centre was opened in 1969 and family units were provided.

Such migrants had to work for two years on government-specified projects, such as the Snowy Mountains Scheme, regardless of their professional training. Of all the European waves of migration, enhanced by chain migration, the post-First World War and particularly post-Second World War, Greeks and Italians were initially the largest groups.

The White Australia policy was gradually opposed in the 1950s. Churches, trade unions and academics were challenging it for a variety of reasons—ethical, political and intellectual—all indicating discomfort with the policy. In 1956, non-European residents could finally become citizens and, in 1958, the dictation test was abolished. With the new Labor Minister for Immigration (starting on 19th December 1972), Al Grassby, the policy changed again, with a quota system being based on personal attributes and occupation, but the Whitlam Government abandoned this policy in 1973, extending migration to include Asians. The policy actively changed from one of assimilation to creating a multicultural society. However, although initially living in enclaves, many migrants by the second or third generation had little interest in speaking their own language or maintaining their culture. They married outside these limitations.

Immigration patterns changed in the mid-1970s with the arrival of Timorese, then Vietnamese, some unofficially by boat as asylum seekers, but most officially. The Malcolm Fraser Liberal Government (1975–1983) generally supported them, as Australia had supported South Vietnam during the long Vietnam War (1955–1975), and NSW received numbers of these new residents. Since then, many 'boat people' have arrived in Australia unofficially, particularly from the Middle East, but also from places such as Sri Lanka. Since 1992, pursuant to Commonwealth law, all are subject to compulsory detention, as 'unlawful non-citizens', pending deportation or permission to stay through the grant of a valid visa.

Notwithstanding the ebbs and flows of immigration policies, the result of all these waves of migration is a very multicultural NSW today.

Among the many pioneering women in NSW who could be included, let's focus on two, notable for their outstanding achievements.

ON THE LAND: *ELIZABETH MACARTHUR (1766-1850)*

Elizabeth Macarthur's contribution to the wool industry has been grossly overshadowed by the public recognition of her husband, John. Yet he was absent from Australia for eleven years, defending himself in a court martial in England for a duel in 1801. Meanwhile, Elizabeth kept developing the experimental sheep breeding program at the Camden Park merino stud which she established. The family had first settled at Elizabeth Farm, Parramatta where Elizabeth created fruitful gardens. Although while in London, John was able to promote their industry, it was Elizabeth's administrative ability in addressing the local and practical problems that led to the successful export of wool. She adjusted to colonial life, raising their eight children and leaving behind an historically important and detailed record of local life.

IN THE CITY: *MARIE LOUISE MACK (1870–1935)*

Louise Mack was raised in a devout Christian household in Redfern, Sydney. She had the good fortune to have a mother who taught her daughters to read and learn, but the misfortune, after her father's early death, to be raised in economically restrained circumstances.

Her determination to become a writer led to her submitting poems to the magazine, *The Bulletin*, using her initials only, to avoid being identified as a woman. The editor of the journal was so impressed when he met her, however, that he offered her a position as a trainee journalist. She married twice, first in January 1896 to John Percy Creed, a Dublin barrister, who passed away in 1914. In September 1924 in Melbourne, she married 33-year-old Allen Illingworth Leyland. He was 21 years her junior, but he passed away in 1932 and she was widowed for the second time.

She left for London where she supported herself by writing romantic novels for serialisation. Her success made her a wealthy woman. When the First World War commenced, Louise was one of a number of journalists stationed at Ostend in Belgium. She later based herself at Antwerp in the same country and, without regard to her own safety, worked near the war front even crossing into German-held territory. She sent back reports of the personal stories of those affected by the occupation, using any means to get her stories back to London's *Daily Mail.* She returned to London after several months and published a book of her experiences. She returned eventually to NSW to live in Mosman and marry a veteran of the First World War, having led a very bohemian life. She had been Australia's first female war correspondent—and indeed the first female war correspondent in the world.

4. *Cities, Towns and Localities*

INTRODUCTION

Providing brief histories of cities, towns and localities is always a compromise as a few hundred words cannot encapsulate the complex and often individual growth and identity of each. Indigenous people tend to exist in the first paragraph and then disappear for the remainder of the discourse. A 'history of progress' is the result as villages become gazetted and towns grow to cities. The following account is no exception to this path. But hopefully it does, in the overall, provide something of the nature of NSW's development as European settlers recreated their places of origin and at the same time found a different environment in which to develop a new society.

SYDNEY

The Indigenous people of the City of Sydney are the *Gadigal* people of the *Eora* nation. They have lived there since the Dreaming and, despite disease and dislocation, continue to do so and it remains their traditional land. Traditional art can still be found on rock faces and confirmation of a people who hunted, gathered and fished in the area is in evidence. There are, however, 28 other clans in the Sydney metropolitan area, all of the *Eora* nation. All of these have felt the impact of European colonisation, but despite this they have retained their family, community and cultural relationships. In the words of the *Darug* elder, Aunty Edna Watson, 'We are here and we have always been here'.

Once colonisation by Europeans commenced, the settlement of convicts and their gaolers started the process of becoming a transplanted society that understood a different organisation of communal living: that of the post-industrial town and city.

Described variously as an 'accidental' town, with 'planning due to the errant goat', Sydney grew in fits and starts. Conceived as a colony of convicts, it was founded on the shores of one of the most beautiful harbours in the world in one of the most remote places in the world—at least from the view of European settlement. Named 'Sydney' for the then British Home Secretary, Lord Sydney, it became the first town and then the first city in the colony.

Its first years as a colony were of cruelty and hardship with inadequate provisioning in all necessities such as clothing and food: the spectre of starvation was never far away in the first few years. But by 1819, Commissioner

John Thomas Bigge (1780–1843), appointed to consider the effectiveness of transportation as a deterrent to felons, could report that it was a thriving town with a good climate. This was due in many ways to the determination of Governor Lachlan Macquarie, and built on the work of both convicts and soldiers.

By the 1830s, it had a standard theatre and a wide range of sporting events, bearing out Bigge's assessment of the climate, one good enough to encourage an *al fresco* lifestyle. Areas such as The Rocks (the original encampment of the First Fleet), with its crooked lanes and rough cottages, were crowded and boasted many small public houses, some of which are still functioning. But the urban fringes boasted a growing number of impressive residences.

Free settlers came in greater numbers; convicts who were emancipated or had become free by serving out their sentences sought ways to avail themselves of their new circumstances. Schools were established as were churches, stores, theatres and libraries. The first bank, the Bank of New South Wales opened in 1817. From 1830, hackney carriages dashed through Sydney's streets which, from 1841, were becoming gas lit. Also by then the *Sydney Morning Herald*, first published in 1831 as the *Sydney Herald*, had become a daily newspaper.

Against the background of arguments concerning the right for emancipists to vote and be nominated for election, *The Sydney Corporation Act* was passed in 1842 and the election for Sydney's 24 councillors took place in October of that year. Sydney had become officially a city. The move was, however, arguably premature, and the effectiveness of the Corporation's Commissioners often proved inadequate.

With the discovery of payable gold in NSW in 1851, firstly in Ophir near the Macquarie River northeast of the city of Orange, people came to the state from all over the world, but especially from China. There was a building boom, unfortunately with a get-rich-quick mentality rather than with any understanding of construction. Parts of Sydney were renowned for wild celebrations. By the 1870s, public health issues, outbreaks of disease, and the development of dangerously constructed slums amid a growing population led to a series of Acts in the next three decades intended to address these problems. However, there was no coordinated or overall attempt to do so.

Despite these problems, Sydney continued to expand with structures using the yellow local Sydney sandstone for material. Public buildings such as the Sydney Observatory, 1845, the Customs House, 1885, and the Town Hall, completed 1889, gave Sydney the makings of a grand city. Commercial ventures were established in the Strand Arcade which opened in 1892; and the Queen Victoria Building was erected in 1898. Magnificent churches such as St Andrew's and St Mary's Cathedrals were built and the Great Synagogue was consecrated in 1878. By the 1860s, horse drawn trams ran down Sydney's streets; two decades later, Sydneysiders could travel through their city by steam trams and in the early 20th century by electric trams.

The bubonic plague of the early 1900s became a spur to the demand for the reform of Sydney. This was also the time when the influence of the 'City Beautiful' movement was felt in NSW. This movement stressed the connection between city design and social issues and sought to increase city pride. A 1909 Royal Commission report into Sydney and its suburbs promoted the idea of beautifying the city; but its haphazard development proved hard, even impossible, to reverse.

Despite the variety of nationalities who came to the colony seeking gold, until the 1930s the population was still mainly from Britain, Ireland or parts of the British Empire, a situation due to some degree to the White Australia policy. There were people from other cultures in Sydney, such as the Chinese, who created a community of market gardeners. There were also Jews, Lebanese and Indians, most of whom lived in Sydney but many of whom did business in rural areas. It was not until the 1940s, and particularly from 1947 to 1970, that people arrived in Sydney from European nations other than the United Kingdom. Since then, there have been further waves of migration from non-European countries which have altered the nature of the city and made it the most multicultural city in Australia. In 2020, the population of the Greater Sydney area was over five million.

In Sydney today, it is the harbour precinct that is most enticing. The Royal Botanic Gardens, envisaged by Arthur Phillip and enclosed by Lachlan Macquarie, plus the adjacent Domain, provide a vast parkland for residents. Between the Botanic Gardens and Circular Quay, overlooking the harbour, Government House, the residence of the Governor of NSW, was built between 1837 and 1843.

Taronga Zoological Park, established as a place of entertainment in 1916 on the northern side of the harbour in Mosman, has become a site for conservation and education. Its site on the harbour is an enviable one, with views over the city and the craft that move on the waters. The Sydney Harbour Bridge, built between 1923–1932 by British firm, Dorman Long and Co., and costing the lives of sixteen men, joined the northern and southern sides of the harbour. Its continuing attraction is reflected in the popularity of the organised Bridge Climb.

The astonishing edifice, the Sydney Opera House, sporting its 'sails', was opened officially by Her Majesty Queen Elizabeth II in 1973, after 14 years of construction. The Danish architect, Jørn Utzon (1918–2008), won the design competition for the building in 1957. It is now a World Heritage Site. Adjacent to Government House and the Botanic Gardens, it is located on Bennelong Point, a place of ceremony and ritual for the *Gadigal* people and known as 'Tubowgule' or 'where the knowledge waters meet'.

The harbour still also contains reminders of the convict past at Cockatoo Island and Fort Denison. Cockatoo Island, known as 'Wareamah' by the Indigenous people, was a place of incarceration for convict escapees where they languished in chains and were cruelly treated. Fort Denison, initially called Rock Island and also a place of secondary punishment, was known as 'Pinchgut' to convicts for its harsh conditions and short rations. It was built on an island known to the Indigenous people as 'Muddawahnyuh', meaning 'rocky island'. It was later fortified as part of Sydney's defences, particularly in 1855–1857 because of the fear of a Russian naval attack during the Crimean war. It was then renamed 'Fort Denison', after Sydney's then Governor, Sir William Thomas Denison.

Sydney has only actually been under attack once, in 1942, during the Second World War. Three Japanese midget submarines entered the Harbour and fired a torpedo at the HMAS *Kuttabul,* a requisitioned harbour ferry, killing nine Australian and two British naval ratings.

ALBURY

Albury is situated on the border with Victoria, on the banks of the Murray River, 553 kilometres south of Sydney. It is in *Wiradjuri* country and was called 'Bungambrewatah' by the Indigenous people, possibly denoting a crossing place. The name was later changed to Albury in honour of a village in Surrey, England.

The *Wiradjuri* nation is the largest Aboriginal nation in NSW by area. Once European settlement of the area commenced, they were variously adversely affected. Initially, many worked on the lands alienated from them and their skills as river men were often called upon. But there were confrontations, such as the 1838 'Dora Dora massacre', that occurred when two stockmen were killed by *Wiradjuri* men on Thologolong station. Settler reprisals resulted in the deaths of at least twelve *Wiradjuri* men, women and children. Further deaths and dislocations resulted; eventually, in the Aboriginal reserves and missions, local people were intermingled with people from other Aboriginal nations.

The area was on the routes taken by white explorers such as Hamilton Hume, William Hovel and Charles Sturt in the mid-1820s. The course of these explorers was quickly followed by squatters with their sheep and cattle, the lands along the river flats proving excellent for grazing. Drovers used this as a crossing place for their stock as they moved further afield. One of the earliest settlers was the Dublin-born blacksmith Robert Brown (1810–1879) who erected a slab hut in 1838 and, in 1841, opened the Hume River Inn, an indication of the growing importance of the place as a transit point for travellers and mail services. By 1847, Albury had a few modest dwellings, two public houses, a blacksmith shop, police barracks and a post office. In 1860, the bridge over the Murray River was completed, enhancing Albury's position as a major junction between cities. The river was named the 'Murray River' in 1830, after then British Secretary of State for War and the Colonies, Sir George Murray. To the *Ngarrindjeri* people it is known as 'Millewa' and to the *Yorta Yorta* people as 'Tongala'.

By 1859, with its own newspaper, racecourse and churches, Albury had grown sufficiently to become a municipality. The town continued to develop with new industries and migrants. Germans comprised the greatest number of migrants outside of Britain, many bringing skills as winemakers. In 1873, the rail line from Melbourne reached Albury and, eight years later, the line from Sydney was completed, although each line used a different gauge for the tracks. In 1962, Albury, which had been the railway break-of-gauge junction for trains from Sydney to Melbourne since 1881, saw the first standard gauge passenger and freight trains simplify and rationalise movement between those capitals.

The Hume Dam, located 11 kilometres east of Albury, was completed in 1936 after a 17-year gestation period. Named after the explorer Hamilton Hume, it holds more water than Sydney Harbour and provides not only water but hydro-electricity and a place for water sports.

Albury's early buildings are an architectural feast. The railway station is a regal Italianate red and brick structure, while the stylish courthouse, built in 1860, has a Palladian facade. The Post Office and the old Telegraph Office are imposing buildings, the latter now accommodating the Murray Conservatorium. Arguably its most famous daughter is Margaret Smith Court, the international tennis player who gained 62 major titles. During the Second World War, there were army camps in the vicinity of Albury. One of these, 18 kilometres south-east of the city centre, was at Bonegilla.

After the Second World War, with the growing number of principally European migrants arriving in Australia, this ex-army camp became a migrant centre, a temporary place for those arriving here to be assessed. For some, it was a place that led to hope and a new life. For others it was a confusing and isolating experience, particularly for those who did not speak English. In its 24 years of existence, it processed more than 300,000 people from over 30 different ethnic backgrounds.

In 1946, Albury was declared a city. In the 1970s, it became a resettlement area for Aboriginal people, many from western NSW, once again creating a mixture of different Aboriginal peoples. In 2020, the city had a population of over 52,000 and is one of the top ten most populated cities in NSW. Positioned between the major centres of Sydney and Melbourne, it considers itself to have the advantages of both city and country. It has easy access not only to these major centres but to the snowfields of the Great Dividing Range and wineries. It was a potential candidate as the capital city of the Commonwealth of Australia, but a separate newly created city, Canberra, in the Australian Capital

Territory carved out of New South Wales, was chosen instead.

ARMIDALE

When British settlers arrived, the *Anaiwan* and *Kamilaroi* people occupied the area that surrounds and includes Armidale. They remain the traditional owners of the region and Armidale has a larger Aboriginal population than most other NSW cities. It is located on the Northern Tablelands in the New England area of NSW, about halfway between the major cities of Brisbane and Sydney. It was named for the city of Armadale on the Isle of Skye by the Commissioner of Crown Lands, George James Macdonald, a Scot whose father held a baronial estate on the Isle. The traditional owners are the *Anaiwan* people.

Squatters moved into the area in the early 1830s and Armidale became the area's administrative centre in 1839. It was then a village composed of slab huts, but on 1st April 1843 opened its first unofficial James Barnet-designed and now heritage-listed Post Office, the same year as the first hotel appeared. The town was badly affected, as were so many NSW localities, by the 1840s depression as banks collapsed and the price for livestock was greatly reduced. However, the setback was short-lived and throughout the 1840s Armidale continued its expansion with shops, schools and a steam-powered flour mill. A contingent of the border police force was located there and the coaching company, Cobb & Co, serviced the area by 1850.

With the discovery of gold in 1852 at nearby Rocky River, the ensuing goldrush led to an expansion of Armidale as a centre not only for the farming and grazing community but also for an ever widening and diverse population. In 1863 it became a municipality. The next few decades saw a consistent and gradual expansion of the town with a courthouse, newspaper, churches, schools and parks established. In 1883, the town was made more accessible by the railway. Its growth and importance was recognised in 1885 when it was declared a city.

In 1938, the nation's first regional university, the University of New England, was established in Armidale, growing from the Teachers' College which had been in the city since 1932. There was also an (obviously abortive) secessionist movement for the New England area to become Australia's seventh state which decided that Armidale becoming a great educational centre would help to achieve its aims. An impressive mansion in north-west Armidale, 'Booloomimbah', had been unoccupied for several years. The home was purchased after much local fundraising and the New England University College was established there as a branch of Sydney University, with Dr Robert Madgwick as its first Vice-Chancellor. In 1954 it became an independent university. While offering many traditional disciplines, it has been at the forefront of research into agriculture.

Residents of Armidale claim, rightly, that theirs is the highest city in Australia, standing 980 metres above sea level.

The city also has many other claims to fame. The notorious NSW bushranger, Frederick Ward (1835–1870), known as 'Captain Thunderbolt', roamed the area during the 1860s. One of the so-called 'larrikin' bushrangers, he inspired local sympathy as he was gentlemanly and non-violent in his behaviour. He is remembered in Thunderbolt's Way, a road that leads the traveller from the Hunter Valley towards Armidale.

Judith Wright (1915–2000), regarded as one of the nation's finest poets, was born during the First World War into a pastoral family whose land, Wallumumbi Station, was near Armidale. She was educated in Armidale at New England Girls' School. During the Second World War, she returned to the area and helped her father run the family property. While her poems reflect many aspects of life, 'South of My Day's Circle' recalls the area in which she grew to adulthood. The renowned cyclist, Cadel Evans, moved to Armidale in 1986 when aged nine and his early education was completed there. Alex Buzo (1944–2006), noted playwright, was educated at The Armidale School.

Armidale's residents and visitors enjoy its close proximity to World Heritage national parks, with many walks amongst forests, canyons and waterfalls. Its architectural heritage too makes visiting it a pleasure. Referred to as a 'cathedral city', with beautiful chapels and cathedrals, it also has many historically and architecturally significant public and commercial structures, some designed or modified by the noted colonial architects James Barnett and Walter Vernon. In 2018, its suburban population was 24,500. It remains a strong regional centre with a modern art museum, Aboriginal cultural centre and 'keeping place' and an arboretum. It is also a noted cultural centre, particularly for music. As well as 'Booloomimbah' it has many grand residences and mansions, such as Saumarez Homestead, a thirty-room mansion built between 1888 and 1906. The city's economy is now largely directed by the University, but it remains a service centre for an area historically pastoral and is a centre that employs many professionals.

BALLINA

Ballina is located on the mouth of the Richmond River, 737 kilometres north of Sydney. At the time of European arrival, the area around Ballina was home to the *Bundjalung* people who had husbanded the area for millennia and who remain its spiritual custodians. The name Ballina is possibly derived from the Aboriginal word 'Bullenah', which refers to the entry to the sea and its wealth. Unfortunately, inter-relationships of Indigenous owners and European settlers were not without terrible consequences and in the 1850s, there was a reported massacre of up to 40 *Bundjalung* people by the Native Mounted Police.

In 1842 cedar cutters, who had been working inland, arrived with their families at today's Ballina by boat on the *Sally*. They established a settlement known as Richmond River Heads, erecting huts, and by 1853 the first sawmill had been built. This was an obvious site to load ships with cedar for Sydney and Melbourne. The next decades saw new businesses such as inns, hotels, general stores and public offices established, most near the riverfront to cater for transient river trade as well as locals. The new industries were often related to servicing the cedar industry, such as shipwrights, sawyers and shopkeepers.

As the settlement expanded, more families arrived and the demand for clergy and schools grew. Ballina Public School, established in 1863, was the first in the area. As well as cedar cutting activities, early settlers produced food for local consumption in mixed farms, with maize as a commercial crop. In the 1860s, there were experiments in sugarcane production on the rich alluvial flood plains and by the early 1880s, a sugarcane mill had been erected. By the turn of the century, shops boasted the sale of 'fine goods' and luxury items and Ballina had its first bank, the Commercial Banking Company. Ballina Co-operative was established in November 1899, producing butter and bacon. Local dairy farmers had found the local soils good for grazing and most of them had pigs as well. As a commercial venture, the co-operative had problems and was bought out by Norco in 1925, which ran it until it closed in 1945.

The town has drawn its population from different ethnic cultures. When gold was found in sand at the mouth of river in the 1850s, a short-lived goldrush ensued. But in the meantime, it had attracted many people to the town, particularly Chinese—market gardeners and store-owners—and Indians who arrived as farm labourers and some became landowners.

Many of the early buildings did not survive, being replaced by Victorian Italianate structures such as the Walter Vernon designed Post Office. An abundance of cedar meant that many Victorian and Federation houses used this timber in their construction. But Ballina still has an impressive 'heritage walk'—particularly along its main street, Norton Street. The area's oldest lighthouse is the Richmond River Light or Ballina Head Light, designed by the NSW Colonial Architect James Barnet (1827–1904). It was established with a temporary light that was installed in 1866 from plans by the then Colonial Architect, James Barnet. In 1920 the light was converted to acetylene gas and automated.

Although Ballina now boasts eight excellent surfing beaches, in the 19th century the beach was for promenading, picnics and playing 'rounders' (bathing being considered immoral). After the First World War, the beach became more a place of local activity and entertainment as laws changed and bathing became more acceptable. From the 1930s to the 1960s, popular beachfront dance halls, jazz concerts and amusement parks drew locals and tourists to the area. In the 1920s and 1930s, chauffeured cars ran commercially, bringing people to Ballina's beaches, especially Lighthouse Beach. During the 1930s and 1940s, Turner's Bus Company brought people from Lismore and met trains carrying people from wider areas. In the 1950s and 1960s, the 'Miss Sun Girl' competition attracted more tourists to the area.

As well as its beaches, Ballina attracts holidaymakers with its waterfront and coastal walks. Remnants of the coastal rainforest still exist in south Ballina, although dairyfarming caused much of the rainforest to be cleared. In east Ballina, the protected 'Chickiba' wetland is a further attraction. For those with an appropriate appreciation of the eccentric, one of the country's iconic 'big' structures can be seen: the nine-metre-high 'Big Prawn', first built in 1989 and refurbished in 2013.

Ballina has its share of notables. Film and TV Actor Simon Baker, known notably for *The Mentalist*, spent his childhood and teenage years surfing at Ballina's beaches. Another is racing walker Kerry Saxby-Junna, born in Young, but raised in Ballina in the 1960s. She competed with the Ballina Athletics Club, an organisation in which her parents remained involved. Among her many athletic achievements she can count a record 27 Australian Championships and 32 world records.

BLUE MOUNTAINS

The Blue Mountains were so named because eucalyptus trees produce an oil that creates, in mass, a blue haze - and this is where it was initially noticed. At one time, every NSW school child was taught that the Blue Mountains were first crossed by the explorers, Gregory Blaxland, William Lawson and William Charles Wentworth in 1813. However, the story is a little more complex than that. Many attempts had been made to overcome the seemingly impenetrable barrier that prevented the colony expanding westwards and potentially finding unknown riches in the hinterland. The success of Blaxland, Lawson and Wentworth came about because they followed the paths of the Indigenous *Darug* people, one of three tribes who called the area home, and who followed the ridges instead of being caught up in interminable valleys. The other two Indigenous peoples who occupied the area were the *Gundungurra* and the *Burra Burra* people. Shortly after this, with the labour of convicts and the assistance of two Aboriginal men, engineer William Cox (1764–1837) constructed a basic road from Emu Plains to Mount York and then to Bathurst on the plains on the western side of the mountain range.

Military posts were established across the route to protect travellers. These were probably located at Springwood, Bull's Camp at Woodford, Wentworth Falls, Blackheath and Mount Victoria. Movement to the 1850s goldrush at Bathurst was facilitated by the road and increased the need to establish railway access. In July 1867, the first train went from Emu Plains to Wentworth Falls where the line terminated. On the other side of the mountains, a 'zig-zag' railway was constructed between 1866 and 1869. Going from the mountain heights to the plains near Lithgow, it was considered an engineering marvel in its day. It was intended to bring coal and produce from the Lithgow area part of the way to Sydney.

Running roughly parallel and north of the road created by Cox, in 1823 Archibald Bell (1804–1883) was shown another pathway across the mountains by *Darug* men. Subsequently he was accompanied by the Government Assistant Surveyor, who marked out the way and named it 'Bell's Line of Road', which became a second road across the Blue Mountains, and led to the development of the towns of Kurrajong, Bilpin, Mount Tomah and Mount Wilson. The road was at first a bullock-driver's nightmare, with its 'jumps' on a steep and challenging section known as 'Jacob's Ladder'. Although it was improved in 1878, it was not until the Second World War that it was further developed as part of the war effort to provide an alternative route over the mountains.

Victoria Pass, the road west from Mount Victoria, descended to Hartley Vale. Until 1904, horse-drawn vehicles made their way slowly down the road. Then motor cars could make the trip—although the first car to travel down to Hartley required a horse to get it back to the top. By the 1920s, motor coaches were bringing visitors to see the Mountains.

The towns of the Blue Mountains progressed to service the traffic on the way to the goldfields from 1851. The mountains also had a reputation for clean, invigorating, healthy air; and travellers started to visit rather than to use these towns as a temporary stopping-off place. Springwood became an early commercial centre. Its original inn, the Oriental Hotel, was built in 1876 and was later replaced by an establishment of the same name in 1891. It is affectionately known today as 'The Orie'.

The best known of the Blue Mountain towns is probably Katoomba, an Aboriginal term for 'shining falling water' or 'water tumbling over hill'. It takes its name from a waterfall that drops into the Jamison Valley. In 1879, the Katoomba Coal Mine opened and a cable car was needed to bring the coal up the precipitous mountainside. The cable car cutting is now the site of the Scenic Railway. This is a major tourist attraction, but the region's most famous drawcard is the remarkable rock formation, the Three Sisters that, according to one Aboriginal dreamtime story, was once three beautiful sisters named 'Meehni', 'Wimlah' and 'Gunnedoo' from the Katoomba tribe. Before a battle, a witchdoctor decided to turn the sisters into rocks in order to protect them, and promised to reverse the spell only after the conflict. However, he was killed and so they will remain as rock formations forever.

The first building in Blackheath, located about 11 kilometres from Katoomba, was an hotel called the 'Scotch Thistle Inn', erected by Andrew Gardner in 1831, and was visited a few years later by the English naturalist, biologist and geologist, Charles Darwin (1809–1882).

Later, the Mountains' reputation as health-promoting led Sydneysiders to escape there for the summer. Sanatoria were built with some very dubious medical practices. Air that was considered invigorating was often more like freezing. However, the reputation remains.

BOWRAL

The original occupiers and custodians of the area around Bowral were the *Dharawal* (*Tharawal*) people, who had been driven from there by the 1870s. Only 118 kilometres south of Sydney, Bowral has been seen as a retreat for the wealthy from the humidity of Sydney's summers to the cooler climate of the Southern Highlands. Its name is thought to derive from the *Dharawal* word 'bowrel', meaning 'high'.

European exploration of the area was as early as 1798, by a party of convicts, and later by the Surveyor-General, John Oxley (1784–1828), who received a large land grant but who did not remain in the area, although his descendants did. The lush green pastures were attractive to settlers, many of those, like the surgeon Charles Throsby (1771–1828) who came to explore and stayed, assisted by generous land grants. He built the Old South Road in Bong Bong, about 7 kilometres from Bowral.

As the railway made its way south, the railway workers stationed in Bowral needed servicing. Stores and public houses were built and although the railway workers left, ten years later the population had tripled. The first church, an Anglican one, was erected in 1863.

A year later that essential service, a post office, commenced functioning. But it was the approach and then arrival in 1867 of the southern railway from Sydney that changed Bowral from a quiet settlement. By the 1880s, the town had a blacksmith, bakery, newsagency and butchery. The arrival of the railway opened the area to increased settlement and allowed existing landowners to benefit from ensuing development. Land speculation became a significant Bowral industry, with land returning ten times its original price by 1890.

By this time, Bowral was first known as 'Wingecarribee', then the property of the sons of explorer John Oxley. Wingecarribee is the current name of the local government area of the Southern Highlands. During the 1870s and 1880s, some of the more wealthy Sydney residents built grand homes in the English garden style in Bowral which, in 1886 was declared a municipality. All the accoutrements of 'civilisation' were established: new churches, a school of arts, schools, police station, hospitals, a court house—and a cricket club, significant because one of its most famous sons, Sir Donald Bradman (1908–2001), lived in Bowral from 1911 to 1924, attending the local Public School.

The town has continued to develop. Its streets were macadamised in the early twentieth century. A reticulated water supply was established in 1922 and electricity illuminated its main streets from 1925, replacing the gas street lamps which had functioned since 1889. By the 1920s, Bowral had public parks, a major sports centre and a greyhound racing track. In 1935 it was the first town in the Southern Highlands to have a sewerage system installed.

The eminent cricketer Donald Bradman is not the only notable to have a connection to Bowral. Jimmy Barnes, lead singer of rock band, Cold Chisel, and his family have lived in Bowral on and off for many years. Theatre and TV comedian and actor Noelene Brown has lived for much of her adult life in Bowral. The proximity to Sydney for people like journalist, businesswoman and 2013 Australian of the Year, Ita Buttrose, makes Bowral particularly attractive. The gracious and up-market yet serene country lifestyle is clearly appealing to those with a busy lifestyle.

Today Bowral has smart galleries, restaurants, stores and guest houses. The general district is also noted for cattle breeding, but it is on the tourists who flock there, visiting the Bradman Museum and the magnificent historic homes and buildings, that the economy depends. The Bong Bong Picnic Races draw a crowd in November each year and the annual September Tulip Festival, boasting over 100,000 blooms, attracts visitors nationally and even internationally. Nearby Fitzroy Falls and Wombeyan Caves are also popular tourist attractions. By 2020, the population of Bowral had reached around 13,600.

Today the Blue Mountains is World Heritage listed and is in easy reach of Sydney by rail or car. The number of bushwalks of different levels of difficulty are a great attraction to visitors. The population of the area in 2020 was 79,400.

BROKEN HILL

The town of Broken Hill, 935 kilometres west of Sydney, and its vast surrounding area (including Menindee and Silverton), had been home to the *Barkindji* people for millennia when the explorer-surveyor, Major Thomas Mitchell (1792–1855), came to the area in 1835. The obsessive search for the non-existent 'inland sea' brought the explorer Charles Sturt (1795–1869) there in 1844 and pastoralists followed with their flocks of sheep. The *Barkindji* were nearly destroyed by the loss of land and water, by conflict with early settlers and by introduced diseases.

The unique quality of the area was not established until September 1883 when a station hand, Charles Rasp, found silver and lead and formed a seven-man syndicate with workers on the same station. Two years later, the Broken Hill Propriety Company Limited (BHP) was formed and the basis for one of the nation's richest companies commenced. Although the area was hampered by its distance from major centres, the company made good profits. The huge silver deposits in particular attracted overseas capital and a fever akin to that accompanying the goldrushes ensued. Stores, shacks, sheds, hotels, blacksmith shops and butcheries were quickly erected, and a town was born. By the end of the 19th century, Broken Hill had attracted a multicultural community—people from Malta, China, Italy, Greece, Yugoslavia, Afghanistan and Cornwall in England.

The wealth of Broken Hill led to the first train arriving very quickly, in 1888, the same year it was proclaimed a municipality. By 1907, it was the second largest settlement in the state, second only to Sydney.

As in mining communities worldwide, miners are a particular kind. They work in some of the most challenging conditions and have become known for their militancy. In 1909, miners abortively struck for better wages and working hours. In 1919 to 1920, they went on strike for a gruelling 18 months and this time had success in their demands for an eight-hour working day and collective bargaining.

During the First World War, a most astonishing local 'war' took place with an attack by two men flying the Turkish flag. On 1 January 1915, a train carrying picnickers was heading to Silverton when it was fired upon, killing four people and wounding seven in what was probably a private war against the British Empire. That evening, vengeful locals burned down the German Club in retaliation.

By 1927, Broken Hill was linked to Sydney by rail although its sense of being closer to Adelaide has persisted. At the end of the Great Depression of the 1930s, which struck Broken Hill severely, BHP withdrew, although some other mining companies, such as Perilya Ltd, remained. A munitions annexe constructed during the Second World War alleviated some of the effects of this withdrawal for locals. Many miners then became contractors to the remaining mining companies. In the mid-1950s, the isolation of local children was alleviated when the Broken Hill School of the Air opened.

At its height in 1929, the population of Broken Hill was 35,000, but in 2019, it had dropped to about 17,450. It is located in an environment that seems quintessentially 'outback'—bordered by desert, semi-arid and located in a vast flat landscape, the horizon so distant that, in the words of one of the nation's eminent poets, Kenneth Slessor, 'you walk on the sky's beach' in his poem South Country. It is this natural phenomenon and its history that brings people to Broken Hill. Artists come for the light, filmmakers for the vastness, scientists for the fauna, and, on those rare occasions when it rains, for the astonishing flora that brings the area to life.

The town has over thirty art galleries housing works of many renowned Australian artists, but in particular those of a group of five artists, formed in 1973, known as the 'Brushmen of the Bush': Pro Hart, Jack Absalom, Eric Minchin, John Pickup and Hugh Schulz. They based themselves there, raising money for various charities through the sale of their creations. Pro Hart (1928–2006) was a local boy and a miner turned painter while the author and adventurer Jack Absalom (1927–2019), born in Port Augusta, also worked in the Broken Hill Mines before deciding that he could and would paint. In 2002, the Living Desert Sanctuary opened, taking in the town's 'Sculpture Symposium'.

The 1971 movie *Wake in Fright* was filmed in the Broken Hill and Silverton areas, taking advantage of the environment. It was followed by several others including cult favourites *Mad Max II* (there's a museum to the film in Silverton) and *Priscilla, Queen of the Desert* which has a memorable scene in what was then Mario's Palace, now the Palace Hotel, in Broken Hill. Much-loved Australian actor, Chips Rafferty (1909–1971), was born at Broken Hill in 1909. In his films, Rafferty presented what was often seen as the typical Australian: laid back, direct and rugged. Equally famous is June Mary Gough, born in Broken Hill and better known for the name she adopted to celebrate her town of origin and the financial support the town people provided to help with her career—June 'Bronhill' (1929–2005). Bronhill sang with the Australian Opera, the Victorian State Opera, the State Opera of South Australia and at the Sadler's Wells Theatre in London. She received an OBE for her services to the performing arts.

In 2015, Broken Hill became the first city in the nation to be awarded National Heritage status.

DUBBO

Dubbo is located on the Macquarie River, by road roughly 400 kilometres north-west of Sydney. Like so many western NSW towns, it is on the traditional lands of the *Wiradjuri* people.

The first European settler in the area was Robert Venour Dulhunty (1803–1854) who arrived after 1829 and chose grazing land which he named 'Dubbo'. It is thought to be named for a *Wiradjuri* word 'Thurro' meaning red cap. Dulhunty eventually grazed his sheep on 80,000 acres in the area. However, he did not live there but dwelt in style at Emu Plains while his convict and itinerant labourers cared for his flocks. It was not until 1847 when free convict labour was withdrawn that he ceased to be an absentee landlord and moved his family to his Dubbo homestead.

Slowly the village grew. By the late 1840s there was a police station and lock-up, its improved version later to hold the infamous bushranger Johnny Dunn (1846–1866), a member of the notorious Frank Gardiner Gang that included Ben Hall and John Gilbert. In addition, a basic courthouse, a post office, an inn and a general store were opened. In the 1850s, churches and schools were built, while the 1860s saw the appearance of a newspaper, bank and hospital. Jean Emile de Bouillon Serisier, who had founded the first general store in Dubbo, also established a vineyard which by the 1870s was one of the colony's largest.

The town continued to expand with the mining of coal, chalk, copper and precious stones. As with so many country towns, the arrival of the railway in 1881 was a significant spur to its growth.

Thomas Alexander Browne (1826–1915) was a police magistrate in Dubbo from 1881 to 1884. While there, and under the pseudonym 'Rolf Boldrewood', he wrote what is arguably one of the best known early Australian novels, *Robbery Under Arms*. Cricketer Glenn McGrath, noted for the astonishing number of 563 Test wickets taken, was born in Dubbo in 1970.

Dubbo services an area known for wool and wheat production. But it also produces timber, fruit and vegetables. The town also has an abattoir, the largest meat processing plant in the country, along with a flour mill and sawmills. Dubbo is famous today for Taronga Western Plains Zoo, which uses moats and ditches with discrete electric fences to allow animals the sense of being free. Like so many NSW country centres and towns, Dubbo's architecture is a combination of Victorian and Federation styles. The Commercial Hotel was designed by architect Hilley using local sandstone. The old Dubbo Gaol, closed in 1966, was also constructed using local sandstone. It remains as a reminder to its past when eight men went to the gallows there. The old Commercial Bank has had a permanent conservation order placed on the building because of its importance to the state's environmental heritage.

Visitors are also attracted to the town because of the nearby Wellington Caves and Warrumbungle National Park. Warrumbungle is an Aboriginal word from the *Kamilaroi* people, meaning 'crooked mountains'. In 2018, Dubbo's suburban population was 38,400 and the population of its statistical area was around 69,000.

LIGHTNING RIDGE

Lightning Ridge is one of the most remote towns in NSW, located in the state's north-west, 770 kilometres from Sydney. Its traditional custodians are the *Gamilaraay* (*Kamilaroi*) and *Yuwaalaraay* people. The Indigenous people were very aware of the wonderful stones to be found in the area and they featured in Dreamtime stories. Although traditionally they did not mine the stones, when various missions closed in the 1930s many moved back into the town from surrounding areas and properties and became opal miners. About 22% of its population was Indigenous in 2016.

The first European settlement on the site was called Wallangulla, an Aboriginal dialect word meaning 'hidden fire stick', possibly a lightning bolt. The town became known as Lightning Ridge in the late 19th century, possibly from the ironstones that litter the area and attract lightning. Local myth has it that, in the 1870s, a local farmer or shepherd, his dog and all his sheep were struck by lightning and died. But it was not until after the First World War that 'Lightning Ridge' seems to have become the official name.

Its European history is largely a 20th century one, although there were known to be opals there by the 1870s. In 1901, it had its first registered miner, Jack Murray, and a year later a professional miner, Charles Nettleton, sank a shaft and discovered the much-prized opals for which the area became renowned. This led to an opal rush and by 1909, there were 1,200 miners in the area. Shortly thereafter it had a hotel, post office, school and church. In 1914, the 11th branch of the Bush Nursing Association was established there in a three-room cottage.

The task of opal-mining was difficult. Until the 1960s, it was manual work, using hand-windlasses and oxhide buckets. It was usually a two-man job, with one man up-top and one underground. Some fortunes were made, others quickly lost. Most managed to make a bare living. The lifestyle was harsh but also attractive, partly because of the thrill of the possibility of great wealth. It was also a lifestyle that provided independence.

The town became multicultural very quickly. Opals and the possibility of 'getting-rich-quick' attracted prospectors from around the world. There were already Germans living at nearby White Cliffs. Recognising the rarity of the black opals the area yielded, they sent samples to what was the gem-cutting capital of the world, Idar Oberstein, in the German Rhineland. More Germans arrived and settled in Lightning Ridge, bringing with them their knowledge of cutting and polishing valuable stones. Indian vendors and

Chinese greengrocers provided the necessities of life to the growing town.

During the Great Depression of the 1930s, the town retained its population due to a government initiative: miners were paid a shilling a foot to sink shafts. Since then the population has varied. The 1940s and 1950s were very calm periods, but in the 1960s, a group of graziers sank a bore which allowed miners to wash the opal dirt and, as a result, output increased. One of the area's many opal fields, Coocoran Lakes, opened in the 1930s and was the site of a renewed rush in the 1980s and 1990s. It produces 80% of the Ridge's black opals.

As well as attracting opal miners, Lightning Ridge is a palaeontologist's delight. Remnants of dinosaurs and mammal ancestors have been found in the surrounding sandstone, which was once the floor of an inland sea. Miners have often assisted scientists in locating such singular and important fossils.

Today it remains a strange and eccentric town. Opals have meant that it shows signs of its wealth in its sophisticated shops and restaurants, for example. Yet it also has houses made from bottles and homes made in the underground mines to escape the extreme heat of the area. It remains one of the few places worldwide where the rare and valued black opals are found and mined. Its population in 2016 was 2,284 people.

The Ridge's most famous son is Paul Hogan, who was born there in 1939. A comedian, actor and screenwriter, Hogan made his international fame in *Crocodile Dundee*. In 1985 he was named Australian of the Year and in 1986 was made a Member of the Order of Australia.

LISMORE

Lismore is a city on the Richmond River, about 40 kilometres from the ocean and 738 kilometres north of Sydney. The local *Widjabul* people of the *Bundjalung* nation had successfully occupied the area from rainforest to the coast. As with so many frontier situations, inter-racial conflict ensued and there were a number of massacres of Indigenous people. Up to 100 were killed at nearby Evans Head in the 1840s.

In 1828, Captain John Rous in the frigate *Rainbow*, travelled up the Richmond River and by 1840, there were reports of squatters in the Richmond Valley and of thousands of sheep grazing in the area. Scottish settlers, William and Jane Wilson, who arrived in the area in 1845, named their property 'Lismore', after a Scottish island they had visited on their honeymoon.

Shortly thereafter, the timber cutters arrived by sea, after crossing the bar at the entrance to the Richmond River. By the mid-1850s, a sawmill was operating and the town's first hotel was in business. In 1855, surveyor Frederick Peppercorne chose one of the paddocks in the

Wilsons' property of 'Lismore' to be the town. A year later the town was proclaimed and its first land sale took place, its first store opening 12 months after that. Following the 1861 Robertson Land Acts, as in so many NSW towns, settlers of moderate means arrived in the area. These Acts permitted free selection of crown land, removing the 'limits of location' decreed by Governor Ralph Darling (1772–1858) in 1836 and breaking the domination by 'squatters' of lands.

Throughout the 1860s and 1870s, churches and schools were built and a bank and newspaper established. In 1879, Lismore became a municipality. This expansion continued through the later 19th century with bridges, a post office and a hospital being built. Amenities such as gas lamps replaced the kerosene street lighting and water was supplied. Farmers were growing a range of foods (potatoes, maize, bananas); and dairying, after a shaky start, was successful once paspalum grass was introduced to the area. In 1881, the Colonial Sugar Refining Company established a crushing mill at nearby Broadwater to process the local sugarcane.

At the time of Federation in 1901, Lismore had a population of 4,542 people. Motor cars became more common and Trevan's bus service ran from Lismore to Casino. By the end of the First World War, the Lismore region had become a major centre for dairy production with Norco Co-operative Limited, an agricultural supply and marketing co-operative, having its headquarters based there.

During the Great Depression of the 1930s, the area was not as badly hit as some areas due to its food production, although a dreadful flood and the collapse of its local bank branch caused distress.

In 1946, Lismore was proclaimed a city. But at this time, its value as a port, reachable by the Richmond River, was declining. Many ships had been requisitioned during the Second World War and the North Coast Steam Navigation company went into liquidation in 1954.

The city was given a new lease of life and, in many ways, a new character following the 1973 Aquarius Festival at nearby Nimbin. People who came for the festival stayed to live in the Lismore area and the town became a centre for creative people with alternative lifestyles, sometimes known as 'hippies'. New local industries of artisans developed: painters, ceramists, woodworkers and designers. And there are now many galleries and theatres in the area. The rich soils continue to produce good crops, but it is now often organic foods that dominate the markets and restaurants.

In 1970, the area became an educational hub with the opening of a Teachers' College at Lismore, which in 1973 became the Northern Rivers College of Advanced Education. In 1989, the Northern Rivers branch of the University of New England was established. In 1993 this became Southern Cross University.

The area, with a population in 2018 of about 28,700, also has the attraction of being surrounded by national parks and nature reserves, including a koala reserve intended to preserve these much loved Australian marsupials.

Julian Assange, of Wikileak's fame, spent several formative years in Lismore, attending one of the locality's public schools from 1979–1983. At age 13 in 1984 Adam Gilchrist, an eminent Australian cricketer, moved to Lismore where his father still resided in 2020. One of the nation's best-loved artists, Margaret Olley, was born there in 1923.

MAITLAND

Many Indigenous peoples and nations live in the Lower Hunter area in which Maitland is situated, although the original inhabitants were probably the people of the *Wonnarua* nation who are represented today on the Mindaribba Local Aboriginal Land Council.

Lieutenant-Colonel William Paterson (1755–1810) of the NSW Corps, the early military regiment, explored the Hunter Valley in 1801 and named the future town's site 'Schanck's Forest Plains'. By 1810, cedar getters were occupying the area, calling their settlement 'The Camp'. The area was opened to settlement in 1818 and several emancipists were granted plots of land, quickly followed by free settlers. One of the ex-convicts was Molly Morgan who, as a secondary offender, had been sent to the penal settlement at Newcastle. When freed, she built the Angel Inn at what is now the centre of Maitland. In 1833, the town was proclaimed 'Maitland' and two years later, the areas of 'East Maitland' and 'West Maitland' were so named. Both East and West Maitland were proclaimed municipalities in 1863.

Slowly these townships developed. Government buildings were erected, bridges built, newspapers established, churches and schools erected. Many of these buildings, made mainly of local sandstone and cedar, remain in Maitland, making it a very gracious city. One example is the heritage-listed Maitland Gaol, first used in 1848 and closing its doors in 1998. It was a maximum-security gaol and saw its share of brutal punishment and riots. It housed, for example, the notorious criminals Darcy Dugan, George Savvas and Ivan Milat.

In 1857 Maitland was connected to Newcastle by rail. Its central situation in the Hunter Valley and its proximity to Morpeth, a shipping port, made it a centre for the area. The fertile flat lands surrounding it attracted free settlers, including Scottish, English, Irish and German.

Coal mining, for which the Hunter Valley area became so well known, commenced around West Maitland in the 1870s. Then J & A Brown commenced mining at Four Mile Creek near East Maitland. In 1886, Antarctic explorer and eminent geologist, Sir Edgeworth David (1858–1934) discovered good coal at Deep Creek in South Maitland, which led to the opening of the area and the discovery of the Greta coal-seam by the use of scientific methodology. By 1924, the Maitland coalfields were producing over 5 million tons of coal annually.

The city gradually expanded, with a steam tram operating from the turn of the century until shortly before the Second World War. In 1922, electricity was supplied to the town and from around 1920 until 1938, a speedway for motorcycles was built and races held in Maitland, allegedly a world first. In 1944, East and West Maitland, together with Morpeth, were combined with Maitland to form the one city of Maitland.

One of Maitland's consistent problems has been its propensity to flood, being situated on the Hunter River on vast floodplains. These floods have affected the environmental, human and social environment. The first recorded flood after European settlement was in 1819. In the 1832 flood, seven people died and in 1893, nine people lost their lives. Since European settlement, Maitland has experienced 15 major floods. The 1955 floods have become legendary. The flood height reached 12.10 metres and 14 people died. Levees, spillways and channels were constructed with the hope of avoiding a repetition. But in 1973, a further major flood occurred and in 2007, 2015 and 2020, storms again led to significant flooding in the area.

Many notable people have been associated with the town. Philanthropist Caroline Chisholm opened a home to shelter homeless female immigrants in a Maitland cottage in 1842. Les Darcy (1895–1917), national heavyweight boxing champion and folk hero, was born in Woodville, East Maitland, along with Ben Hall (1837–1865), bushranger, born in Maitland in 1837. He became a member of the notorious Frank Gardiner gang, but also became something of a popular figure as his violence was always against that figure of authority, the police force. John Bell, eminent actor, director and founder of the Bell Shakespeare Company, was born in Maitland in 1940. He has been recognised for his contribution to the theatre by numerous awards.

Ruth Cracknell (1925–2002), much loved actor of radio, theatre, film and TV, was born in Maitland, gracing Australian theatres and screens for over 55 years and was noted as both a comic and dramatic actor. Well-known political figure, Herbert Vere Evatt, was born in East Maitland in 1894. He became the third President of the United Nations General Assembly, 1948–1949, was Justice of the High Court of Australia, 1930–1940, and Chief Justice of the Supreme Court of New South Wales, 1960–1962.

Maitland is about 165 kilometres north of Sydney. It still has a local brickworks, many light industries and is a centre for tourism. The life of its open-cut mine is likely to be short-lived, given increasing environmental concerns about such mining, but the region is refashioning itself as a centre for wine and food production. In 2020, the population of Maitland was about 86,000.

NEWCASTLE

The *Awabakal*, *Worimi* and *Mindaribba* peoples are the traditional custodians of the land and waters of the present-day city of Newcastle on the Hunter River. Their presence was noted by early colonists and they mounted a strong defence against the occupation of their lands.

Possibly due to its reasonable proximity to the penal settlement at Port Jackson, Europeans went to the area, albeit somewhat haphazardly, from a very early date. In 1791, William and Mary Bryant with their small children and other escaped convicts, stole a longboat and got as far as Timor. On the way they rowed into a small creek near the present Newcastle. In 1796, a group of fishermen brought coal samples from the Hunter River back to Sydney and in 1797, Lieutenant John Shortland, returning from Port Stephens, noted good coal at Nobby's Head at the mouth of the river, which he named after Governor John Hunter.

Shortland's reports inspired action and good quantities of coal were first sold in Sydney and then, in 1799, sent to Bengal, probably the first export of a commodity from the colony. By 1801, a penal settlement was established at Coal River, and more Europeans arrived in the area after coal and cedar, both commodities vitally needed by the new colony. The official settlement was abandoned the same year. In 1804, however, and with the name Coal River changed to Newcastle in imitation of the English coal port of that name, Governor Philip King sent over 30

Irish prisoners there as a place for the harsh punishment of recidivists.

For almost two decades, the settlement remained a place of notoriously harsh punishment. Particularly cruel was the occupation of burning oyster shells, first from the Aboriginal middens near Stockton, to make lime used in the building of many of Sydney's structures. The lime was corrosive and affected the eyes and hands of the convicts, many of whom had already been subjected to whipping. Other convicts were sentenced to hard labour in coal mining, salt-making and timber-cutting.

In 1815, a more humane commandant, Captain James Wallis, was appointed and the town was graced with new streets and buildings such as a school, church and hospital. Work was also commenced on the breakwater. In 1822, the penal settlement closed and a year later the remaining convicts were sent to Port Macquarie. The period's horrors are presented in the 1844 novel, *Ralph Rashleigh*, written by ex-convict James Tucker.

The ending of Newcastle as a place of secondary punishment led to a new phase in the city's development, as it was now freed from the ignominy of its origins. New settlers arrived and it commenced its long history as an industrial and harbour city.

In 1828, the huge private firm, the Australian Agricultural Company, although better known for its work in the wool industry, gained a monopoly of the coal in the area and opened its colliery in 1831. The same year it opened the nation's first railway in Newcastle. Throughout the last few decades of the 19th century, the city saw the establishment of local industries and the building of substantial structures providing a rich heritage of Victorian architecture. By the turn of the century, its population was more than 50,000.

Newcastle's position as a port city and its mineral resources increased its wealth and standing. In addition to its basis for coal mining and transport, its importance was increased when Broken Hill Proprietary Limited (BHP) decided to open its steelworks there in 1911. With the steelworks up and running in 1915, the government made available roads and port amenities. The steelworks proved profitable, benefiting from the lack of German competition due to the prohibition on trading with the enemy during the First World War. The town now centred on steel production and during the Second World War this industry was significant in the war effort. However, in 1997, BHP announced its intention to abandon steel operations in Newcastle within three years. The city does, however, remain an important port for the shipment of coal.

Newcastle has faced a number of challenges over the years. In 1942, it was bombed by a Japanese submarine and in 2007, as a result of heavy storms, a bulk carrier ship ran aground at Nobby's Head. But possibly the event that caused the most damage, both physically and psychologically, was the 1989 earthquake in which 13 people died and 162 were injured. The damage to the city and its heritage buildings was considerable.

Today Newcastle is the second largest city in the state. It has had to be reinvigorated since BHP withdrew at the turn of the 21st century and has done so by modernising its foreshore with restaurants and a boardwalk to exploit the tourist potential of its beaches. The freeway has made the 168-kilometre journey from Sydney a relatively pleasant and easy trip. Among its notable sons and daughter are Jane Turner (born 1960), actor and comedian, and particularly known and popular for the TV series *Kath & Kim*. Also born in Newcastle were singer, composer and pianist, Daniel Johns, and Jennifer Hawkins, winner of Miss Universe 2004. Newcastle's population in 2019 had reached 450,000.

ORANGE

Two hundred and fifty kilometres west of Sydney is the important regional centre of Orange. The traditional custodians of the area in which Orange is located are the *Wiradjuri* people, the most populous Indigenous people in the state. Sites in the area indicate the long association of the *Wiradjuri* with the land for which they care and which is their spiritual and physical home.

The site of Orange was visited by a number of surveyors and explorers during the early part of the

19th century. In 1823, for example, the surveyor and engineer Lieutenant Percy Simpson (1789–1879) went through the area on his way to Wellington. His companion was John Blackman and the name of the first settlement was 'Blackman's Swamp'. But it was not until 1829 that the name 'Orange' appears as a village on maps. It is thought to have been named by Sir Thomas Mitchell (1792–1855) in recognition of the Prince of Orange with whom he had served during the Peninsular Wars (1807–1814). The Indigenous connection is maintained, however, in the naming of the mountain to the west of Orange: Mount Canobolas meaning 'twin heads'.

The soil was fertile and settlers quickly purchased and sub-divided their areas, leasing to tenants. By 1845, a village to the north-east of Orange had a number of inns, a blacksmith, a wheelwright, two stores, a tannery and a flour mill. It also had a local medical practitioner. Orange itself had a number of slab and bark huts, some of them administrative buildings, but it was not until the 1861 Robertson Land Acts that the area started to expand. Settlers took up the good land avidly and, by 1880, it was one of the major wheat producing areas in the state. During the 1880s, orchards were also established with great success.

It was not only the rich soil that attracted people to the area. In 1851, gold was discovered at nearby Ophir. New goldfields were found to the south and west of

Orange and the town population increased, sometimes through new businesses, at other times through itinerants and occasionally by disappointed miners who returned to Orange as settlers. In 1860, the town became a municipality. Cobb & Co. coaches ran through Orange from Bathurst to Forbes on the way to the goldfields and in 1877, the railway reached the town. Orange then became a railhead for goods and produce for export but also for goods moving to towns further inland.

Gradually services were provided for the population of Orange. A gas company was established in 1877, water was provided in 1890, a sewerage system was completed in 1919 and, in 1923, electric lights illuminated the streets, replacing gas lights. So important was the location that it was one of the towns considered as a possible national capital at the time of Federation. In 1946 it was proclaimed a city.

Today Orange is a very graceful town with tree-lined avenues and many Federation houses and exceptional parks. It has a wonderful show of autumn colours, although its winters are very cold, between June and August having lows of between 1 and 2 degrees. It often snows and locals will ask one another if 'the old man has his hat on', a reference to Mount Canobolas. It remains renowned for its fruit growing and, by 1970, was producing more than half the state's supply of apples. Although 'Orange', it has not produced citrus; but, in addition to apples, it produces olives, grapes and berries. It has more recently established vineyards and the district now has over 40 of these. In 2020, it had a suburban population of about 38,800.

A number of well-known Australians are associated with Orange, possibly the best-known being Andrew Barton (Banjo) Paterson who, among his many writings, penned 'Waltzing Matilda'. He was born in 1864 in the home of John Templer, 'Narrambla', 5 kilometres from Orange. Another of Australia's poets, Kenneth Slessor, was born there in 1901, although the family moved shortly thereafter to Sydney. Also born in Orange in 1914 was Frederick Hanson, a former Commissioner of the NSW Police Force.

WAGGA WAGGA

Wagga Wagga is situated in the traditional lands of the *Wiradjuri* people and is in south-west NSW, about 460 kilometres from Sydney. The area was known to Indigenous people for its rich flora and fauna, especially birds, and its rivers and streams. This heritage is recognised in the name of the town and of the river on which it is situated. 'Wagga Wagga' indicates a place where many crows gather and 'Murrumbidgee', the name of the river, means 'big water'.

Squatters moved into the area in the 1820s and, in December 1829, Captain Charles Sturt journeyed from Gundagai down the Murrumbidgee River, passing through the site of the future Wagga Wagga. Settlement swiftly followed.

In the 1850s and 1860s, stores, hotels, churches and banks were established. In 1858, the first newspaper was started, the *Wagga Wagga Express*, and is still in circulation today. In 1860, the first public school under the national system was built. Until 1862, the river had to be crossed by punts, but in that year, a new bridge was opened. The town started to attract professionals, such as medical practitioners and solicitors. This was also a period in which Frank Gardiner and his gang of bushrangers roamed the area.

Possibly the most infamous event in early Wagga Wagga was a case of perjury. In 1868, a butcher, Tom Castro, claimed to be Sir Roger Tichbourne, heir to estates in England. Tichbourne had, it was believed, drowned when the ship he was travelling in disappeared. With his family, Castro went to England to make good his claim. It was not until 1874 that his claim was proved false. For his troubles, he was sentenced to 14 years imprisonment. The case attracted such international notoriety that when Mark Twain came to Australia, he specifically visited Wagga Wagga.

In 1870, the town was gazetted as a municipality. At that stage it had a population of about 1,000. It was also the year of a big flood, a problem that affected many NSW towns situated as they were on rivers and flood plains. There had already been considerable flooding on the Murrumbidgee in 1852–1853.

By 1881, with the expansion of the railway system, the population had grown to around 4,000, and gas lighting was installed throughout the streets of in the same year. The town continued to grow, with Federation buildings such as the Court House built in 1903. Electricity reached the town in 1922 and, in 1946, it was declared a city.

Today, Wagga Wagga is a service centre for the fertile Riverina district of south-western NSW, known for its wheat, cattle, and sheep. It is also a commercial and administrative centre. Secondary industries include timber and flour mills, dairy-products factories and engineering works. It is a beautiful city with elegant buildings and exceptional galleries and parks. It is home to one of the campuses of Charles Sturt University, whose history dates back to the establishment of the Bathurst Experiment Farm. After a series of reincarnations (Teachers College, College of Advanced Education), it was incorporated in 1989.

Wagga Wagga has a number of notable people associated with its history. William Farrer, whose research into cross-breeding of wheat types to produce strains suitable to Australia, conducted many of his experiments at the Experimental Farm at Wagga Wagga. Sir Thomas Blamey (1884–1951), deputy to the American General Douglas MacArthur, was born at Lake Albert near Wagga Wagga in 1884. He attended Wagga Wagga Superior School where he was later a pupil-teacher. Blamey became Commander-in-Chief of the Australian forces and the nation's first Field Marshall. When he was eight years old, cricketer Mark Taylor's family moved to Wagga Wagga where he attended school and played cricket for the Lake Albert Cricket Club. Later in life, when about to surpass Bradman's Test record, Taylor famously closed his innings to improve his team's chances of winning. Another cricketer, Michael Slater, who also played test cricket for Australia, was born and raised in Wagga Wagga. Lex Marinos, actor, broadcaster, writer and director, was born in Wagga Wagga into a family of Greek café-owners. He was awarded an Order of Australia for services to the performing arts. Steve Mortimer, a rugby league halfback for Australia, was also born in Wagga Wagga.

While most of Wagga Wagga's population was born in Australia, it also has residents born in China, India, New Zealand and Germany. In 2019, its city population reached 66,000.

WOLLONGONG

Wollongong, the third largest city in the state, covers a long coastal strip of 85 kilometres south of Sydney. It is situated on the traditional lands of the *Wodi Wodi* people who are part of the *Dharawal* (*Tharawal*) nation. The area is threaded with walking tracks that the *Wodi Wodi* travelled, reflected in songlines. The lakes and rivers provided abundant food and even inland there were small fish, eels and yabbies to be caught. The name 'Wollongong' is thought to come from the *Dharawal* language, although its meaning is debated. One interpretation is 'five islands/clouds', another is that it means 'ground near water', yet another that it means 'sound of the sea'. The town is affectionately known as the 'Gong'.

In 1770, Captain James Cook had attempted to land in the Illawarra area in which Wollongong is situated but was prevented by heavy seas. In 1796, George Bass and Matthew Flinders made their historic voyage in the rowboat *Tom Thumb*, down the south coast from Port Jackson. A year later, the area was traversed on foot by the ill-fated crew of the *Sydney Cove* on their epic journey along the coast to Port Jackson. After being shipwrecked on an island to the north of Tasmania, they took to their longboat and headed north, only to be wrecked again on the mainland at the northern end of what is now Ninety Mile Beach, about 260 kilometres north of Melbourne. The three survivors reported coal in the area and George Bass (1771–1803) made a further trip to the area to verify this.

Possibly due to its proximity to the Port Jackson settlement, the area was investigated by a number of different people. In the early part of the 19th century, cattle were shipped there, explorers and scientists visited the area and cedar cutters were illegally felling trees and shipping the timber to Sydney. In 1815, some of the traditional custodians reportedly led European settlers and their cattle down the escarpment and into the area. This may well have been the party of Charles Throsby, who had noted the area, created a track for his cattle and set up a hut in what is now the centre of Wollongong.

The town of Wollongong was more clearly defined when the soldiers' barracks was moved there in 1829 to address the general lawlessness of the area and the confrontations with the *Wodi Wodi* people. The next three decades saw the town take shape with churches, hotels, a government school built, and the commencement of a local newspaper. When the harbour was improved and paths down the escarpment made the area more accessible, Wollongong kept expanding. It became a town in 1843 and a municipality in 1859.

Mid-century, cedar cutting and grazing were declining and being replaced by dairying as the local staple activity. But it was coalmining in the hinterland that really opened the area; and the colonial demand for coal was voracious. Most factories depended on coal, as did railways and steamships. Port Kembla, a few kilometres south of Wollongong, became the centre for its shipment in 1883. The completion of the railway line down the south coast in 1888 meant that Wollongong and all its produce was connected to Sydney and all centres between.

Port Kembla became a centre for smelting and metal manufacturing by the end of the First World War. When Cecil Hoskins (1889–1971) moved the family's Iron and Steelworks to Port Kembla from Lithgow, the area was given a further boost. In 1935, Broken Hill Proprietary (BHP) purchased the works, which established Greater Wollongong as a large-scale industrial area. In 1947, Wollongong was amalgamated with other municipalities to form the City of Wollongong, extending for 50 kilometres along the coast.

In the latter part of the 20th century, however, steel production and coal mining declined. However, the area's economic activities now included construction and manufacturing of metallurgical products plus an active fishing fleet.

The city has become an education hub with many schools, TAFE colleges and the University of Wollongong (UOW) established 1975, developing from a division of the NSW University of Technology (1951). At first, the UOW focused on producing engineers and metallurgists for the local steel industry. It now offers a wide range of courses in different disciplines and education has become a major employer in Wollongong.

The current population is very multicultural. In 2016, 21.5% were born overseas compared to 11.2% for the regional average. The places of origin include the UK, China, North Macedonia, Italy, New Zealand, India, Germany the Philippines, Vietnam and countries of the former Yugoslavia. In 2019, Wollongong's population was 217,000.

Many notable people from the worlds of politics, arts, the media and sports (particularly rugby league and soccer) have had a close relationship with Wollongong. The 27th Governor-General of Australia, His Excellency General the Honourable David John Hurley AC DSC (retired), was born (in 1953) and educated in Wollongong, as was Anthony Warlow, born in 1961, star of opera and musical comedy.

5. *Agricultural and Pastoral Industry*

Early farms were established by the colonial government to feed the inhabitants and occupy the convicts. As the history professor, Grace Karskens, has pointed out, the supplies sent with the First Fleet reflect this: tools, seeds and plants were all indicative of a vision of a self-sufficient colony based on subsistence farming; no commerce, no treasury. The first government farms, however, suffered from a critical lack of expertise and understanding of their new environment. Those convicted of urban crimes did not make the best farmers. Tools intended for English soils and trees were quickly blunted and the first crop failed. Many of the few animals Governor Arthur Phillip brought with him on the First Fleet either died or were lost in the bush. However, Phillip persisted with the establishment of government farms, felling and clearing areas with convict labour and, slowly, the amount of produce from government farms increased, as did the stock being raised.

Once grants of land, seeds and labour were made to officers, both civil and military, these independent farmers were no more successful. Captain Watkin Tench, for example, complained of the poor soil and the resulting failure of his potato and wheat crops. This general pattern of an inability to understand and accommodate to the local environment was a frequent story in much of the history of early NSW. Most settlers and squatters brought with them the traditions of British agriculture, if they had any knowledge—many early colonists had little or no knowledge of agriculture. They did not understand the local soils or harsh climate and so they cleared land and overgrazed it. After devastating Hawkesbury floods in 1806, soon after his arrival to the colony, Governor William Bligh organised the distribution of flood relief and promised settlers that the government stores would buy their crop after the next harvest.

The poet, Dorothea Mackellar (1885–1968), described this land as one of 'drought and flooding rains' in her poem, 'My Country', published in 1908. The early settlers did not yet have knowledge of the climatic swings captured by Mackellar, nor of the devastation that bushfires could bring, and the introduction of cloven-hoofed animals unfortunately compacted the soils. In both June and August 1809, for example, the Hawkesbury River again flooded the surrounding area causing major destruction to crops and stock. A correspondent of the *Sydney Gazette* described the scene: 'All is uncertainty and dread, all terror and astonishment'. They also had to deal with caterpillar plagues that caused devastation to crops from 1799 onwards.

There were some positive signs, however. The first independent agricultural venture was at Experiment Farm at Rose Hill, 23 kilometres west of Sydney's CBD. Ex-convict James Ruse (1760–1837), who actually came from a farming background, received the first land grant in the colony, an amount of 30 acres (12 hectares) and produced grain seed which was then used productively. This tiny beginning led the way for Australia to become one of the world's most important agricultural nations. Once land was granted in areas where the soil was more fertile, such as Parramatta, there was improvement in agriculture. However, lack of transport to these areas, combined with inappropriate farming methods, reduced viability

By the end of Macquarie's tenure in 1821, less than 750,000 acres (300,000 hectares) of land had been granted to convicts, emancipists, military and civil officials, and free settlers. Once a way had been found over the Blue Mountains in 1813, settlement was no longer confined to the Cumberland Plain and the coastal areas north and south of Sydney, although it was some time before farmers and pastoralists availed themselves of this opportunity for expansion. These people were the founders of the colony's rural industry and the providers of food for its inhabitants.

Those who were not impressed with life as small-scale farmers left their land, providing larger proprietors with an opportunity to take advantage of the situation. People like the Reverend Samuel Marsden (1776–1838) ruthlessly pursued the acquisition of land by purchasing these early grants. One of the greatest success stories was that of Alexander Berry and his 'Coolangatta Estate', established on the rich alluvial soils of the NSW south coast. Berry, like a number of early free settlers, fancied himself as a squire and, with the help of partners and family, built up a landed empire based on an initial 10,000-acre (4,050 hectares) land grant in 1822. Berry had quadrupled his holdings by 1863, providing himself not only with land and its produce but with lifestyle and status. The Estate was soon exporting horses to India, cedar to Europe and cattle, tobacco, cheese, potatoes and wheat to Sydney. As land passed from small grants intended to create a self-sufficient agricultural society, the nature of the colony changed. Agriculture became commercial.

Through the system of land grants, many settlers and ex-convicts became pastoralists, grazing sheep and sending their fleeces to England. The colony's 'ride on the sheep's back' commenced with the entrepreneurial John Macarthur, who imported merino sheep from South Africa. These he cross-bred with fat-tailed meat-producing sheep, generating a fine wool which was met with delight by woollen goods manufactories in England. His wife Elizabeth played an important role after John's enforced departure for England in 1809. She was responsible for the care of the merino flocks, and for eight years successfully managed the Camden Park estate where she took charge of its convict labourers, assisted by her nephew, Hannibal Macarthur.

'Remittance men', sent to the colonies and paid to stay there by their families, became gentleman farmers. Others, who were less than competent at home, came to NSW to make their personal fortunes. The Blaxlands, Gregory and John, both farmers who had fallen on hard times in Kent, took advantage of the offer of passage, land and labour to bring their families to New South Wales. They became pastoralists, but involved themselves in a range of commercial activities, some successful, many not.

As more settlers arrived, many with capital, cattle and particularly sheep stations developed on land outside the designated area for settlement, the 'limits of location' decreed by Governor Ralph Darling in 1826. These 'squatters' simply took (and eventually were allowed to lease) the lands on which their animals grazed. By 1840, the colony was producing over two million kilograms of wool annually with the wool industry's success generating personal wealth for many squatters and pastoralists.

After much argument, animosity and division, the 1846 Waste Lands Occupation Act and the 1847 Order-in-Council accepted the squatters' rights to land they had 'owned' by occupation. They were allowed leases, the right to purchase leased land and the renewal of leases, all on generous terms.

The 'squattocracy's' control of land and the power and position associated with it was challenged in NSW by the Robertson Land Acts of 1861. These Acts allowed settlers with little capital to select and purchase small areas of land intended for agriculture, and not to produce wool. The Act, introduced as The Alienation of Crown Lands Bill, proposed 320 acres (129 hectares) per farm at one pound per acre at auction. This led to a rush for land by both selectors and squatters. There was frequent abuse of the system with, for example, those with capital using agents to purchase land for them with the intent of increasing their holdings or on-selling lands at a good profit.

Agriculture did not need huge capital to get established. It could be small-scale and depended on family labour and assigned convicts. Pastoralists, conversely, needed greater capital investment. Their profits were greater as they not only exported wool but produced meat, sold stock and speculated in land sales. It became the pursuit of wealthy settlers, particularly merchants.

To improve local sheep stock by importing merinos, and petition for release from British import duties, local pastoralists formed the Agricultural Society of NSW in 1822. The Society held an annual fair at Parramatta to exhibit its members' produce.

The need to preserve food, particularly for excess livestock, was assisted in NSW by French engineer, Eugene Nicolle, and his committed backer, Thomas Mort, who was involved in a lengthy list of projects as an entrepreneur and financier. Nicolle spent much of his time working on refrigeration techniques and in 1867, with Mort's support at the renamed New South Wales Ice Company, Nicolle demonstrated that, using his machinery, food could be frozen for long periods, thawed, cooked and eaten. However, while their efforts had some success on trains, they were a failure on sea voyages. It fell to Andrew McIlwraith and Andrew McEacharn, both from Scotland, to develop a system which would prove successful and economic. In 1879, due to their efforts, the pioneering *Strathleven* left Sydney with a cargo of colonial meat and butter, bound for London via Melbourne.

The Australian Agricultural Company was established in 1824 by an Act of the British Parliament. Its purpose was broad: improve flocks of merino sheep for fine wool production, move into cattle farming, and develop crops for export such as tobacco and flax. By 1826 it held one million acres (400,000 hectares) in the Port Stephens area on the NSW coast. Settlers and stock followed and, by 1830, nearly 600 farms and gardens were established in the surrounding area, as well as 23 'stations' (large farms). This was in return for an initial capital investment of one million pounds.

What is significant about this early development is that market considerations were secondary to patronage and bureaucracy in the allocation of land. In addition, the later consolidation of land in the hands of wealthy pastoralists created a potential pool of labour. Early farmers not only provisioned the colony but employed convict and free labour.

Wheat proved to be a very successful commercial crop and machinery was being used in its harvesting by the 1890s. Its expansion had been advanced by the development of the railways. The depression of the 1890s had affected the price for wheat, but this was alleviated by two things. First, government assistance, in the form of leasing land to settlers at a small rent to allow for capital to go to improvements, was introduced by the government of George Reid (1845–1918), the fourth Prime Minister of Australia during 1904–05. Secondly, the world price for wheat increased. Between 1896 and 1906, the amount of land devoted to wheat doubled, and New South Wales became one of the leading international exporters of wheat. It was, however, affected by what has been called 'The Federation Drought', from 1895 to 1903, when extended drought caused many rivers to dry up. This affected crops, stock and river transport, the latter so important for the movement of goods to inland towns; and it led to greater focus on planning for irrigation.

From the late 19th century, various NSW government departments promoted Australian products, like wool and wheat, by means of brochures, booklets and posters. The overproduction of wheat worldwide at the outset of the Great Depression of the 1930s had its impact, but a series of crop failures in the USA diminished this and, by the late 1930s, Australian wheat was again receiving high prices.

Fruit growing and viticulture also have a long history in NSW. Governor Arthur Phillip obtained seeds and plants of fruit trees on the way from Rio de Janeiro and the

Cape of Good Hope. These were planted at Farm Cove in Sydney when he arrived, but with little initial success. One of the earliest successful viticulturalists was James Busby (1802–1871), a government employee with a land grant of 2,000 acres (800 hectares) in the Hunter River district that extends from 120 to 310 kilometres north of Sydney. He was knowledgeable about viticulture and published several books on the subject. As the population increased, settlers were both a market for fruit and suppliers of the same as they cultivated their own orchards and vineyards. Improvements in irrigation, canning and drying techniques all led to the industry's success.

As rural communities developed, agricultural societies were important for bringing them together and providing the necessary support in isolated settings. These have often been local, but the one which has been most responsible for bringing the bush to the city is Sydney's famous Royal Easter Show, which showcases rural skills, livestock and produce. This show commenced in 1822 but underwent a series of reincarnations until it was declared 'Royal' in 1891 by permission of Queen Victoria. By this time the Agricultural Society of NSW had expanded its show to include manufacturing and arts as being representative of wider rural pursuits.

Sheep farmers found that they needed assistance in their ventures, particularly in herding sheep. At first, Scottish sheep dogs, Collies, were imported but interbreeding throughout the 1800s, including with the native dog, the dingo—confirmed by DNA testing—resulted in better suited working dogs. In NSW interbreeding with dingoes eventually led to the Blue Heeler. The Hall family, on cattle stations in the upper Hunter Valley, needed a droving dog that could manage long distances through rugged bush and mountain ranges. The pastoralist Thomas Hall (1808–1870) crossed dogs used by drovers in Northumberland, England with dingoes, resulting in dogs that by 1840 were known as 'Hall's Heelers'. Only in 1870, after Hall's death, did the dogs become freely available and, in 1903, the 'Blue Heeler', or 'Australian Cattle Dog', was established. George Robertson, a Scot, also created a new breed, in the 1870s at 'Warrock Station' near Casterton in Victoria, and called his dogs 'kelpies', after the water spirit of Celtic folklore. The Australian Kelpie was recognised as an official breed in 1905. Farmers generally acknowledge the incredible competence of the breed as a working dog and its contribution to the success of their ventures.

Organisations such as the Country Women's Association (CWA) of NSW, formed in 1922, helped to develop better welfare and conditions for rural women and their families. Medical services also developed, such as the Bush Nursing Association of NSW, formed in 1911 on the initiative Lady Rachel Dudley (1868–1920), wife of the Australian Governor-General William Humble Ward, 2nd Earl of Dudley (1867–1932). It was disbanded in 1975 when the Health Commission took over management of the Bush Nursing Centres, with many being converted to Community Health Centres.

Another important step in medical assistance was the Royal Flying Doctor Service, founded in 1928 by the Reverend John Flynn (1880–1951), substantially improving health facilities and services in rural and remote areas.

Life on the land had problems. The 'soldier settlement scheme', instituted after the First World War, allocated blocks of land to returned servicemen. As with many of the land grants given to convicts and early settlers, little regard was given to the preparedness of these men for lives as farmers. Additionally, government organisation of the scheme was equally unsystematic. In Yenda in NSW, one soldier settler arrived with his family to find that none of the promised provisions were supplied. For many of these soldier settlers, life on the land was one of increasing debt until sadly many of them simply walked off their blocks.

In an example of innovation on the land, in 1916, Raimond Squire, a farmer from Quirindi, NSW, invented the spring tine drill cultivator, which increased the speed of soil cultivation.

One of the problems for the growing wool industry was to compress the product into handy units. In 1887, the manufacturer and inventor Christian Koerstz (1847–1930), a Dane, arrived in Sydney and formed a business partnership with Frederick Mason, a grain and produce merchant based in Sussex Street. Together, the two men developed improvements to the wool press, water pump and motor, as well as an improved rotary pump. The company achieved fame both at home and overseas. Koerstz's wool presses had evocative names such as 'Little Wonder' and 'Conqueror'. He established a factory at Pyrmont, Sydney, later expanding to Rosebery, where he produced a range of agricultural tools.

A further innovation important to the pastoral industry was shearing by machine. Early patents for such a machine in NSW were granted in 1868 and 1870. But the real honour goes to the inventor and wool grower Frederick Wolseley (1837–1899), who had interests in a number of NSW sheep properties. He developed a working powered shearing machine by 1868 and, with the contribution and modification of other interested parties, the new labour-saving shearing machine was successfully exhibited and adopted within a decade at a number of stations, although manual blades predominated for some time.

RURAL WORKERS

While cattle could look after themselves to some degree, sheep required tending and protecting. The role of the shepherd—mainly a 19th century phenomenon—was an important one. On sheep stations, their life was lonely and isolated. Accommodation for a few shepherds and a hutkeeper was usually in a 'wattle and daub' hut, in which a woven lattice of wooden strips, 'wattle', was 'daubed' with a sticky material, combining things like clay, animal dung and straw. In the daylight hours they were accompanied in their monotonous tasks by their dogs. During the 19th century and until the development of the kelpie, this was usually a collie dog and it was an occupation in which some did quite well.

Henry Burke arrived in NSW from Ireland in 1858. He worked for ten years as a shepherd on a property near Armidale in northern NSW, after which he selected land in nearby Salisbury Plains, calling his station 'Ballbyne'. When he died in 1915, his two sons inherited a successful 3,000-acre (1,200 hectares) merino and cattle station.

There were many occupations on rural properties, all essential to the success of the pastoral industry. Fence building and maintenance was critical. Post and rail fences were widespread, but in NSW the dry stone wall was common. Hedge fences were experimented with and the hawthorn, sweet briar and furze were grown and used as fences in NSW. One plant, introduced as a hedged fencing plant in the Hunter Valley, was the disastrous 'prickly pear', which was later declared a noxious weed. The Australian Agricultural Company, for its Warrah Estate on the Liverpool Plains, favoured imported wire fencing which, when used as wire netting, had the perceived advantage of excluding another introduced pest, the rabbit.

Many other rural workers helped comprise the backbone of the pastoral industry. Woolclassers on merino stations were part of the scene in NSW. Shearers were always essential and took on iconic status in the outback.

With their swags and 'billies' (cans for water that could be boiled on a fire), they moved from station to station, carrying out backbreaking work. The 'jackeroo', a generalised term for someone engaged in a variety of rural activities, was often a type of apprentice, learning all aspects of running a station. Stockmen and drovers, at first involved in a range of work, became known for their ability to manage herds, especially when droving or overlanding stock, often over vast distances.

DIFFICULTIES OF FARMING

As part of the acclimatisation movement in the colony, a range of flora and fauna was introduced. This was partly due to nostalgia for England and partly out of despair at the perceived poverty or peculiarity of local varieties. Foxes and rabbits are two such notable examples and their depredations or destruction of the land brought misery to both farmers and pastoralists. Rabbits were introduced by the First Fleet as a food source, but by the 1880s had become so prolific that landowners resorted to any means to eradicate them: trapping, poisoning, explosives, disease, rabbit-proof fencing. Bounties were set on rabbit scalps. One associated problem with many of these methods was that rural dwellers frequently depended on the rabbit for their basic food. In 1950, a virus called myxomatosis was introduced to combat the growing problem. At first it was very successful, but as rabbits became resistant to it, its initial success fell away. Rabbits remain a problem, competing with sheep for pasture, damaging vegetation and contributing to the decline of native animals and plants.

A further problem was, and is, that of finding sufficient water. For many scientists who considered the need for augmenting water supplies in a very dry environment, the idea of artesian bores was very attractive. The first native born NSW Government Meteorologist, Henry Russell (1836–1907) was convinced that much of the rainfall in the Darling River catchment area went underground. During the late 19th century, the river was a major transportation route with pastoralists of western NSW using it to send their wool by shallow-draft paddle steamer from river ports including Bourke and Wilcannia to the South Australian railheads at Morgan and Murray Bridge.

In the 1880s, cattle farmers explored Russell's idea and, particularly in north-western NSW, commenced boring for artesian water. By the commencement of the 20th century, there were 158 such bores in NSW. Windmills were also in use with varied effectiveness, many being improvised by landowners.

FARMING IN NSW TODAY

The grain production areas of New South Wales are mainly located in the slopes and plains regions to the west of the Great Dividing Range and on the northern coastal floodplains to the east of it. In both regions the dominant winter crop is wheat with canola, barley, triticale and a variety of winter pulses including chickpea, lupin, faba bean and lentil. In the north, summer crops consist principally of sorghum, cotton, maize, mungbean, sunflower and soybean. Irrigation has enabled the cultivation of many grain crops in both the north and south of the state.

While the north coast of NSW produces most of Australia's soybean crop, sugar cane is grown on the coast. The coastal region usually receives sufficient rainfall to allow double cropping of summer and winter grains or grain production in rotation with pastures or fodder crops.

6. *Politics*

From its inception, the colony of New South Wales had a central government that controlled planning and provisioning. The early governors of New South Wales had virtually unfettered official powers in the colony. They were Captains-General and Governors-in-Chief and their actions were not initially limited by any council. They appointed officials, could order punishments for misdemeanours, institute martial law, grant land and disburse public monies. Essentially, they exerted legislative, executive, judicial and administrative control. They were answerable to the British Government and had to act within the terms of their commissions, but distance could make that problematic. As the colony developed and settlers asserted themselves, however, the governors found that they were serving two masters, local and imperial—a difficult task.

The developing colony of NSW offered to different groups the opportunity to exploit the distance from England and challenge the political power of the governors.

This could be done by building up a powerbase, such as the New South Wales Corps, which exploited periods in which they controlled the colony in the absence of a governor. These men built fortunes based on illegal trade. When Governor William Bligh (1754–1817) attempted to curb their excesses, they challenged and arrested him—on 26 January 1808, although the day at that time probably had little significance—and had him removed from office in what has become known as the 'Rum Rebellion'. That the Corps was disbanded, and Bligh exonerated, does not diminish the significance of local power bases. A much later governor, Sir George Gipps (1790–1847), met a similar challenge when he attempted to curb the growing power of the Pastoral Association. Their influence was based on connections in Britain and not on military power.

One of the issues troubling the developing political scene—and there were many—was the role that ex-convicts could play, particularly while convicts were still being transported to the colony. This was played out in the 'exclusives versus emancipist' debate with the former supported by conservative free settlers, officials, and military officers, and the latter by former convicts, demanding full civil rights. The liberal governor, Richard Bourke, replaced military personnel as jurymen in criminal cases with citizens—including ex-convicts who met the property test to sit on such juries.

From 1823, the governor had a council of appointees— that is, appointed in England—of five men, extended in number over time. The first partly elected NSW Legislative Council met in 1843. Two-thirds of its members were elected, and one-third appointed by the governor. Ex-convicts who met the qualification were allowed both to stand for and vote in this election. Once transportation finished, and gold was discovered near Bathurst in 1851, the position of New South Wales as an independent entity changed.

The Constitution of NSW has an interesting history. In 1853, under the leadership of William Charles Wentworth—the son of Dr D'Arcy Wentworth and a convict, Catherine Crowley—a clause involving an Upper House not unlike the British House of Lords was proposed by Wentworth. This House would be the domain of the important and wealthy who would hold the position for life. At a public meeting, he was condemned for trying to create a 'Bunyip Aristocracy' and the offensive clauses were removed from the proposal. By 1856, a bicameral legislature was introduced with an elected Assembly and an appointed Council.

In 1850, the Port Phillip settlement on the southern end of NSW became a separate colony, Victoria, through the Australian Colonies Government Act. The Act also enfranchised male citizens over 21 years of age with landholdings valued at 100 pounds and householders whose dwelling had an annual value of 10 pounds— aimed at including squatters on pastoral leases as well as free settler tradesmen.

The secret ballot was introduced in NSW in 1858. In 1893, 'plural voting' whereby a man could vote both where he lived and where he held property, was abolished and 'one man one vote' was achieved. These changes created a comparatively progressive liberal democratic parliamentary system. At first, election was on a simple majority system. But in the decade from 1910, this was modified by holding a second ballot between the two most successful candidates.

WOMEN IN POLITICS

Despite the numerous competent women in various fields of endeavour, the idea of women running a country or even being allowed to vote would have invoked hearty 19th century ridicule. During the 1880s women began forming rights groups, including the Women's Christian Temperance Union, the Women's Suffrage Society, and the Women's Suffrage League, all designed to promote women's suffrage. In fact, women could not be lawyers or members of Parliament and it was not unusual for them to receive half the male wage rate for any work. When women married, all their possessions were owned by their husband, and a man could abandon his wife and children, leaving them in poverty. In 1888, the poet and author Louisa Lawson (1848–1920), born in Gulgong, NSW, started a newspaper for women in NSW. She employed only women and pushed for women's rights.

Women in NSW were enfranchised in 1902, but it was not until 1918 that women could nominate for the NSW Legislative Assembly and, in 1925, the feminist Millicent Preston Stanley (1833–1955) was the first woman elected to that body. It was 1926 before women could be appointed to the NSW Legislative Council. The process has been slow, but since that time an increasing number of women have been involved as members of parliament or as leaders of their parties. In 1981, Franca Arena became the first woman from a non-English speaking background to be elected to the NSW Parliament and in 2003, Linda Burney was the first Indigenous woman to be elected to the NSW Legislature. In 2001, the state had its first female Governor, Professor the Hon Dame Marie Bashir AD CVO, and in 2009, its first female Premier, Kristina Keneally. The first elected female Premier was Gladys Berejiklian in 2019, although she had been Premier since January 2017. In mid-2019, the NSW Legislative Council had 12 of 42 (29%) members who were women, while 33 of 93 (35%) Members of the Legislative Assembly were women.

ROLE OF NSW IN CREATING THE COMMONWEALTH/FEDERATION

The call for a united nation was proposed as early as 1854 in the *Sydney Morning Herald* newspaper. In 1857, a Select Committee of the New South Wales Legislative Council considered the need for Federation, while accepting that state rivalries would possibly oppose such a move. This proved to be a valid assessment and the move for unity was countered many times by states' self-interest. The driving positive factor, however, was the need for tariff uniformity and the recognition of the need for a unified defence system.

In November 1883, a convention was held in Sydney. It was attended by representatives of the seven colonies—and Fiji. Less than a year later, this body presented a request to the Crown asking for a Federal Council Act. This had been opposed by New South Wales and by the major proponent of Federation, Sir Henry Parkes (1815–1896), who considered that a federal council would not assist the progress. The council was established but lasted less than 15 years.

Parkes convened the Federation Conference of February 1890, taking the first steps towards Federation. In May he and three other member delegates were appointed to the Sydney 1891 National Australasian Convention. When it met on 2nd March 1891, Parkes was appointed as its president. The group then set about debating of a series of resolutions proposed by Parkes with a view to laying down some guiding principles. It was at this convention that the first draft of a bill to constitute the Commonwealth of Australia was framed, with Parkes proposing the name of 'Commonwealth of Australia' for the new nation.

From 1895 to 1896, the different colonial parliaments, including Western Australia, but not at this stage

Queensland, passed the Enabling Acts that could lead to unification. As a result, a 'People's Federal Convention' was held at Bathurst, New South Wales, in November 1896. This set the date for the election of federal representatives and led to discussions on different aspects of a working federation, such as finance and judiciary. A resulting Bill was put to popular vote twice. The first time, NSW voters were in favour, but the majority was insufficient. On the second occasion, NSW voters quadrupled their vote in favour of Federation. By this time, Queensland had decided to join the party (although New Zealand opted out).

A delegation went to England to present the Commonwealth Bill to the Imperial Parliament. NSW was represented by Protectionist Party member Edmund Barton (1849–1920), who became Australia's first Prime Minister (1901–1903). Royal assent was given on 9th July 1900 and Queen Victoria declared that, as from the first of January 1901, the Commonwealth of Australia should come into existence. Barton, one of 11 children, resigned to become a founding member of the High Court of Australia, presiding until his death.

PREMIERS OF NSW

The first Premier of NSW was Stuart Alexander Donaldson (1812–1867) who took office on 6th June 1856. His term lasted little more than two months, ending on 25th August 1856, although he remained active in the state's political scene. He was followed by Charles Cowper (1807–1875) who served as Premier an astonishing five times, although not consecutively, finishing his final term on 15th December 1870. While many issues distinguished the policies of the pre-Federation Premiers from one another, the biggest issue was free trade versus protection. The first NSW Premier in the post-federation period was the politician and police magistrate John See (1844–1907) who held the role between 1901 and 1904. The issue of tariffs was now a federal one and See was described as a 'Progressive'. The next few Premiers (Thomas Waddell, Joseph Carruthers and Charles Wade) were either Progressive or Liberal. The first Premier from the Australian Labor Party (ALP) was James McGowen, a man with working class credentials and a background in the Union movement, but not a particularly inspiring or competent Premier. He was replaced by William Holman (1871–1934) who served first as an ALP Premier but who changed loyalties over the conscription issue in the First World War and formed the Nationalist Party. He was followed by two ALP Premiers, John Storey and James Dooley, but in December 1921, Holman's Nationalist Party gained office with Sir George Fuller (1861–1940) as Premier.

Then followed one of the great characters and icons of NSW politics, John (Jack) Thomas Lang (1876–1975). Lang was Premier twice, once from 1925–1927 and then during the difficult years of the Great Depression, 1930–1932. Brother-in-law by marriage to the equally iconic poet and writer Henry Lawson, Lang was ambitious and self-interested. He shrewdly observed the ALP factionalism following Holman's defection in 1916. Ideologically he is difficult to pin down. He was staunchly opposed to the influence of communists in the labour movement, but he appeared to take on a socialist stance with his insistence that 'Capitalism must go'. While in no way a unionist, he courted the support of the unions— and gained it possibly by some of the social legislation that he supported such as the Widow's Pension Act in 1925. His physical presence earned him the nickname of 'The Big Fella'. His actions when faced by the financial problems of the Great Depression inspired the slogan of 'Lang is greater than Lenin'.

After Lang, premiers Bertram Stevens and Alexander Mair were members of the United Australia Party, a coalition of Nationalists and right-wing Laborites. With the outbreak of World War Two, and until 1965, all governments were ALP and so naturally were all Premiers. Since then, the Premiers have vacillated between Liberal and ALP, serving two or three terms. The first woman Premier was Kristina Keneally, ALP, who served for fifteen months before a change of government. The second woman Premier was Gladys Berejiklian, a Liberal, who became Premier at the commencement of 2017. A list of the NSW Premiers from 1988, and their time in office, is shown in Table 6.1

Table 6.1 List of NSW Premiers since 1988

Premier	Political Party	Time in office
Nick Greiner	Liberal	25.03.1988 – 24.06.1992
John Fahey	Liberal	24.06.1992 – 04.04.1995
Bob Carr	Labor	04.04.1995 – 03.08.2005
Morris Iemma	Labor	03.08.2005 – 05.09.2008
Nathan Rees	Labor	05.09.2008 – 04.12.2009
Kristina Keneally	Labor	04.12.2009 – 28.03.2011
Barry O'Farrell	Liberal	28.03.2011 – 17.04.2014
Michael Baird	Liberal	17.04.2014 – 23.01.2017
Gladys Berejiklian	Liberal	23.01.2017 – present

GOVERNORS OF NSW

The NSW Governor, appointed by the British Sovereign, is the Sovereign's representative in the state and is the formal Head of State in NSW. The role of Governor has changed greatly over the years, now having an important constitutional, ceremonial and community role in New South Wales. With regard to constitutional matters, the Governor acts on the advice of their Ministers.

The Governor's primary task is "to perform the Sovereign's constitutional duties on their behalf, acting within the principles of parliamentary democracy and responsible government as a symbol of stable government and a nonpartisan safeguard against the abuse of power". The Governor represents NSW at special occasions, such as ceremonies or visits by foreign Heads of State. A list of the Governors of NSW from 1946 is shown in Table 6.2.

Table 6.2 List of NSW Governors since 1946

Governor	Term of office
Lt-Gen Sir John Northcott KCMG, KCVO, CB, KStJ	01.08.1946 – 31.07.1957
Lt-Gen Sir Eric Woodward KCMG, KCVO, CB, CBE, DSO, KStJ	01.08.1957 – 31.07.1965
Sir Arthur Roden Cutler VC AK KCMG KCVO CBE	20.01.1966 – 19.01.1981
Air Marshall Sir James Rowland AC, KBE, DFC, AFC	20.01.1981 – 20.01.1989
Rear Admiral Sir David Martin KCMG, AO	20.01.1989 – 07.08.1990
Rear Admiral Peter Sinclair AC	08.08.1990 – 29.02.1996
The Honourable Gordon J Samuels AC, CVO, QC	01.03.1996 – 28.02.2001
Professor the Honourable Dame Marie Bashir AD CVO	01.03.2001 – 01.10.2014
His Excellency General the Honourable David Hurley AC DSC (Retd)	02.10.2014 – 01.05.2019
Her Excellency the Honourable Margaret Beazley AC QC	02.05.2019 – present

POLITICAL PARTIES

Minor parties, such as the Greens and One Nation, are a relatively new phenomenon in NSW politics, and a plethora of them, plus independents, can be seen at each election—especially in the Legislative Council. This has not always been the case.

The earliest political division was that of 'exclusives' versus 'emancipists', the former generally opposed to change and the latter, particularly through the Australian Patriotic Association, advocating liberal reforms. Both, however, represented the wealthy of colonial society.

Formed in the 1890s by trade unions seeking a greater voice in government, the oldest of the extant political parties is the Australian Labor Party. The term 'Liberal Party' has been used a number of times in Australia's history, but the present Liberal Party was established by Robert Menzies (1894–1978) from a coalition of free enterprise parties in 1944. The Country Party was established at the federal level in 1920 to represent the interests of farmers, graziers and rural people in general. In 1975 it changed its name to the National Country Party, before adopting the current name National Party in 1982. The Liberal and National Parties have formed government by means of a coalition in both NSW and federally. The Nationals are the second oldest political party in NSW and in 2019 celebrated 100 years of representation in State Parliament.

7. *Education*

SCHOOLS

The idea of the reformative nature of education was evident in the books carried on the First Fleet and the basic schools that were run on many of the transports. There was, however, no allowance made for a government schoolmaster or a school in the early colony, although Governor Arthur Phillip was instructed to reserve land for the eventual construction of schools.

Born in 1754, the former laundress Isabella Rosson was the first teacher to be appointed in the colony. She had been sentenced to seven years' transportation for theft and arrived on the First Fleet transport, the 'Lady Penrhyn'. She established a school in her home in 1789 (a 'dame school'), married another convict and teacher, William Richardson, and together they taught for Reverend Richard Johnson until they returned to England in 1810.

Governors John Hunter and Philip Gidley King fostered the idea of improving the morality and utility of the children of convicts. Schools were opened in Sydney, Parramatta, Norfolk Island and the Hawkesbury, with early teachers drawn from the ranks of convicts and ex-convicts. The school focus was on religion, morality, reading, writing and arithmetic. Despite these early establishments, Governor William Bligh complained in 1807 that the only school was the orphan school, which accommodated about 54 girls, and a small missionary school.

While early educators brought with them ideas from Britain, the circumstances of the colony were bound to refashion such concepts. Early schoolmasters, for example, were of varied religions and not necessarily Anglican, due to the lack of literate or educated free people. The Society for the Propagation of the Gospel in Foreign Ports was active in funding colonial schools and teachers' salaries and there were also private ventures in their establishment. Under Governor Philip King, customs duties began to be used as a source of revenue for schools.

The fact that the colony was established as a penal settlement made it an obvious focus for using education as a means of social control or reform and government initiatives in schooling were soon made a priority. Education, however basic, might reform the second generation. As the colony's population grew exponentially, the Colonial Office's earlier demands to instruct the young of convicts to create a moral society, now became a general need to educate the children of the lower social orders.

It was assumed that convicts abandoned their children, often referring to them to as 'vagrant infants' or 'urban urchins'. Consequently, an orphanage was established in Sydney in 1818 by Governor Lachlan Macquarie, replacing Governor Philip King's Orphan School. Apart from basic reading, writing and religion, these children were taught useful trades. Much the same happened at the Native Institution, an attempt by Macquarie to provide Aboriginal children with a basic education in the three 'Rs' plus agriculture, and turn them into labourers and, therefore, 'useful'. These approaches indicated aspects of social control in education.

From 1820–1860, religious schools opened as numbers and support became available. In 1833, the Church and Schools' Corporation, which encapsulated the Anglican monopoly of government funding for education, was dissolved by Governor Richard Bourke. Bourke then attempted to introduce a similar scheme to the Irish National System, but the prefix 'Irish' aroused opposition to its implementation through its association in Protestant thought with Roman Catholicism. He therefore acquiesced and gave a pound-for-pound subsidy for all denominational schools.

Early education was assumed to be the responsibility of the church, assisted by the various missionary societies:

the London Missionary Society and the Society for the Propagation of the Bible. The expansion of educational facilities and focus was bound closely to the colonial role and power of religious institutions. Although initially support for Anglican education was favoured, opposition by Catholics, Presbyterians and Methodists in particular, and changes in England, led to a broadening of support for general church education regardless of denomination

Governor Gipps proposed a similar system to that of the church but was forced, like Bourke, to use the pound-for-pound subsidy. The Anglican Church, although not the established church of the colony, was nevertheless a powerful force. In early schools, the curriculum was utilitarian and moralistic. In addition to basic literacy, boys learned useful trades and girls learned domestic skills.

By 1840, a multiplicity of private schools had developed. Three secondary schools had been established: Sydney Grammar School (founded as the Sydney Free Public Grammar School, non-denominational, 1825), the King's School Parramatta (Anglican, 1831) and the Presbyterian Australian School. Household tutors and governesses were also in demand, indicating the changing nature and wealth of the colonials. Trade, and the entrepreneurship of colonials, created this wealth, which was welcomed in Britain as an indication that the colony would soon be financially independent. However, the Depression of the 1840s weakened the ability of the government to stay committed to the pound-for-pound subsidy. Churches found that they could not maintain their existing schools, let alone establish new ones. The Anglican Church removed its opposition to the Irish National System, which then commenced alongside the government subsidised denominational schools. In 1847, the NSW Legislative Council allocated money specifically for the new schools modelled on the Irish National System. And so, two systems and two administrative Boards were established to deliver education: the Board of National Education and the Denominational School Board. The state now subsidised and provided education.

William Wilkins (1827–1892) was appointed the new superintendent of the Board of National Education in 1854. He had been trained in a system of apprenticeship and schooling as a teacher and introduced these ideas in NSW schools. He believed that teaching had standards and aptitudes, and teachers were professionals. In 1848, the Kempsey National School became the first government school in NSW. National Schools were established when thirty local children could attend, and the community was expected to contribute to the financial and administrative running of the schools. By mid-1851, 37 schools had been established by the Board of National Education, with Fort Street Model School being established as a model school for teacher training.

Robert Lowe (1811–1892), a liberal thinker and solicitor nominated by Governor George Gipps to the Legislative Council, led an inquiry into education which resulted in new public funding of education. While Lowe advocated for secular education, this was not in opposition to religion which, in the form of enlightened Protestantism, he considered had a rightful place in both education and society. But, while being a decided Anglican, he was opposed to what he considered to be unenlightened and ambitious clerics—and to denominational education. The inquiry argued that the funding of denominational schools had led to an unnecessary proliferation of schools, fuelled by denominational rivalry, rather than the provision of needed education. In 1866, under the sponsorship of Henry Parkes, then in the NSW Legislative Assembly, the new Public Schools Act replaced the two boards (which had proved a divisive and inefficient system) with a Council of Education. This Act also established the idea of 'travelling teachers' in areas where the numbers of children did not justify the provision of buildings and full-time teachers. These were referred to as 'half-time schools' and contributed greatly to the education of children in remote areas who would otherwise have remained uneducated.

The number of both government and church schools in the colony began to grow. Table 7.1 shows the explosion in government (mostly one-teacher) schools between 1866 and 1871, while the number of denominational schools decreased.

Table 7.1 No. of schools and pupils in NSW schools in 1866 and 1872

Year	No. of Government. Schools in NSW	No. of students	No. of Denominational Schools in NSW	No. of students
1866	259	19,258	317	35,306
1872	691	46,458	211	33,564

Parkes also became a force behind the new 1880 Public Instruction Act that established non-sectarian teaching, with a limit of one-fifth of each day given over to religious instruction. This was hardly secular, but it removed state aid to denominational schools. Throughout this period, particularly in rural areas, the dame schools persisted, as did the employment of governesses.

The state support of denominational schools was being frequently challenged with the mantra that education should be 'free, compulsory and secular', with the state paramount in its control. The Public Instruction Act withdrew state financial support to denominational schools and introduced compulsory education for children aged six to fourteen years. The Act also replaced the Council of Education with the Department of Public Instruction (renamed the Department of Education in 1915), recognising the importance of the state's role in the provision of general education. State secondary schools were also established—Superior Public Schools, High Schools and Evening Public Schools. The half-time schools were replaced with house-to-house schools, with a teacher going to the different homes of children within relatively close proximity to one another. In its official history of education, one hundred years later, the NSW Department of Education described it as follows:

"The Public Instruction Act 1880 has provided the framework for education in New South Wales ever since. By this act the state assumed full responsibility for primary education and for the first time accepted some responsibility for secondary education; authority was transferred. . .to a minister of public instruction heading a department. . .answerable to the parliament."

The first six state high schools opened in 1883, one for each sex at Sydney, Bathurst and Goulburn. The following year two more opened at Maitland. While the schools at Sydney and Maitland prospered, the two high schools at Goulburn and the boys' school at Bathurst closed by the end of 1886.

During the 1880s, many of (what are now) the GPS schools were established, including: St. Ignatius (Catholic) in 1880, St. Joseph's (Catholic) in 1881 and Sydney Church of England Grammar in 1886. Newington College had already been established in 1863. Privately provided education for girls in NSW also proliferated in this decade, including Methodist Ladies College in 1886, Ascham in 1886 and Presbyterian Ladies College in 1888. Abbotsleigh (Anglican), for example, was founded as a superior or high school by Marian Clarke (1853–1933) in 1885, first in North Sydney, then Parramatta and finally at Wahroonga, where it remains today. Clarke believed firmly in a full and stringent education for girls. Due to ill health, she sold the school to another proprietor-principal, but eventually it was purchased in 1924 by the Anglican diocese of Sydney.

At the end of the 19th century and during the early part of the 20th century, more interest was shown in the importance of secondary education as a means of providing the expertise needed for a growing industrial society. There was a belief that, by the age of twelve, it could be determined how a child would then develop academically and for their role in the workforce.

Working as apprentices in schools, potential teachers had been exploited and received little understanding of pedagogical principles. They were poorly paid, and they focused their educational delivery on a narrow system of training rather than educating. With the creation of the Commonwealth of Australia in 1901, there was a new concern for improved public education, although it remained a state responsibility. A developing and central theory was that education could stabilise and order society. In 1904, a Royal Commission was established to inquire into the methods of public instruction in NSW.

NSW was fortunate in the early part of the 20th century to have several forward-thinking advocates in the field of education. Arguably most important was Peter

Board (1858–1945), who was the Director of Education 1905–1922. He encouraged education that focused on the interests of the child, established Intermediate and Leaving Certificates, stressed that schools must prepare students for responsible citizenship as well as for the workplace. Fees were removed from schooling, and when the Nationalist-Country Party reintroduced them in 1922, Board resigned in protest.

Aboriginal children were little considered in these changes with the boys being prepared for farm work and the girls for domestic service. Aboriginal children could also be excluded from schooling if non-Indigenous parents demanded it. At the Cootamundra Girls' Home and the Kinchela Boys' Home, Aboriginal children, usually those of mixed parentage, were trained after being taken from their families.

In 1906, 19 district schools were established in rural areas to bring the advantages of secondary education to remote areas. Over the next few decades there were other changes. Secondary education was delivered by staff with university qualifications in their specialised subjects. After passing the Qualifying Examination at the end of primary school, academically able students were channelled into high schools. Others were offered pre-vocational courses in technical drawing, woodwork and metalwork for boys, and domestic science for girls. In rural areas, courses offered were agriculture, farm mechanics and horticulture.

The curriculum, however broadened from the colony's earlier years, was still dominated by the concept that all that was important had occurred elsewhere, particularly in Britain. Children were taught to be proud of the amount of pink—indicating the British Empire—on the map.

At the same time, teachers were being prepared more for the life of a professional when in 1906, the Sydney Teachers' College was established with educationalist Alexander Mackie (1876–1955) as its principal. Mackie was also made a professor at the University of Sydney, thus implying that teaching was not just to be learned by apprenticeship but was a discipline to be learned academically. This Institution continued under the NSW Department of Education until 1974. With the expansion of tertiary education after the Second World War, one consequence was the enhancement of the training of teachers and the development of professional teachers, for whom educational theory and its attendant disciplines were important.

From the end of the 19th century, but particularly during the early 20th century, new ideas were stirring about the need for a more liberal and general education rather than simply rote learning. Towards the end of the Great Depression of the 1930s, this was furthered by the New Educational Fellowship conference which was held in Sydney in August 1937. It advocated a holistic approach to education rather than simply academic ability or vocational preparation. The later Director of

Education, Sydney-born Harold Wyndham (1903–1988), was involved in this conference.

From 1930s to the 1960s school children in the Sydney metropolitan area undertook an intelligence test to decide who would attend which type of secondary school. This form of testing discriminated on more than intelligence, as working-class children were less likely to have the language and knowledge background than their middle-class counterparts.

In the 1940s, the 'leaving age' was raised to 15 years and, in 2010, to 17 years. Aboriginal schools were established when assimilation became Government policy after 1940. By the late 1950s, comprehensive schools were established, catering for all in an inclusive way. After 1962, the Wyndham Scheme consolidated the idea of comprehensive co-educational high schools in NSW. Although a few schools remained selective, the idea of the comprehensive school was allied with the idea of local community. Simultaneously, secondary schooling was extended from five to six years starting with the entry year of 1962. Since that time, government schools have attempted to accommodate a range of expectations: distance, gender and ability. In addition, pedagogical changes have been reflected in teacher training and educational structures.

One of the specialised areas was named 'Schools for Specific Purposes', with an early such school being established in 1927 at Glenfield, which was a school for slow learners. The recognition of the need for such schools was not really realised until the 1950s and 1960s, while some special needs students now go to regular schools but attend special classes within those schools.

In the period following the Second World War, government involvement has grown in providing and financing education beyond the elementary. However, in the period after the early 1970s, federal government aid has gone to both government and private schools with many parents in more affluent areas sending their children to private schools while government schools are more patronised in regions of social disadvantage.

UNIVERSITIES

There are 42 universities in Australia: 40 Australian universities (37 public and 3 private) and two international private universities. Of these, the three Australian private ones all have campuses in NSW: the University of Notre Dame Australia, Torrens University Australia and the University of Divinity. Eighteen of the public universities have a campus in NSW, with ten having their main campus there. A selection of largely NSW–based universities is discussed below.

In 1850 the explorer, politician, author and journalist William Charles Wentworth (1790–1872), the son of a convict Catherine Crowley (1772–1800) and her husband

D'Arcy Wentworth (1762–1827), proposed a university. Just two years later the colony had its first such institution, the University of Sydney, and its founders were particularly keen that it should be based on merit rather than the accident of birth. It was a completely non-religious institution, funded by the state, providing both a liberal education and a professional one. In 1881, it allowed women to attend.

The University of Sydney was not only Australia's first, but is now regarded as one of the world's leading universities, spreading across the inner-city suburbs of Camperdown and Darlington. Until 1949, the University of Sydney remained the only such institution in the state and is now one of the 'Group of Eight' research-intensive universities in Australia. By 2020 it had more than 70,000 students and 7,500 staff.

The University of New South Wales in Sydney was incorporated in 1949, after it commenced life as the NSW Institute of Technology, using part of the Sydney Technical College as its campus. It expanded its site in Kensington, where it is today, and now has over 59,000 students enrolled. It also increased its academic disciplines from the original engineering and science to include humanities, and is also one of the 'Group of Eight'.

Macquarie University was established in the north-west suburb of Ryde in Sydney in 1964 and concentrated on providing a range of cross-disciplinary studies. It opened its doors to undergraduate students in 1967 and today it has over 40,000 students and around 1700 Academic Staff. In 1969, the Macquarie Graduate School of Management (MGSM) was opened and later became the most prestigious business school in the country. Macquarie was also the first university in Australia to own and operate a private medical facility in 2010, when it opened a $300 million hospital on its campus.

Created in 1968, the NSW Institute of Technology (NSWIT) in 1988 became the University of Technology Sydney (UTS). Located in the southern end of Sydney's CBD, it currently enrols about 46,000 students. The other Sydney-based university is the Australian Catholic University (ACU), a public university which has its main campus in North Sydney.

These growing universities were complemented by a number of Colleges of Advanced Education (CAEs) until the latter were given new status and incorporated into the state's university system between 1989 and 1994. Examples include Armidale CAE (part of the University of New England in 1994), Mitchell CAE (Charles Sturt University in 1989) and Ku-ring-gai CAE (combined with the New South Wales Institute of Technology to form the University of Technology, Sydney in 1990). Reflecting the movement of population to the west of Sydney, the University of Western Sydney (now Western Sydney University) was established by the union of three organisations, Nepean CAE, the Hawkesbury Agricultural

College and the Macarthur Institute of Higher Education, in 1989. It currently has more than 28,000 students enrolled across four campuses.

There are several other universities in NSW that are not located in Sydney. These include (main campus location in parentheses) Charles Sturt University (Bathurst), Southern Cross University (Lismore), University of New England (Armidale), University of Newcastle (Newcastle) and University of Wollongong (Wollongong).

In the second half of the 1980s, Australian universities, including those in NSW, were affected by education becoming a commercial commodity when full fee-paying international students were encouraged to gain tertiary qualifications in Australia. By the end of the 20th century, NSW was the state with the largest proportion of fee-paying international students.

The 'lockdown' response to the COVID-19 virus in 2020 played havoc with university enrolments and in turn bottom lines. Not only was all teaching essentially performed online, but with international students unable to begin their studies here, there was a massive blowout in the budgets of those institutions who had a great reliance on their fees, some in the order of hundreds of millions of dollars.

ADULT AND TECHNICAL EDUCATION

The 'Mechanics Institute' and 'School of Arts' movement seen in Britain in the 1820s was replicated in New South Wales. They were established principally for adult working men, many of whom had no formal schooling, to provide an alternative pastime to gambling and drinking in pubs. They provided practical subjects such as landscape gardening along with morally uplifting lectures on intemperance. The Sydney Mechanics Institute was founded in 1843 and in 1878 became Sydney Technical College, whose aim it was to teach and apply knowledge. It enrolled apprentices and those commencing technical education. In 1892, the George Dibbs colonial government commenced a new Sydney Technical College and during the Second World War it was particularly involved in the war effort. In 1949 it became the Department of Technical Education and gained new standing, eventually becoming TAFE.

8. *Infrastructure and Transport*

The building of infrastructure—roads, bridges, wharves, buildings—was usually a public initiative often later taken up by private entrepreneurs. Infrastructure in a prison colony is purpose built. Buildings and roads that commenced with Governor Lachlan Macquarie's building program indicated a growing sense of a penal colony becoming a settlement colony. The construction of roads and buildings was the chief employment of convicts.

BUILDINGS

The first colonial buildings were tents, then small huts of wood and stone, and in 1805 in Parramatta, convicts built a brewery. When Governor Lachlan Macquarie embarked on a vigorous public works program, granaries, stores, a new hospital and barracks, schoolhouses, burial grounds and the Parramatta Female Factory all appeared under his direction. He was assisted in this by Francis Greenway, the first Government Architect of the colony (and ex-convict forger). Greenway was responsible for many Sydney colonial buildings including the Hyde Park Barracks, St James Church, the Macquarie Lighthouse and Government House, whose stables now house the Conservatorium of Music.

Anyone who has entered Sydney Harbour today will see Fort Denison, still referred to by its earlier title 'Pinchgut'. The architect, George Barney (1792–1862), oversaw its construction which was completed in 1857, the idea being born of the fear of Russian attack at the time of the Crimean War.

The Sydney General Post Office (GPO) building, located in Martin Place, Sydney, was first opened to the public in 1874, and was constructed in two stages over 25 years, beginning in 1866. By the time of its final completion in 1891, the structure was hailed as a turning point for the colony, and historians have since noted the building's significance as a force for driving prosperity and for the country's Federation. Its architectural expression, including its Pitt Street carvings, has since been described as 'the beginning of art in Australia'. Many major cities in the country used to mark distances from the location of their GPO, and some still do so. In 1942, the clock tower was disassembled to reduce the visibility of the GPO in case of an air attack on Sydney, it later being rebuilt in 1964. Today, the GPO is occupied by the five-star Westin Hotel.

The Sydney Opera House has become one of the best-known symbols of the city. Located on Bennelong Point, named for the Indigenous man who was friend to Governor Arthur Phillip, the area had been a military base and then a tram depot. The Danish architect, Jørn Utzon, won the competition (from 233 entries) to design the building whose architectural sails overlook the Harbour and are a constant drawcard for international visitors. Construction began in 1959 and was expected to take four years with a cost of $7 million. In fact, it took fourteen years to build, opening in 1973, at a total cost of $102 million.

Barangaroo

Barangaroo, named after the wife of Bennelong, who was a senior man of the *Eora*, is an inner-city suburb of Sydney, located on the north-western edge of the CBD and the southern end of the Sydney Harbour Bridge. It is part of the local government area of the City of Sydney and was part of the territory of the *Gadigal* people, the traditional owners of the Sydney city region. The area was used for fishing and hunting by Indigenous Australians prior to colonial settlement.

Upon completion, with a new Metro rail station by 2024, more than half of Barangaroo will be dedicated public space encompassing a continuous Sydney Harbour promenade, expansive parklands and plazas.

TRANSPORT AND TRAFFIC

Early transport was often by river or sea. The Parramatta, Hawkesbury and Georges Rivers were the conduits for trade and communication in the early colony and linked settlements to Sydney. With the advent of an engineer as Governor in 1838, Major George Gipps, the building of the semi-circular quay of Sydney progressed. It was built on the Tank Stream's estuary and the work was supervised by the Colonial Engineer, George Barney. This improved the port facilities in the colony.

Up to 1875, transport by road was largely on bullock wagons and Cobb & Co. coaches. The latter provided a fast and reliable service to the colony, travelling 45,000 kilometres per week by 1870. Sydney's first trams had been introduced to Pitt Street in 1861, being horse-drawn and providing an important link between the ferries and ships at Circular Quay and the main railway terminus, then located at Redfern. However, this mode of transport did not last long and in 1879 the steam tram appeared in Sydney, running along Elizabeth Street, from Hunter Street to Central Railway. The first extension out to Randwick racecourse was built the following year.

Historian Professor Robert Lee wrote that the steam trams of 1879 were 'immensely popular', with the system growing rapidly through the 1880s – mainly because they were much cheaper to build than suburban railways.

In far west NSW, at Broken Hill, camels were the dominant means for transport of goods until 1900. The iconic 'Afghan' cameleers, as Muslims and non-drinkers, were permitted to carry alcohol from the railhead to hotels.

On 13th October 1933, Australia's first traffic lights were established in Sydney at the corner of Market and Kent Streets. The Minister for Transport, Colonel Michael Bruxner (1882–1970), opened the event, although it took another four years before more such lights were installed. The date of the first pedestrian-activated traffic lights is debatable, but was possibly in 1949 at Pacific Highway near Lindfield Railway Station on Sydney's upper north shore. In 1959, the then Department of Motor Transport established the first coordinated traffic light systems in Australia, both sets on Parramatta Road, Petersham. The Sydney CBD was advantaged by computerised regulated traffic lights in 1964.

Roads

Early roads in the colony were a haphazard affair, following bullock tracks or the tracks of explorers. Governor Lachlan Macquarie, arriving in NSW in 1810, addressed the problem with the establishment of toll roads, first from Sydney to settlements at Parramatta and the Hawkesbury River. Once the colonists had found a way over the Blue Mountains in 1813, roads became necessary to exploit the richer pastures of the immediate inland. The road over the Blue Mountains created by William Cox and his party was a major feat. It opened the whole interior to the land-hungry pastoralists whose flocks had grown and who had exhausted the feed available on the eastern seaboard near Sydney. Road improvements in the colony were essential for the movement of goods and people.

The more important roads were 'macadamised', a technique developed by the Scottish civil engineer, John McAdam (1756–1836). This involved laying a finer top course of broken stone over a coarser base course on a convex earth base, providing good drainage. In 1822, the government contract to improve the road from Prospect to Richmond (later known as Blacktown Road), specified that it was to be macadamised—the first road built in NSW using this method.

The customary bullock drays were slow, the drivers often walking beside the dray. Horse-drawn vehicles became more utilised on the macadamised roads for the transport of the goods so necessary on the diggings. As the colony developed, and particularly with the influx of population following the discovery of gold in the 1850s, the condition of roads deteriorated. In the 1830s and 1840s, NSW had legislated for road trusts run by local government organisations. These bodies could enforce tolls and were expected to construct and maintain roads. Cobb & Co. transferred some of their coaches from Melbourne to NSW in 1862, with Bathurst, 200 kilometres north-west of Sydney, as the centre of their new enterprise. Until the late 1860s, the company depended on the trusts' roads to move goods and people. But road travel remained slow and painful and, prior to 1900, roads were not funded by any level of government, instead receiving funding on a sporadic basis.

The arrival of motor vehicles posed a new problem for road building. Existing roads were rough and narrow, and the tyres of cars damaged the existing surfaces. Nobody wanted to pay for their upgrade. Administrative structures were needed to deal with the issue and in NSW, the Main Roads Board, later the Department of Main Roads, was established in 1925. Its first major task was to build a coastal road from Sydney to Newcastle. This road opened in 1930, considerably reducing the distance and time of the journey between the two main centres.

The year 1970 was a turning point in the creation of a modern road system in NSW, with significant progress being made on expressways, and financial support for the roads program was greater than it had ever been. In September 1983, a $5 billion five-year program announced by Premier Neville Wran revitalised road making in NSW. The most ambitious of the Roads 2000 program for the Sydney region was the orbital, a new freeway/motorway route around Sydney, aiming to link all the radial and inter-city freeways, while bypassing busy urban centres. From 1995–96 a ten-year upgrade of the Pacific Highway was financed, largely by the state but with assistance from the Commonwealth Government.

Today, the NSW road network is almost 185,000 kilometres long and carries more than 60% of the freight moved in the state. Important road freight corridors include the Pacific (M1/A1) and Hume (M31) Highways, which carry most of the 81 million tonnes of interstate freight between Melbourne, Sydney and Brisbane.

Bridges

Prior to 1830s, bridges were mainly timber constructions such as the first bridge that was built in 1788 over the 'Tank Stream', the fresh water supply for the early days of Sydney prior to 1837. Its 'stronger' replacement collapsed after three years. Timber log bridges, called 'corduroy bridges', were the simplest method of crossing rivers and essential for the movement of food and people throughout the colonial period. These bridges consisted of long logs topped by small crosswise logs. Side logs formed kerbs either side of the bridge. After a while, planks replaced logs, making traversing the bridges a more comfortable ride for coach passengers. In order to recoup the costs of construction, turnpike (toll) roads were built.

The arrival of David Lennox (1788–1873) in the colony in 1832 marked a change, as he was an engineer who introduced scientific bridge-building. The Lansdowne Bridge, 1834–36, was one of his triumphs and was both functional and elegant. The bridge, crossing Prospect Creek between Parramatta and Liverpool, was made of stone quarried nearby and punted to the site.

As stone was extracted by convict labour, it was a cheap material. Once transportation finished in 1840, timber again became the preferred material because of the cheaper cost of the labour required. The timber bridge remained the mainstay of bridge-building in NSW until after the Second World War. Stone, concrete and iron supports gave strength and durability to these constructions, which numbered over 4,000 by this time.

There are many other major bridges, not the least of which is the Australian heritage-listed Sydney Harbour Bridge that was opened by NSW Premier Jack Lang on 19th March 1932. Spanning Sydney Harbour, it carries vehicular, rail, bicycle, and pedestrian traffic between the Sydney CBD and the North Shore. It is nicknamed 'the coathanger' because of its arch-based design. Construction commenced in 1924 and took 1,400 men eight years to build at a cost of $4.2 million and 16 lives. Made of steel, the bridge contains 6 million hand driven rivets, is 502 metres long, 48.8 metres wide and weighs 52,800 tonnes. The highest point is 134 metres above sea level.

Other early prominent NSW bridges include Pyrmont Bridge (Darling Harbour, 1858), Glebe Island Bridge (Glebe Island, 1861), Fullers Bridge (Chatswood West, 1918), Roseville Bridge (Roseville Chase, 1924), Tom Ugly's Bridge (Blakehurst, 1929) and Ryde Bridge (Ryde, 1935).

The eight-lane ANZAC Bridge, with a span of 345 metres, is the longest cable-stayed bridge in Australia. Opened in 1995, it is the main link between the Sydney CBD and Glebe Island, forming part of the western suburbs of Sydney. It replaced the former Glebe Island Bridge.

Tunnels

There are also some important road tunnels in NSW, including the Airport Tunnel (Mascot, 550 metres), Border Tunnel (Tweed heads, 1600 metres), Bylong Rail Tunnel (Bylong, 2000 metres) and the Sydney Harbour Tunnel (2800 metres). March 2007 saw the opening of the Lane Cove Tunnel, a $1.1 billion, 3.6-kilometre twin-tunnel tollway in Sydney which connects the M2 Motorway at North Ryde with the Gore Hill Freeway at Artarmon. Opening in 2020, the North Connex is a 9-kilometre motorway tunnel in northern Sydney. It connects the M1 Pacific Motorway to the M2 Hills Motorway and is both the longest and deepest road tunnel in Australia. It is 90 metres below ground at its lowest point.

An interesting pedestrian link and tunnel between Wynyard station and Barangaroo in the Sydney CBD is the Wynyard Walk. It is 180 metres long and was officially opened on 20th September 2016. When Central Station was completed in 1906, a pedestrian tunnel was opened beneath the railway, running between Devonshire Street and Railway Square. In the early 1970s, the Sydney City

Council and the NSW Government combined to build an 80-metre extension to it under Railway Square. It has a length of 300 metres.

Railway tunnels include the heritage-listed Woy Woy railway tunnel located between Wondabyne and Woy Woy stations on the Main Northern railway line. The dual-track, 1,690-metre tunnel was opened on 16th January 1888. Opening on 23rd February 2009, the 13-kilometre Epping to Chatswood Rail Link runs completely underground and includes three intermediate stations: Macquarie University, Macquarie Park and North Ryde. On 26th May 2019, it formed part of the Metro North West link. The Sydney Metro is the first fully automated driverless metro rail system in Australia and is the biggest urban rail infrastructure investment in Australia's history. The Metro North West has 13 metro stations and 36 kilometres of twin tracks, mostly underground, operating from Tallawong Station to Chatswood via Macquarie Park, supported by over 4,000 commuter car parking spaces.

In 2024, Sydney Metro will be extended from the North West, south under Sydney Harbour, through new CBD stations and beyond to Sydenham and Bankstown. Sydney will have 31 metro railway stations and a new 66-kilometre long standalone metro railway. At the time of writing design studies are underway to extend Sydney Metro to the upcoming Western Sydney Airport, as well as additional lines between St Marys, Liverpool and Macarthur via the new airport.

Open to traffic in August 1992, the Sydney Harbour Tunnel is a twin-tube road tunnel providing a second vehicular crossing of Sydney Harbour, alleviating congestion on the Sydney Harbour Bridge. It is one of two tunnels under the harbour, the other being a set of rail tunnels for the Sydney Metro.

The WestConnex in Sydney is a 33-kilometre predominantly underground motorway scheme that first opened in December 2016 and is still currently under construction, with various links and extensions. In all, it will create around 16 kilometres of new tunnels.

Railways, trams and buses

Early British settlers in New South Wales were used to the convenience of British railways that had started back home in the 1820s. They pushed for railways to be built in the colony and, in 1849, a railway was planned linking Sydney to Goulburn. Unfortunately for the growth of the rail system, when gold was discovered near Bathurst in 1851, the privately-owned Sydney Rail Company found that its labourers either deserted or demanded higher wages. The Company turned to the colonial government for assistance. Railway workers were brought from England and their wages paid. As a result, a line was constructed from Sydney as far as Parramatta Junction. The original Sydney terminal station was sited near Redfern; and Parramatta Junction was near the present Granville Railway Station.

The *Sydney Morning Herald* announced the opening of the railway in September 1855 in glowing terms, declaring that 'With the introduction of railways will follow in quick succession a series of moral, social, and material advantages which few have hitherto been led to contemplate'. But railways were slow to develop, with distance, cost and often inept company leadership hindering progress. In the 1860s, the driving force for expansion of railways was the need to connect major hinterland settlements with Sydney.

John Whitton (1819–1898) was selected as the Engineer-in-Chief of NSW Railways, serving between 1856 and 1890, and is sometimes referred to as 'the Father of NSW Railways'. The line linking Sydney to Goulburn was finally opened in 1869, offering great commercial opportunities to local farmers, pastoralists and produce generally. It connected the Southern Highlands to the city commercially and psychologically. In the decade following 1870, the numbers travelling by rail increased sevenfold and the miles of rail line more than doubled. The Great Western Railway joined Sydney to Bathurst in 1876.

One of the greatest engineering challenges to this endeavour was crossing the Blue Mountains. The 'zigzag' rail system was used to facilitate the movement of locomotives up the steep slope by a series of traverses. Trains alternated going forward for the first part of the slope, then backwards for the next section. In this way, inland centres were linked to the port of Sydney.

Rail development was hampered between states by each having its own rail gauge – the width between the rails. But in 1883, Sydney was linked to Melbourne by rail and six years later to Brisbane. In the 1880s, NSW was building 275 kilometres of rail per year. Towards the end of the 1880s, the NSW colonial government had overseen the construction of over 2,700 kilometres of railway throughout the colony. The 1890s depression and a decade of severe drought brought hardship to rural communities. With this change, Sydney's suburban railway network expanded dramatically. The first suburban railway, the North Shore Line going from Hornsby to St Leonards, opened in 1890.

Dr John Bradfield (1867–1943), chief engineer for railway construction in NSW, is well-known for his designs of the Sydney Harbour Bridge and the Circular Quay Railway Station. But during the 1920s, he had a forward-thinking plan for Sydney to have a grand electric railway system. The first of these was the Illawarra Line in mid-1926 and, later in the same year, the city underground system linking St James and Museum Stations. Once the Harbour Bridge was opened in 1932, the North Shore Line was continued to Wynyard Station. In 1956, Circular Quay station opened completing the City Circle, and the Eastern Suburbs railway was opened through to Bondi Junction on 23rd June 1979, about 50 years after it was first planned and 31 years after construction began.

Between 1879 and 1961, the Sydney tramway network served the inner suburbs of Sydney, with electrification starting in 1898 and most of the system converted by 1910. At its peak during the 1930s, it was the largest in Australia, the second largest in the British Commonwealth of Nations (after London), and one of the largest in the world. The network was heavily patronised in its heyday, with about 1,600 cars in service at any one time (compared with about 500 trams in Melbourne today). During 1945 there were 405 million passenger journeys. In 1923 its maximum street trackage totalled 291 kilometres.

The tram system was closed down with the withdrawal of the services completed on 25th February 1961 when R1 class tram 1995 returned from La Perouse to Randwick Workshops just before 4:40pm. Nearly sixty years later trams of a different sort made their re-appearance on the streets of Sydney. The Sydney light rail network (or Sydney Light Rail) is a light rail system serving Sydney with the network consisting of three passenger routes, the L1 Dulwich Hill, L2 Randwick and L3 Kingsford lines. A separate light rail network serving Western Sydney called Parramatta Light Rail is also under construction and is scheduled for completion in 2023. After some initial problems, the light rail system appears to be working well and has been embraced by the general public.

The development of the internal combustion engine led to both private and public buses competitively using this new technology from 1930. The first Government bus service went from Manly to Cremorne Junction and opened on Christmas Day 1932. The introduction of trolley buses introduced a further element into the transport scene during the inter-war years.

After the Second World War, the railway system was expanded and improved and, as a result, the trams were removed, and the tram-tracks torn up or covered over in the 1960s. Buses have, however, remained a major people mover in many areas of Sydney and major country towns. Early buses were double-deckers, but in the early 1970s, these were replaced with single-decker buses (they've now made a reappearance on the northern beaches). The increasing amount of road traffic in Sydney has led to some areas having designated bus-only lanes.

Shipping/maritime services and water transport

In 1805, convicts were deployed in making several ships seaworthy, repairing punts and building longboats. In colonial times, large numbers of ships, travelling in virtually all-weather conditions, were frequently wrecked along Australia's coastline. There are a number of wrecks that occurred in the waters off Booderee National Park, approximately 200 kilometres south of Sydney.

In 1789, the marine craft 'Rose Hill Packet' inaugurated the first ad hoc Sydney ferry service, moving passengers and produce from Sydney Cove along the Parramatta River to the farming settlement of Parramatta. A trip to Parramatta and back could take a week. In June 1831 steamships enabled timetabled ferry services on Parramatta River. Punts were constructed close to Sydney near the current location of Gladesville Bridge.

Billy Blue, commemorated in the naming of Blues Point, arrived as a convict in 1801 and set up a business in the 1820s ferrying people across the harbour from Dawes Point, where the southern end of the Sydney Harbour Bridge now stands—Sydney's first regular ferry service. By 1830 a regular ferry service was set up between Balmoral Beach and Balgowlah, and other enterprising rowboat ferrymen transported people across the harbour.

Further commercialisation of the harbour ferry services saw the establishment of the North Shore Ferry Company in 1861; and Manly, promoted as a resort area on the northern side of the harbour, developed as a result of the access provided by ferries. Many of the suburbs on the north side of the Harbour owe their establishment and development to the work of the ferries. Where transport was available, settlement followed.

In 1907, the Port Jackson and Manly Steamship Company was established, consolidating many of the smaller runs and later the government took over the harbour ferries when they were in financial difficulty. Until the building of bridges across the harbour made many ferry routes redundant, ferries were a critical part of the transport system in Sydney and wherever rivers ran throughout the colony of NSW. Ferries now have become a tourist attraction, or a more picturesque way of travelling on the Harbour, as well as a key component of commuter travel.

The romance of the Sydney ferry has been celebrated in poetry from Henry Lawson's *Sydney-side* to Kenneth Slessor's *Five Bells*. As Grace Karskens, a professor of history, has pointed out, the earliest means of transport in the colony was by water. The local Indigenous people, saltwater people, used their canoes to traverse the coast and its inlets. Early non-Indigenous settlement was around the harbour, bays and inlets and consequently so was early transport. Ferries have been an essential part of Sydney life and transport ever since, even after the Sydney Harbour Bridge was opened in 1932. A popular Australia Day tradition is the ferry race from Barangaroo Wharf to Shark Island and then back to a spectacular finish at the Sydney Harbour Bridge.

The Waterways Authority was formed in 1995, taking over the remaining functions of the Maritime Services Board of New South Wales, which existed between 1936 and 1995. On 1st September 2004, NSW Maritime became the trading name of the Waterways Authority, and the name of the Waterways Authority was officially changed to the Maritime Authority of NSW in June 2006. In November 2011, NSW Maritime was merged with the Roads and Traffic Authority to form the Roads and Maritime Services.

UTILITIES

Power supplies

The first public use of electricity took place in 1863 when a single arc lamp was illuminated on Sydney's Observatory Hill to celebrate the marriage of the Prince of Wales, the eldest son of Queen Victoria. In 1879, NSW imported several generators and had arc lighting installed at the Domain so that construction of the Garden Palace, being built for the first International Expo, could continue at night.

On 9th November 1888 Tamworth (population 3000) switched on arc and incandescent lighting in the main street, becoming the first NSW town to use electric power supply. It was quickly followed by other major towns. It was not until 8th July 1904 that Sydney joined the illuminated ones when Pyrmont Power Station provided electricity to Sydney streets. At the Powerhouse at Pyrmont, The Lady Mayoress, Olive Lees, turned the ceremonial golden key, declaring "I have much pleasure in switching on the electric light for the city of Sydney; I trust it will be a boon to the citizens and an encouragement to the enterprise of the City Council." It brought to an end almost 50 years of gaslight. Electricity could now be purchased for domestic and commercial use.

The Electricity Commission of New South Wales commenced operations on 22nd May 1950 as the statutory body responsible for the generation of electricity and its bulk transmission throughout NSW. It 1992 it adopted the trading name Pacific Power and in 2018 TransGrid Services (TGS) was established to provide connections for renewable generation, telecommunications and other contestable services.

The Snowy Mountains Scheme, a joint project by the NSW and Victorian governments, was completed in 1974. It is the largest hydro-electric scheme in the country, diverting the waters of the south-flowing Snowy River westwards, beneath the Great Dividing Range. In doing so it provides electric power and additional water for the Murray and Murrumbidgee Rivers which is heavily used for irrigation.

By 2020 NSW was experiencing a solar power boom and, across the state, record numbers of households installed small-scale solar photovoltaic (PV) systems. The NSW government's aim is to have net zero emissions by 2050 and switching to solar can help achieve this target.

Communications networks

In 1838, the Colonial Postmaster-General of New South Wales, James Raymond (1786–1851), introduced the world's first pre-paid postal system and in the same year a regular postal service was introduced between Sydney and Melbourne. In 1949 postal prices were made uniform across all the Australian colonies and during the 1850s pre-paid adhesive stamps were gradually phased in.

Towards the end of 1857, NSW's first telegraph line was opened linking Sydney and Liverpool and, a year later, a line was completed between Sydney and Albury. Overseas telegraph links commenced in Adelaide and, in November 1872, Sydney was linked to the overseas network. This must have seemed miraculous to a colony so divorced from its European origins. Within 48 hours it could receive news from the world. In 1882, Sydney's first telephone exchange was opened.

Prior to Federation of Australia in 1901, each of the six Australian colonies had its own telephony communications network. The Australian networks were government assets operating under colonial legislation modelled on that of Britain.

On 9th April 1962 the Sydney–Melbourne coaxial cable was officially opened with the infrastructure supporting the introduction of subscriber trunk dialling between the cities and live television link-ups. The cable also carried telegraph and telephone traffic and provided the first inter-city television transmission in the country, allowing simultaneous television broadcasting in Melbourne and Sydney for the first time.

The Australian Bureau of Statistics' website states that the number of households with access to the internet at home increased to 7.7 million in 2016–17, representing 86% of all households, the same as in the previous year.

Australia's National Broadband Network (NBN) was announced in 2009 by the Rudd Labor Government. The aim was to address Australia's broadband availability and performance and to facilitate the structural separation of Telstra by providing an optic fibre alternative to its copper access network. It was originally planned to reach 93% of premises with an optic fibre connection with the remaining 7% of premises being served by either a new satellite service or terrestrial fixed wireless service.

About 36% of Australians, the greatest number, will be connected to the NBN by Fibre To The Node (FTTN). Hybrid Fibre Co-Axial (HFC) is the second-most-common method which will connect (22%). This is typically used to connect properties to the NBN where an existing pay TV (Foxtel) or cable network (Telstra or Optus) is available.

The initially promised Fibre To The Premises (FTTP), the most desirable, will be used by only 17% while Fibre To The Curb (FTTC) will connect to 12%.

Water supply and treatment

The early settlement relied for water on the Tank Stream that ran through Sydney into the harbour. It was so-called for the tanks that Governor Arthur Phillip had cut into the stone during a drought in 1790, to capture the water which flowed from the springs. Despite various Governors' attempts to keep the stream clean, by the 1840s it was little more than a sewer and, 20 years later, it was covered. From

1827 to 1837, civil engineer James Busby (1765–1857) built a tunnel from the Lachlan Swamps (now Centennial Park) to Hyde Park where it was released to the public by a valve on the corner of Elizabeth and Park Streets. This was referred to as 'Busby's Bore' and addressed the immediate problem of providing clean water to Sydney. In 1844, reticulation pipes connected residences to the bore at the cost of ten shillings per annum.

Although they were investigated as early as the 1840s, dams would take longer to become part of the water supply. Other shorter-term projects were preferred. Busby's Bore had steam pumps installed to assist its efficiency and the Botany Swamps Water Supply Scheme commenced operations in 1859. Water was pumped to reservoirs at Crown Street and Paddington. These systems required frequent maintenance and improvement as the population grew. In 1888, the Board of Water Supply and Sewerage was formed to manage the problem comprehensively. By this time, the Upper Nepean River, by using gravity feed, was filling reservoirs downstream. But this too proved inadequate for the growing population, particularly during several severe droughts.

In the early 20th century, four new dams were constructed as part of the Upper Nepean Scheme, the Cataract Dam being the first of these, completed in 1907. As each of these dams was a huge construction project, cottages and barracks were built nearby to house the workforce and their families. In this way new settlements were created with all the attendant commerce of a town. More dams were constructed leading to the building of Australia's largest urban water supply dam, Warragamba Dam, which opened in 1960. It has a total capacity of with total capacity of 2,031 gigalitres. By comparison, the capacity of Sydney Harbour is about 500 gigalitres which is about 200,000 Olympic size pools. Since then, most dams have been upgraded, particularly using post-tensioned anchors and replacement of valves.

9. *Manufacturing and Industrial Development*

By 1800, male convicts were employed in building trades from brickmakers to plasterers. Women spun wool, picked oakum (a tarred fibre used to seal gaps, usually in ships or plumbing), worked in dairies or as nurses. People worked in small industries as potters, hat-manufacturers, tanners, brewers, shoemakers, tailors and tinsmiths. Flourmills, public and private, were established; windmills were built by 1797 and a steam mill was functioning in Sydney by 1813.

Whaling and sealing efforts made the sale of oil and sealskins profitable and these industries expanded during the 1820s. Ex-convicts were particularly active in these industries. James Underwood (1771–1844) became a builder of ships for sealers; Henry Kable (1763–1846), a convict transported in the First Fleet, arranged the work gangs; and the renowned merchant Simeon Lord (1771–1840), convicted for the theft of cloth in England and arriving in Sydney in 1791, sold the produce—oil and skins—to England. After varied fortunes and investments,

Lord became a wholesale merchant and manufacturer, financing various endeavours of other entrepreneurs.

All three of these men were typical of the early entrepreneurs—shrewd and devious. The skins were used for shoes and the oil lubricated machines, lit lamps and enhanced foods. Several freemen, who were merchants, invested in whaling. The firm of Jones, Riley and Walker was established by three free merchants (Richard Jones, Edward Riley and William Walker). Jones and Walker, in particular, had fingers in most local enterprises, owning many of the whaling ships that sailed from Sydney. For the sailors who worked the boats, it was a hazardous profession. Sperm whales were large and dangerous, growing to a length of up to 21 metres and weighing up to 80 tonnes.

Industrious ex-convicts were major contributors to developing industries. Chief Constable and farmer, Andrew Thompson (1773–1810), for example, established a granary and built a saltworks north of the Hawkesbury River—and a bridge to facilitate the movement of his commercial endeavours. Convicted of stealing cloth from a shop, Thompson had been sentenced to fourteen years transportation and arrived in Sydney on the *Pitt* in February 1792.

Colonialism and economic exploitation were inextricably entwined. Initially, manufactures were only intended for local demand or requirements such as textile and clothing production, and the capital invested was small. The development of the wool industry in NSW was intended to supply the mills of England, but the expansion of local industries was treated warily by British interests that considered that the colony should import from them.

The immediate impact of the goldrushes of the 1850s was to rob the colony of many of its small manufacturers who, lured by the promise of wealth from the diggings, abandoned their businesses.

Until Federation in 1901, NSW was largely agricultural, and manufacturers were often geared to primary production or immediate consumers. There were mills, tanneries, boiling-down concerns, cloth manufactories and brewers and distillers. Very successful were manufacturing businesses producing ready-made clothing. The invention of the sewing machine, replacing laborious hand-sewing, had led to the proliferation of this industry.

With the establishment of a federal government, tariffs between the states were eliminated and goods from NSW could be sold freely in other states. In addition, import duties protected and strengthened local manufacturers. Manufacturing industries became major employers of labour.

Interstate railways, despite the varied gauges, grew with increased freight.In turn, manufacturing gained impetus from the development of infrastructure. The expansion of the railways, for example, led to the local manufacture of locomotives, wagons and carriages. This also provided employment for tens of thousands of workers.

There had been iron works since 1848 in NSW, slightly west of Mittagong, but these had not been profitable. The Broken Hill Proprietary Company Limited, known as BHP, was proposed in 1885 to exploit silver and lead. Despite vicissitudes, it was extremely successful and profitable, later expanding into iron and steel. In the 1870s, the Eskbank Ironworks was established at Lithgow on the far side of the Blue Mountains, about 150 kilometres from Sydney. For a time, it was very productive and provided, for example, the ironwork for the Wagga Wagga Bridge, but it eventually proved unprofitable. In 1908 the Hoskins family purchased the operation and turned it around.

Before long Hoskins' steelworks was in competition with a newly developed BHP steelworks which opened in Newcastle in 1915. BHP had the advantage of having high-quality iron deposits and coal nearby. The First World War cut off supplies of overseas imports—a blow to NSW generally as it was heavily reliant on imported goods—but which greatly advantaged the early native steel industry. In the period between the two world wars, BHP produced cheaper iron and steel, which generated advances in other industries. By 1939 manufactures contributed nearly two-fifths of the annual value of production in NSW, almost double the proportion of 1911.

Mining ventures could have unanticipated consequences for the NSW environment. Sand mining for rutile and zircon, for example, was conducted on the NSW coast from Sydney to the Queensland border (and beyond). The water blasting and digging up of the sandy beaches, followed by attempts at restoration, caused damage to many beaches. The industry, especially on the east coast, suffered from conservationist and anti-mining movements during the 1970s because it operated on or near the coastline where the majority of Australians live or seek their recreation. As a result, restrictions have been placed on mining activities and exploration in NSW and they must be conducted under a relevant authority.

Car manufacturing gained ground during 1925, when Ford set up a plant in Granville, Sydney. Components were imported but assembled in local factories, which reduced the price of cars to local consumers. A year later, General Motors (GM) established its assembly plant at Marrickville, Sydney. In 1936, Ford extended its assembly plant, opening a workshop in Homebush, while GM opened a new plant at Pagewood. These activities dramatically increased the use of cars and trucks locally.

Australia's largest airline, Queensland and Northern Territory Aerial Services Limited, or 'QANTAS', was founded in Queensland, in 1920, and moved its headquarters to Sydney, in 1938, from its former base at Longreach. It made a great contribution to transport in areas not served by road and rail. By 1939, QANTAS Empire Airways had its own workshops at Mascot and, in 1947, it effectively became government owned. By 1957, when it opened new headquarters in Sydney, it was one of the largest businesses in the country. In the 1990s, it ceased to be government owned and was sold via a share float, being gradually privatised between 1993 and 1997.

In the period between the two world wars, the Australian policy, including that of NSW, was to develop manufacturing by continuing the wall of import tariffs that had been commenced at the end of the previous century. This policy and practice continued for several decades after the Second World War which stimulated the production of a wide range of manufactures. The need to manufacture all areas of munitions led to a new era in the development of associated industries, such as precision engineering. Tanks, ships and aircraft, such as the Beaufort Bomber, were constructed in NSW as a contribution to the war effort.

The period after the Second World War was character-ised by an increasing presence of multinational companies in many areas of manufacturing in NSW. Prevalent were companies from the UK and USA, but multinationals who became involved in the state's manufacturing industries also came from Germany, the Netherlands, Switzerland and France. This increasing involvement with overseas networks meant that manufacturing was much more affected by global events.

NSW has always, to greater and lesser extents, been a centre of innovation. The technology of the lawn mower was transformed in 1952 when Mervyn Victor Richardson (1893–1972), born in Yarramalong in NSW, invented (in his backyard in Concord, Sydney) and patented a mower with rotary action blades: the 'Victa' lawn mower. His business expanded dramatically and his product became an integral part of many households. The Victa mower, along with the Hills Hoist (a height-adjustable rotary clothesline developed in Adelaide in 1945), had routines dedicated to them during the opening ceremony of the Sydney 2000 Olympic Games.

In 1958, at Lucas Heights near Sydney, the Australian Energy Commission established a uranium mining and research centre with a view to investigating the use of atomic energy for industry and defence. Although Australia has an estimated one-third of the world's uranium deposits, it has no nuclear power station, relying instead for power on extensive coal and natural gas reserves. With a reassessment of coal and gas power in the context of climate concerns, there is renewed interest in the potential for nuclear power. In 1969 there was a proposal for a nuclear power reactor in Jervis Bay, 200 kilometres south of Sydney, but it did not eventuate.

Today, the New South Wales manufacturing industry is one of the driving forces behind the state's economy and employs over 240,000 people, representing 7% of all employees in the state and produces a wide range of goods that are integral to NSW workplaces and households.

10. Health

Nine naval surgeons (including surgeon's mates) sailed on the First Fleet, of whom four (John White, William Balmain, Thomas Arndell and Denis Considen) were pre-chosen to establish a medical service for the colony. All had seen the appalling and inhumane consequences of the Poor Law and workhouses in Britain. John White (1756–1832) was the head of the medical service established in the new colony. Despite the hard work of these doctors, and those who followed them, the convict hospitals were places of ill-health and poor provisioning. It was not uncommon for staff at the General Hospital, for example, to sell food or goods intended for patients who then had to depend on the charity of others to assist them. The levels of mortality, illness and disease made the task of caring for the health of convicts and early settlers a difficult one.

When Lachlan Macquarie was appointed Governor of NSW in 1810, he turned his attention to the construction of a new hospital in what became Macquarie Street. The hospital was Lachlan Macquarie's first public works project, although he had been denied the necessary finances to build it. As a result, he made a deal with merchants Alexander Riley and Garnham Blaxcell, and colonial surgeon D'Arcy Wentworth, that in exchange for a monopoly on the importation of 45,000 gallons of rum to the colony, they would build the hospital. And so, it was initially known as the 'Rum Hospital'. At first a convict hospital, Sydney Hospital (as it was called later) serviced the whole community. Well-constructed permanent buildings, hospitals were later erected at major rural centres.

As there was no provision for support staff for the four initial surgeons, medical workers had to be drawn from convicts, with variable results. During Macquarie's governorship, this became better regulated and the Principal Superintendent of Convicts was responsible for the appointment of staff to the hospitals. The organisation varied, but once the medical service came under the control of the military in 1836, patient-carer ratios were set at one carer to every 10 patients.

Medical services were free, whether you were a convict or civilian pauper, and so treated in a hospital, or an official who was treated at home by the various medical superintendents. For assigned servants, the first 14 days hospitalisation was free and thereafter the cost was to be borne by their masters. But in 1839, this system changed and charges were levied.

As it was a penal settlement, all medical care was initially through the Crown. The first full-time private practitioner was William Bland (1789–1968), a Sydney-based emancipist who had previously been convicted of killing a ship's purser in a gun duel but pardoned when he arrived in the colony. While his career could be described as colourful—he was not averse to criticising people of high status and was politically active—he was known for his excellence in medical practice and surgery. He removed cataracts and kidney stones and performed a remarkable procedure, binding the subclavian artery to cure an aneurysm. This was only the seventh time such a procedure had been reported world-wide. Bland also founded the Australian Medical Association.

By 1808 an examination board had been established to list professional qualifications as a requisite to practise, and the concept of a professional Medical Board, with powers of registration and accreditation, was established by law in 1838.

Those suffering from 'mental derangement' were often housed in jails where they were inevitably abused. Asylums were established for them, the first at Castle Hill, but due to constant bickering between surgeons and non-medical superintendents, they became neglected. There were other such asylums established at Liverpool and Tarban Creek (later Gladesville Asylum) in 1826 and 1838 respectively, and at Callan Park, an area on the shores of Iron Cove in Lilyfield, in 1873. The rationale was confinement and restraint, for the protection of society, rather than any great care for the welfare of the individual 'lunatic'.

With the ending of transportation to NSW in 1840, many of the convict hospitals became voluntary hospitals under civilian control. Their reputation for care was poor and many languished. In 1888–1889 the Second Royal Commission on Public Charities established that the Government would inspect and have financial control of hospitals and the organisation of administrative health services. The First Royal Commission into Public Charities 1873 had led to changes in the treatment of delinquent and destitute children.

In an attempt to keep at bay introduced diseases from ships arriving in Sydney, disembarking passengers were housed at an isolated spot, the quarantine station at North Head. The site was first used for this purpose in 1828 when the convict transport 'Bussorah Merchant' arrived with a number of crew infected with smallpox. Accommodation, as the site developed, reflected social class differentiation, even to the extent of housing some patients in a hulk, *Faraday*, in the bay. By the time it closed in 1984, 16,000 people had passed through, most to recover and enter the colony (though not all, as the cemetery and modern museum there testify).

In 1881, a smallpox epidemic broke out in Sydney. Disease and associated death were routine in lower social orders in crowded living conditions, threatening all and leading to panic. The quarantine station at this time was providing no real medical treatment. Infected and non-infected residents mixed, patients were left unattended and lived in their own filth. As a result of the general epidemic, an isolation hospital for people with infectious diseases was reorganised, and a new infectious diseases hospital was built at Little Bay in 1881. It was the NSW government's first public hospital, later becoming the Coast Hospital and, in 1934, Prince Henry Hospital, named after Prince Henry (1900–1974), the Duke of Gloucester and the third son of King George V. The Duke had visited Sydney that year. Its position reflected contemporary belief in the necessity for isolating those with infectious diseases in areas where fresh air would assist their recovery. A year later, the Royal Prince Alfred Hospital was established.

General health was affected by contaminated food supplies and water supplies polluted with sewage. An awareness of this and as a reaction to the smallpox epidemic, the Board of Health was formed. It was responsible for the management of hospitals and for such matters as checking diseased animals and meat, inspecting dairies, and overseeing noxious trades and cattle slaughtering.

An offshoot of public health, particularly as industrialisation grew apace, was the concern for the health and wellbeing of workers. In NSW, Farmer & Company and the NSW Railways Department's workshops in Sydney established first aid rooms in that workplace. These were part of the developing welfare mentality at the end of the

19th century. The First World War gave a boost to this idea of receiving welfare, which became general practice after the Second World War.

In 1859 and 1861, two public Turkish bathhouses opened in Sydney's Spring Street and Bligh Street, before any such were opened in the United States or England. The climate may well have contributed to this: it may have reflected a growing awareness of the social need for cleanliness. Appropriate to growing appeal of the Blue Mountains to those wishing to improve their health by exposure to clean and bracing air, a Turkish bathhouse opened at 'Wynstay' at Mount Wilson in the 1890s, on the estate of the Irish born Richard Wynne (1822–1895). In Turkey, these baths were part of the process of religious purification; in non-Muslim countries they implied a growing awareness of health and hygiene. Their promoters, such as Dr John Le Gay Brereton (1827–1886), who brought the idea to Sydney in 1859, claimed for them the most astonishing array of curative properties for diverse ailments. It was even considered that they cured drunkenness and so gained the support of the temperance movement. Whatever their advantages, they remained popular for over a century, expanding in number with some being built in private establishments.

During the early 19th century, anyone in the colony could claim to be a medical practitioner. The first NSW Medical Board was constituted in 1838 and was responsible for examining and approving the qualifications of those wishing to be declared 'legally qualified medical practitioners'. It required a register of such persons to be maintained and their names published each year in the Government Gazette. The 1838 Act underwent various amendments throughout the century with professional associations and journals such as Sydney's Australasian Medical Gazette (established 1881 and later merged to form the Medical Journal of Australia in 1914) appearing. These, combined with growing population and wealth, led to an increased confidence in the efficacy of scientific medicine and consequently an increasing demand for medical care. The Medical Practitioners (Amendment) Act 1900 (Act No. 33) imposed penalties on persons using titles including Surgeon or Physician if they were not appropriately registered.

At the end of the 19th and the early 20th centuries, tuberculosis (TB), known at first as 'consumption', was prevalent. This was an infectious bacterial disease that mainly affected the lungs and in which the mortality rate was high. Founded before the First World War by a group of philanthropists and relevant professionals, the National Association for the Prevention and Cure of Consumption opened the first anti-tuberculosis dispensary in September 1912. In the early 1930s it became The Anti-Tuberculosis Association of New South Wales and in 1973 altered to the Community Health and Anti-Tuberculosis Association. In mid-2001 the name was again changed to Community Health and Tuberculosis Australia (CHATA) reflecting the association's concentration on respiratory disease in the international context, with particular interest in the Western Pacific Region. In 2006 it became the Australian Respiratory Council (ARC).

In its beginning, the organisation provided medical as well as social solutions and remediation for the disease and its attendant problems. In the 1940s, it began using mobile chest X-ray units for the detection of TB throughout NSW. Sanitaria were also established, two in particular at Wentworth Falls in the Blue Mountains. The first anti-tuberculosis clinic was opened in Hay Street, Sydney. Dispensaries expanded throughout Sydney, financed by Government grants and public donations. During the Great Depression of the 1930s, the role of the dispensaries expanded to general charitable work, providing food, housing and clothing for those who might be subject to the disease. During the 1950s, the ARC, in concert with the NSW government carried out a mass screening campaign to identify and so control and possibly eradicate tuberculosis. Thereafter, the campaign transcended state boundaries and became a national concern.

There have been many great innovators and researchers amongst the state's medical practitioners. In 1918, Dr Norman Gregg (1892–1966), a Sydney ophthalmologist, discovered the connection between birth defects and rubella in pregnant women. In 1926, the medical pioneer in anaesthesiology, Dr Mark Lidwell (1878–1969) of Sydney's Royal Prince Alfred Hospital, together with physicist Edgar H. Booth of Sydney University, invented the world's first electronic pacemaker. In 1960, scientist Neil Moore of Sydney University successfully transferred frozen embryos into sheep. A year later, the obstetrician Dr William McBride (1927–2018) declared thalidomide, a drug frequently used by pregnant women to counter nausea, to be the cause of many severe birth defects. The same year, an ultrasound scanner was built by two researchers, David Robinson (1939–2010) and George Kossoff, of the Commonwealth Ultrasonics Institute, Sydney.

In 1895, the first ambulance service in NSW was established in Railway Square, Sydney, in a borrowed police station. Nothing was mechanical and patients were transported on handheld stretchers. Vehicles were horse-drawn until 1912, and it was not until 1976 that advanced intensive care vehicles were in use. The railways established an ambulance service in 1882, which lasted until the 1980s. Known as the NSW Railways Ambulance Corps, it boasted 10,843 trained members by 1941. To maintain their service, they held competitions involving stretcher drill and oral exams. It provided services to many commuters and at times of rail accidents.

The first NSW Minister for Health was Frederick Flowers (1864–1928). Arriving in the colony with his family in 1882, he served as an active member of the Labor Party, both within the community and as a Parliamentarian. In 1914 he undertook the Health portfolio, a role in which he supervised the introduction of health centres for mothers and children.

During the later 20th century, private organisations became active in investing in health care. At one time four major groups, Affinity Healthcare, Benchmark Healthcare, Healthscope and Ramsay Healthcare, owned and/or operated 117 hospitals, but only two have continued past 2004. Not for profit groups, often with religious affiliations, have also been involved in the provision of hospitals. For example, St Vincent's in Sydney's eastern suburbs has a long history of being at the forefront of HIV/AIDS care, in 1985 opening the first dedicated AIDS Ward, named Ward 17 South, in Australia.

EPIDEMICS AND DISEASES

In the first few years of settlement, mortality rates were high mainly through dysentery and typhus, malnutrition and scurvy. For several decades, dysentery remained a prevalent disease due to poor hygiene. But the diseases that beset the population were many and varied. Venereal disease was common, as was oedema and the skin infection, erysipelas, and there were recurrent bouts of influenza and tuberculosis. Children suffered from measles and whooping cough. For women, puerperal fever was a common concern after childbirth, and cancer rates rose in the second half of the 19th century for both men and women.

Epidemics may be defined in terms of morbidity, but also relate to the panic and distress they cause to a community—and often a search for a scapegoat. The 1789 smallpox or chickenpox epidemic, which affected so many Aboriginals, was often attributed to the French on La Perouse's ships (at a time when the French and British were at war). In the later smallpox epidemic of 1881–82, the Chinese community were labelled the scapegoats. This was born of fear and hysteria stirred up by the press, and of a growing concern at the number of Chinese in the colony following the goldrushes. The Chinese were boycotted and humiliated as a result. From 1913 to 1917, a further smallpox epidemic occurred. Quarantine was the immediate response, although there were few deaths. This outbreak led to a public debate concerning the importance of vaccination and was the last such smallpox epidemic in the state. In 1980, the World Health Organization (WHO) declared smallpox had been completely eliminated globally.

Measles has occurred many times both in colonial and modern periods. In 1866–67, an outbreak occasioned many deaths, mainly of children. With the 1875–76 outbreak of scarlet fever, a known disease which led to the death of 1,500 infants and children in New South Wales, quarantine was the major official response. But it also led to a concern for the living conditions that were associated with it. Following the First World War, the global influenza epidemic known as the Spanish Flu, also affected the state's population with 42% of deaths in 1918–1919 a result of the condition. Panic gripped people and schools; cinemas and public halls were closed; people had to wear masks in public. Australia's swift action to curtail the spread meant that its death rate was lower than many other countries.

In the end, the flu killed around 13,000 Australians (and around 50 million people worldwide).

Severe acute respiratory syndrome (SARS) is a disease that can cause severe pneumonia. An outbreak of SARS spread from China to several other countries in 2002–2003, but there have been no outbreaks since then. There was only one case of SARS in Australia, in someone who became infected in her home country and visited New South Wales.

The disease COVID-19 is caused by a recently identified strain of coronavirus in humans. The virus first appeared in Wuhan city in Hubei Province, China, at the end of 2019 and has since spread to many other countries, including Australia. Symptoms of COVID-19 range from mild illness to pneumonia and while most people recover easily, others become quite ill very quickly. Victims may experience fever, a sore throat, fatigue and shortness of breath. At the time of writing, COVID-19 is causing a major disruption to life, not only to NSW but around the world, while a vaccine is being sought. Globally, nearly 20 million people have been infected and there have been nearly one million deaths, although these figures are expected to increase significantly. Australia is coping relatively well with the outbreak, as it did with Spanish Flu, with only a fraction of expected cases/deaths compared to incident rates in the rest of the world. It is strange to this author to be writing history in such immediate terms.

NURSING

Early nursing care in the colony was haphazard and generally provided by untrained convicts, with midwives providing some services. Traditionally, men cared for male patients and women for female patients. In 1816, the Rum Hospital in Sydney became the first public hospital in Australia, and in 1845 the Sydney Infirmary and Dispensary, a charity instituted the previous year to provide medical care to the poor, moved into the building. In 1894 it was renamed Sydney Hospital.

In the early years nursing care was provided with little understanding of hygiene or medical procedure. A major change occurred with the appointment of the first of the Nightingale nurses, Lucy Osburn (1836–1891), in 1868. She arrived with five other nurses, all trained in the Nightingale technique, and her actions saw nursing training introduced and hygiene standards raised. She had to contend with opposition from many sections of local society, particularly medical men who found her assertive nature confronting. Nursing was, after all, the 'handmaiden' of the medical profession. But Osburn was constantly supported and defended by Henry Parkes who at the time was the Colonial Secretary.

In 1924, the NSW Nurses' Registration Board confirmed the status of nursing in the state, regulating their training and certification. At that point nurses were still single women who lived in nurses' quarters attached to hospitals. In the 1940s, a growing shortage of nurses led to many changes in the profession. Married women were allowed to train, nurses' aides (now called enrolled nurses) carried out many routine procedures, thus freeing nurses for more complex activities, and men started to join the cohort. In the 1980s, progress was made towards more professional training when the NSW Government moved to tertiary training for nurses in institutions rather than hospital-based training.

Growing concern for occupational health and safety emerged after the First World War, but particularly after the Second World War. This is evident in the often-hidden role of industrial nurses. These nurses were situated in factories and workplaces, often located in first aid rooms. Their professional life was isolated, unlike that of nurses working in hospitals. Their role was to treat injured and sick workers, along with educating those in the workplace about their health and safety. One of the many problems for such nurses was that they were caught between their responsibility to employers and employees. While part of management, they also saw first-hand some of the less than perfect conditions in workplaces.

A good example of such nursing is provided in the experiences at Sydney's Eveleigh Railway Workshops. Industrial nurses were appointed there from 1946. The best known of these was Agnes Mary Lions (1908–92) who worked at Eveleigh between 1947 and 1968. She saw the role of industrial nurse as more than providing bandages and aspirin and she visited sick workers at home and listened to them voice their problems.

Agnes was, however, a very determined and authoritative woman who found herself at odds with the men who had undertaken first aid training, considering, rightly, that her nursing training was superior to any first aid instruction. Educated at Sydney's Petersham Girls' Intermediate High School and trained at Royal Prince Alfred Hospital, Agnes was a hard-working, capable and devoted nurse. The data she collected on industrial nurses led to the first industrial award being granted to them by the NSW Industrial Commission in 1948.

11. *Entertainment*

STAGE, SCREEN AND RADIO

Early theatre and music

In January 1796, Sydney's first playhouse opened with a company of convicts presenting 'The Revenge' and 'The Hotel'. It began with the recitation of the 'Barrington Prologue', reportedly spoken by the former pickpocket and author, George Barrington (1755–1804), of Henry Carter's poem:

> *'From distant climes, o'er wide spread seas we come,*
> *(Though not with much éclat, or beat of drum)*
> *True patriots all; for be it understood,*
> *We left our country for our country's good'.*

In 1825, in Emu Plains west of Sydney, convicts presented three plays: 'Barissa or the Hermit robber', 'The Mock Doctor or the Dumb Lady Cured' and 'Bombastos Furioso'. In a convict society, the role of theatre centred on the issue of morality and the necessity to provide uplifting performances in which the good were rewarded and the evil overcome. These were amateur productions, but in 1833 the first regular theatre productions opened in Sydney. For a long time, performances were held in the saloon of the Royal Hotel and elsewhere, but London-born promoter Barnett Levey received the first theatre licence granted in the colony on 22nd December 1882 and built the Theatre Royal. The NSW Governor Sir Richard Bourke patronised his enterprise.

Schools of Arts in different centres also provided diverse entertainments and educational activities. At the 1857 inaugural event at the Maitland School of Arts, for example, the contribution of science to all aspects of human endeavour was lauded. The speaker supported twice-weekly functions at the venue, combining serious presentations with musical evenings.

The idea of entertaining, rather than just being entertained, was apparent in the development of bush ballads. Their importance lies in their commemoration of historical events and personalities. Many of them were set to well-known music from Britain indicating the duality of the early colony: the tunes were British, but the subjects were colonial.

At the time of the 1879 International Exhibition in Sydney—the first World's Fair in the southern hemi-sphere—the amount of time available for the enjoyment of local recreational activities was commented on favourably. Schools of Arts and free libraries were well frequented, and social gatherings with accompanying music and dance were regular occurrences. Theatres were popular and holiday excursions were enjoyed by all.

Nineteenth century theatre revelled in Shakespeare and Gilbert and Sullivan, indicating the continued reliance on Britain as a source of matters theatrical and cultural. The antipodean rights to the latter had been purchased in 1879 by J C Williamson (1845–1913), an Australian theatrical entrepreneur. In 1881 he leased the Theatre Royal in Sydney and expanded from there to own more theatres at which the French stage actress, Sarah Bernhardt, and the Australian operatic soprano, Nellie Melba (1861–1931), appeared. Although the depression of the mid-1890s affected attendances, by 1902, Williamson had leased Her Majesty's Theatre in Sydney and produced 'Ben Hur', a four-hour extravaganza complete with chariot races and galloping horses. His theatrical empire provided operas, plays, pantomimes and concert tours until 1976.

One of Sydney's most enduring theatres is the State Theatre which opened on 7 June 1929. It was the vision of Stuart Doyle, owner of Union Theatres, and the renowned architect Henry White. It was billed as 'The Empire's Greatest Theatre' and was designed as a picture palace in the grandest and most spectacular style.

The Sydney Theatre Company began in December 1978, following the closure of The Old Tote Theatre Company the previous month. The company initially operated out of several rented premises around the city, producing 38 productions in five separate venues. Eventually, after an extensive search, it found a new home, at the derelict Walsh Bay Wharf 4/5, that met all its capacity and location requirements.

Based in Surry Hills, Sydney, since 1984, the Belvoir has become one of Australia's most distinguished theatre companies. It began when a group of 600 theatre-lovers came together to buy a theatre to save it from becoming an apartment block,

The Sydney Lyric opened in 1997 and has hosted many international performers and productions. Acquired by Foundation Theatres in 2011, it has now become an important part of the NSW musical theatre scene, hosting a number of world premieres.

Live music and dance

Sydney has been the home to a magnificent array of live music, including the Bondi Lifesaver between 1971 and 1980. Notable Sydney venues have included the Coogee Bay Hotel which had a large stage and a mezzanine level for the really big shows, and the Bexley North Hotel, an iconic pub venue during the 1980s.

Between 1954 and 1970 the Sydney Stadium was frequently used to stage concerts by visiting overseas performers, particularly the "Big Show" package tours promoted by expatriate American entrepreneur Lee Gordon. It was the only large-capacity indoor venue in Sydney during that period. In 1970 it was demolished to make way for the Eastern Suburbs railway line. Located in Haymarket, the Sydney Entertainment Centre (later known as Qantas Credit Union Arena) was a multi-purpose arena, opening in May 1983. It hosted many notable musical performers, including Queen, Elton John, John Farnham, the Wiggles, and Paul McCartney among many others. It closed on 20 December 2015.

There are a number of annual music festivals held in NSW, including Splendour in the Grass, held at North Byron Parklands, Byron Bay, which also hosts the annual Byron Bay Bluesfest. The Tamworth Country Music Festival is a popular annual music festival held for 10 days from Friday to Sunday in mid to late January each year. It sometimes includes Australia Day and is a celebration of country music culture and heritage with live performances.

There are a number of orchestras located in the state, including the Sydney Youth Orchestras, the Sydney Symphony Orchestra and the Australian Chamber Orchestra. Others located in Sydney include the Australian Brandenburg Orchestra and the Sydney Youth Jazz Orchestra.

The Sydney Opera House is a multi-venue performing arts centre at Sydney Harbour and is one of the world's most famous and distinctive buildings. The building comprises multiple performance venues, which together host well over 1,500 performances annually, attended by more than 1.2 million people. Among its performance venues are the Concert Hall, the Joan Sutherland Theatre, Drama Theatre and Playhouse.

Radio/wireless

Radio brought the world into people's households and provided entertainment for those who were not so mobile. Radio serials were very popular, such as 'Blue Hills', created and written by Gwen Meredith (1907–2006) who was born in Orange, NSW. It was broadcast by the ABC for 27 years, from 28th February 1949 to 30th September 1976 and ran for a total of 5,795 15-minute episodes. It was at one time the world's longest-running radio serial, set in a typical though fictional Australian country town called *Tanimbla,* and listeners were glued to their radios for the experience of keeping up with the lives of its protagonists and the lives of their families. Prior to Blue Hills, Meredith also wrote the scripts for the long-running radio serial 'The Lawsons' which ran between February 1944 and February 1949, comprising 1299 episodes. It finished the week before the commencement of Blue Hills and included several of the same characters.

There were many other popular local shows, including 'Life with Dexter' whose main character was played by Willie Fennell (1920–1992), born in Bondi, NSW. The show ran from 1953 to 1964 and followed the life of Dexter Dutton, his family, and neighbours. The popular quiz show *Pick-a-Box*, hosted by Bob Dyer (1909–1984) and assisted by his wife Dolly Dyer (1921–2004), ran on radio from 1948 until the early 1960s and was originally produced in the studios of Sydney's 2GB. It was launched on television in 1957 and continued until 1971.

Cinema

During the 1930s, 1940s and 1950s, Saturday entertainment was usually going to the 'flicks' at the local cinema. Most suburbs had at least one cinema house that became family entertainment and social hubs. They provided the escapism of movies but also the information of the newsreel. These were typically one-screen cinemas housing many people at one sitting and usually showing two films per session with an interval for refreshments. The Civic (later Hoyts Civic), in the Sydney suburb of Auburn, for example, had 2,271 seats. Moviegoers could purchase front row, back row or dress circle tickets. Opening in 1934, its elaborately ornamented structure was enhanced by the Wurlitzer organ that entertained people before and during the show. It closed in 1967 and was demolished in 1973.

The first Sydney cinematic experience was much simpler and was introduced by cinema and theatre entrepreneur brothers Charles McMahon (1861–1917) and James McMahon (1858–1915). In 1890 James displayed a model of Edison's phonograph and obtained a new model for the Sydney Tivoli in 1899. In 1891 Charles exhibited an electric weighing machine and in 1895 toured a demonstration 'Kinetoscope parlour' where people could view 'Anna Belle' performing her butterfly dance, 'Caicedo Dancing on the Tight Rope', a blacksmith shoeing a horse, a cockfight and a comic barbershop routine. In 1896-97 James opened the Salon Cinématographe in Pitt Street, Sydney, introducing a new cinématographe with special colour effects and payment by a coupon system.

In 1906 the world's first feature-length film 'The Story of the Kelly Gang' was produced in Victoria and opened at the Palace Theatre at 230 Pitt Street, Sydney, in February 1907. In that year, many permanent halls were established in Sydney, and by 1909 Sydneysiders could be entertained at the Colonial Theatre at 525 George Street, where a continuous cinema ran from 11 a.m. to 11 p.m., all for the price of threepence. On 24th June 1912, the Crystal Palace at 526 George Street in Haymarket, a thing of architectural beauty, was opened. Audiences flocked to see the new films that were being produced with Australian settings and stories, such as 'Captain Midnight' and 'Australia Calls'. Two films of the early 20th century which are still extant have gained iconic status: 'The Sentimental Bloke' and 'On our Selection'. Famed documentaries shown included those of Frank

Hurley's 'Grip of the Polar Ice' which dealt with Douglas Mawson's Antarctic expedition.

During the 1920s, filmgoers were entertained by an increasing influx of American films. The local industry that had been so prolific was now challenged by the technology of the American film industry and the role of American film distributors. This led to increasing exposure to American behaviours, values and preoccupations. Sydney's Lyceum and Prince Edward cinemas grossed record amounts showing the American 'talkies', 'The Jazz Singer' and 'The Red Dance'.

The first public screening of a 'talkie' (a sound synchronous motion picture) was on 10th June 1929, in a Sydney suburban cinema, the Wintergarden Theatre, Rose Bay. The theatre was demolished in 1987 but is commemorated by a plaque.

During the 1930s, actuality films, many based on Australian events, were enjoyed by audiences. Charles Chauvel (1897–1959), for example, produced the part-documentary, part-drama, 'In the Wake of the Bounty' in 1933. It attracted the attention of the censors, however, for the bare-breasted Tahitian women pictured. In this film, viewers gained their first exposure to a new young actor in the leading role: the 24-year-old Errol Flynn (1909–1959) as Fletcher Christian (1764–1793) seizing control from Bligh. Born in Tasmania, Flynn attended the secondary school Shore in Sydney, but this came to an end when he was reportedly expelled for theft. He later claimed it was for a sexual encounter with the school's laundress.

Following the Second World War, moviegoers could see their local environment in a number of American films that were shot in Australia, such as 'The Sundowners (1960), and 'The Overlanders' (1946). The first Australian-made colour feature film was Charles Chauvel's 'Jedda' in 1955, exploring Indigenous and non-Indigenous relations. But Australian films were not what were generally presented by cinemas controlled by foreign distributors.

In the 1960s and 1970s, the Australian film industry underwent a renaissance and moviegoers could be entertained by representations of familiar life. Often these films presented the comical 'ocker' image. Born in Broken Hill, NSW, one of the more prolific Australian actors was Chips Rafferty (1909–1971), who was widely regarded as an 'archetypal Aussie' of his day.

But the sophistication and variety of genres improved and directors such as Peter Weir, Gillian Armstrong and Bruce Beresford have provided both the local and international market with films of great distinction. A typical example is that of the Sydney-born Peter Weir, a NSW based director, who was responsible for noted films such as 'Gallipoli' (1981), 'The Year of Living Dangerously' (1982) and 'Picnic at Hanging Rock' (1999). He has also directed a range of international films such as

'Witness' (1985), 'Dead Poets' Society' (1989) and 'Green Card' (1991).

Television

Black and white test transmissions commenced in Sydney on TCN-9 on 13 July 1956. Two months later, on 16 September, TCN-9 Sydney had its official launch at 7.00pm when announcer John Godson was the first voice heard and Bruce Gyngell (1929–2000) the first person seen on camera introducing the first program *This is Television*. The ABC is a national public television network in Australia and was launched on 5 November 1956.

Some of the more popular Australian television shows based in NSW include Home and Away (1988-present), a soap based on the fictional coastal town of Summer Bay and Rake (2010–2018) based on a Sydney criminal defence barrister. Long-running and much-loved Australian productions have included Pick a Box (1957–1971), Mr Squiggle (1959–1999), Playschool (1966–present), Skippy (1968–1970), Hey Hey It's Saturday (1971–1999), No. 96 (1972–1977), Countdown (1974–1987), The Don Lane Show (1975–1983), The Sullivans (1976–1983), Prisoner (1979–1986), Sale of the Century (1980–2001), A Country Practice (1981–1994), Mother and Son (1984–1994), Kath and Kim (2002–2007), and Wentworth (2013 – present).

MUSEUMS

New South Wales is the home to many of the country's most famous museums. Australia's first public museum, the Australian Museum, was established in Sydney in 1827 with the aim of procuring 'many rare and curious specimens of Natural History'. Two years later, a carpenter William Holmes (1797–1831) was appointed the first custodian of the collection, then principally housed in the old post office building in Macquarie Place. Initially known as the Sydney Museum or Colonial Museum, it was not formally named the Australian Museum until 1836. It was also specified that the Museum and Botanic Gardens be jointly governed by a 'Committee of Superintendence' made up of 'eminent men of the colony'.

The museum's collections were initially housed in various buildings around Sydney, until the construction of a dedicated building. Designed by colonial architect, Mortimer Lewis (1796–1879), construction work began in 1846 on a site in William Street near Hyde Park. The new museum opened to the public in 1857, although with only a single exhibition gallery. Since that time, the site has undergone several modifications to accommodate the expansion of exhibitions, collections and staff. In 2008 a new wing to the east of the site was built to house scientific staff and collections.

The beginning of what is now known as the Powerhouse Museum took place in 1879, when the

Sydney International Exhibition was held in the Garden Palace, a purpose-built exhibition building situated in the grounds of the Royal Botanic Gardens. When the Exhibition concluded, the Australian Museum appointed a committee charged with selecting the best exhibits to display them permanently in a new museum to be situated within the Garden Palace. The intriguing name selected for this was 'The Technological, Industrial and Sanitary Museum of New South Wales', and its aim was to exhibit the latest industrial, construction and design innovations. Unfortunately, in September 1882, with the opening imminent, the Garden Palace was completely destroyed by fire, including almost all of the selected artefacts. The only ones that remained included a Ceylonese (the former name of Sri Lanka) statue of an elephant carved in graphite that had astonishingly managed to survive the inferno, despite dropping five stories to the ground.

During the following decade, while the museum was rebuilt and more exhibits were acquired, it was temporarily housed in a large tin shed in The Domain, a dwelling it regrettably shared with the morgue of Sydney Hospital. The stench of decaying corpses became unbearable and, after intense lobbying, the museum was later relocated to a three-storey building in Harris Street, Ultimo. It was then rebadged as the Technological Museum.

The new museum was situated adjacent to the Sydney Technical College, intended to provide inspirational material to the nearby students. Its name was later changed to The Museum of Applied Arts and Sciences, establishing branches in the NSW country towns Broken Hill, Albury, Newcastle and Maitland, among others. Before long, it outgrew the main Harris Street site and by the late 1970s, many of the exhibits were stored in its attic, away from the public.

The situation was so serious that, on 23rd August 1978, then NSW Premier Neville Wran announced that the decaying Ultimo Power Station, several hundred metres north of the Harris Street site, would be the museum's new permanent home, along with the adjoining former Ultimo Tram Depot. In 1982, it incorporated the Sydney Observatory. On 10th March 1988, the newly named Powerhouse Museum was opened, with the main building containing five levels, three courtyards, a cafeteria and several offices. The museum is continually expanding and maintains offsite storage facilities.

Located at Darling Harbour in Sydney, the Australian National Maritime Museum is the national focus for maritime collections, exhibitions, research and archaeology. The museum, which opened on 30th November 1991, presents a changing program of exhibitions and events to highlight Australia's maritime past and chronicle the stories, objects, people and places that are part of the country's history. It has over 850,000 visitors annually and 13,000 members support the museum and regularly enjoy special events and activities. The museum has one of the largest floating historical vessel collections in the world, featuring the celebrated replica of Captain Cook's *HMB Endeavour*, the former Navy destroyer *HMAS Vampire*, the former Navy patrol boat *HMAS Advance* and former Navy submarine *HMAS Onslow*.

THE OUTDOORS

Parks

Parks, as public domains, have played an important role in both passive and active entertainment. In industrialised Britain, they had been viewed as a means of providing the increasing numbers of urban dwellers living in cramped conditions with sites to improve moral and physical wellbeing. This philosophy, known as 'euthenics', recognised that inner wellbeing could be achieved by altering the external environment.

The roots of the earliest public park in the early colony go back to 1800, although it didn't become so until much later. The 'Old Government House' in Parramatta was the former country residence of 10 early governors of NSW between 1800 and 1847. During the 1840s, local residents successfully lobbied for the grounds and surrounding area to be declared a 'people's park' for their health and recreation, and in 1858 Parramatta Park was opened for public use.

Hyde Park in central Sydney was, however, the earliest of such areas to be formally dedicated. It was set aside by Governor Arthur Phillip but not proclaimed a public park until 1810. Its most popular early use was as a horse racing course, although it was also used for cricket matches and general family games. In 1854 it was made more inviting when the newly formed Hyde Park Improvement Committee created formal paths and gardens and installed monuments. It became a place where the public could be entertained by processions and oratory, along with featuring a bandstand. After the upheaval to Hyde Park occasioned by the construction of the underground railway system in the 1920s and 1930s, it was reconstructed with two major new works being included, one at either end of the park.

At the northern end, that allegorical fantasy, the Archibald Fountain, was unveiled in 1932. Its full name is the J F Archibald Memorial Fountain and is named after Jean François (J F) Archibald (1856–1919), owner and editor of *The Bulletin* magazine, who bequeathed funds to have it built. There is now a giant chess board near the Fountain which entertains both players and observers. At the opposite end, two years later, the ANZAC Memorial opened to commemorate soldiers lost in First World War.

In 1816, Governor Lachlan Macquarie established the Royal Botanic Gardens and 'The Domain', on land that Governor Arthur Phillip had set aside as the 'Governor's Demesne'. Over time, the area of the Botanic Gardens consolidated, and the area known as the Domain contracted, with areas taken for roads, for the Art Gallery of NSW and the State Library.

Initially, the Botanic Gardens was to be a place of scientific research, with the first Colonial botanist, Charles Fraser, appointed in 1817, but in 1831 Governor Richard Bourke opened the Botanic Gardens to the public. In 1879, a grandiose Garden Palace exhibition building was constructed. It celebrated government, commerce and the arts and under the central dome stood a bronze statue of Queen Victoria. Built of iron, glass and wood with brick foundations, it reportedly cost £192,000 at the time of the opening, with the ground floor covering two hectares to which, if the areas of the basement, galleries and tower floors were added, made a total area of 3.4 hectares. On the morning of 25th September 1882, it was totally destroyed by a huge fire in circumstances that were possibly suspicious. The Botanic Gardens is the oldest scientific institution in Australia and also remains an area for sport and strolling for the people who work and live in the city.

The remaining parts of The Domain, a 34-hectare area of open space, opened as a public area in the 1830s. In its time the grounds have been a site for weddings, balloon ascents, commemorative events, outdoor cinemas and theatre, music concerts, sporting events, political and religious spruikers and family outings—and occasionally as an (unofficial) haven for the homeless. The 1850s Inter-colonial Cricket Match, between New South Wales and Victoria, was played there, and more recently, The Domain has been the site of concerts such as 'Opera in the Park', continuing its role as a place for public entertainment.

A particular aspect of the Domain's history is 'Speakers' Corner', established in the eastern end, near the Art Gallery of NSW, in 1878. On Sundays, speakers on soapboxes expressed their views on wide-ranging subjects—religion, politics and social reform. In 1916, during the First World War, the Domain was the site of anti-conscription rallies and, in the 1960s, for large anti-Vietnam War 'moratorium' demonstrations. It was the place for demonstrations and conflicts between rival political factions in the 1920s and 1930s, between communists and the New Guard—a short-lived Australian monarchist, anti-communist organisation that emerged from the Sydney-based Old Guard in 1931, during the Great Depression.

Aboriginal speakers were also active in Speaker's' Corner from the late 1930s, including civil rights campaigners such as Jack Patten, Tom Foster, Pearl Gibbs and William (Bill) Ferguson. One of the more prominent soap box orators between the early 1950s and late 1980s was John Webster (1913–2008) who delivered his proclamations beneath the Moreton Bay Fig trees.

Some parks have been artificially constructed rather than taking advantage of the natural environment. Centennial Park is such an example. Dedicated to commemorating the centenary of establishment of the colony in 1788, it had the dual purpose of protecting the central ponds and swamps which formed early Sydney's water supply, known as 'Lachlan's Swamps', as well as being a park accessible to everyone. It was opened as Centennial Park on 26th

January 1888 by Sir Henry Parkes who said: 'this grand park is emphatically the people's park, and you must always take as much interest in it as if by your own hands you had planted the flowers, the park will be one of the grandest adornments to this beautiful country.'

The layout and landscape design of the park is attributed to the botanist Charles Moore (1820–1905), the Director of the Botanic Gardens from 1848–96. It features formal gardens, ponds, grand avenues, statues, historic buildings and sporting fields. Renewal of Centennial Park throughout the 1990s included the involvement of John Lennis (1952–2015), then an Aboriginal Education Officer with the Royal Botanic Gardens & Domain Trust.

A feature added to Centennial Park to mark the centenary of Federation is the Federation Pavilion. It was erected on the site of the official ceremony to mark the Federation of Australia and the inauguration of the Commonwealth of Australia on 1st January 1901. The Pavilion encloses the 'Commonwealth Stone', almost the only remnant of the original pavilion used by the British aristocrat and statesman, Lord Hopetoun (1860–1908), the first Governor-General of the Commonwealth of Australia, at the ceremony in 1901.

Another example of an early 20th century park is Nielsen Park (established 1912), located in Vaucluse on the southern side of Sydney Harbour, created and named in honour of the Secretary for Lands, Niels R W Nielsen (1869–1930). It provided places for safe swimming and boating as well as venues for Sunday band performances.

Created by the state and federal governments during the 1980s to celebrate Australia's Bicentenary in 1988, Bicentennial Park is a 40-hectare suburban parkland located 16 kilometres west of the Sydney's CBD in the suburb of Homebush Bay.

National Parks were also important for recreation such as bushwalking. The Royal National Park (151 square kilometres), about 29 kilometres south of Sydney, was formally proclaimed on 26th April 1879 and is the second oldest national park in the world, after Yellowstone in the United States. 'Royal' was only added to its name in 1955, after Queen Elizabeth II passed by the park on the train during her 1954 tour of Australia. Even before the opening of a connecting railway line in 1886 the park would regularly receive more than 50,000 visitors a year and that figure increased considerably once visitors could come by train. Families used the area for picnics, boating and general amusements. Today there are more than 225 national parks and reserves in NSW, including the Blue Mountains, Ku-ring-gai Chase, Kosciuszko and Mungo national parks.

Swimming

With a mild climate and a long coastline with many beaches, it is not surprising that swimming and surfing have long been popular entertainments in NSW. Although harbour baths provided safe sea bathing, such as in Manly and at Nielsen Park, by the late 19th century Sydney Harbour had become highly polluted and swimmers gravitated towards ocean pools. Early such pools were constructed in Newcastle and Wollongong, but it was the pools on Coogee, Bronte and Bondi beaches in Sydney that are regarded as playing significant roles in nurturing Australia's swimming cultures and surf lifesaving movement.

Club swimming carnivals at the Bondi and Bronte baths in the 1890s included men's swimming, diving events, water polo matches, and other events. (Women's swimming events were a novelty in colonial NSW.) State government schools and private schools began offering learn-to-swim programs for boys and girls in the late 1800s and instruction in swimming was included in the school curriculum in NSW in 1897.

More elaborate swimming pools were soon being constructed around Sydney Harbour, sometimes adjacent to where harbour baths had been. The oldest in Australia are at Balmain. Constructed in 1882, since 1964 it has been called the 'Dawn Fraser Baths' to honour one of Australia's greatest swimmers. Dawn Fraser, born in Balmain, won eight Olympic medals, including four golds, and six Commonwealth Games gold medals. The first game of water polo in Australia was played there around 1888.

Sunbathing and surfing are longstanding popular pastimes. During the early 20th century, particularly at Manly and Bondi beaches in Sydney, mixed bathing became lawful, although surfers over eight years old were expected to be covered from neck to knee.

The iconic North Sydney public pool was completed in 1936 (the year after the opening of the nearby Luna Park) as the Great Depression was easing. The precursors of the Domain baths, located just to the east of the Royal Botanic Gardens, can be dated back to around 1840. The pool was named after Andrew 'Boy' Charlton in 1968, after the famous Sydney freestyle swimmer Andrew Charlton (1907–1975) who won a gold medal in the 1500-metre freestyle at the 1924 Summer Olympics in Paris.

After the Second World War, most country towns and urban neighbourhoods soon had, or had easy access to, public pools.

LUNA PARK

Amusement Parks were a turn of the century phenomenon. One of the most recognised, Luna Park, is situated in Milsons Point on the north side of Sydney Harbour close to the Sydney Harbour Bridge. The first Australian 'Luna Park' opened in St Kilda in Melbourne in 1912. When a second opened in Adelaide's Glenelg in 1930, the residents objected, and several years later a venue was sought in Sydney. A site was found at Milson's Point near the harbour and construction, including reassembly of the rides from the Glenelg operation that had been placed in voluntary liquidation, cost £60,000, taking place over a three-month period. It opened to the public on 4th October 1935, at a time when the worst of the Great Depression was fading, and was an immediate hit. Its entrance, in the shape of a cavernous mouth, has welcomed over 100 million people over the years. The 'circus' atmosphere was enhanced by its slogan: 'just for fun'.

Luna Park was closed in mid-1979 immediately following the Ghost Train fire, which killed six children and one adult. Much of the original park was demolished, and a new amusement park was constructed, initially under the name of Harbourside Amusement Park, but later restoring the Luna Park name. The park was closed again in 1988 as an engineering inspection determined that several rides needed urgent repairs which were not carried out before a NSW government deadline. Ownership was passed to a new body and it re-opened in 1995.

However, Luna Park closed again after thirteen months because of noise and pollution complaints from clifftop residents about the Big Dipper rollercoaster. As a result, the ride's operating hours were heavily restricted, leading to a significant drop in attendance that made the park unprofitable. After another redevelopment lasting 14 months, it reopened in 2004 and has been operating since. The Luna Park Precinct was listed on the NSW State Heritage Register on 5th March 2010.

PINBALL MACHINES/VIDEO ARCADES

From the early 1900s to about 1970, most notably during the 1930s, penny arcades, venues for coin-operated entertainment devices, were very popular. They fulfilled desires for both entertainment and gambling. These were replaced by pinball machines in the 1970s and 1980s in pubs, milk bars and shopping centres across NSW. In turn, video games invaded arcades, entertainment centres and eventually private homes.

EVENTS

In the first half of the 20th century, 'Back to town' events were very popular in rural areas. These were held both to celebrate the founding of an area but also to encourage the return of 'lost' residents. Pageants, processions and carnivals attracted attendance as did sporting events.

NSW is home to many annual events that attract great crowds. The Toyota Country Music Festival in Tamworth is an ungated event of ticketed and free shows and rated among the best in the world. In January each year this, the largest music festival in the southern hemisphere, attracts over 300,000 visitors across 10 days, with over 700 artists featured in 2,800 scheduled events across 120 venues.

Other major events in NSW include the Hunter Valley Wine and Food Festival and 'Pie Time', in the Southern Highlands in June, with 30 days and 100s of ways to enjoy pies. The Wupa@Wanaruah is a free Aboriginal art and culture exhibition that is annually facilitated by Ungooroo Aboriginal Corporation, in conjunction with venues located throughout the Hunter Valley Wine and surrounding region. 'Yulefest' in the Blue Mountains is held between June and August when many venues offer traditional Xmas style celebrations.

Since 1998, the annual Sydney Royal Easter Show has been held at the Sydney Olympic Park precinct at Homebush Bay (the previous 116 were held at Moore Park). The Show, first held in 1823, is open for two weeks during the Easter period. There are many other annual shows held in towns across NSW.

Held annually in Bowral, 'Tulip Time' is one of Australia's oldest floral festivals, attracting tens of thousands of visitors. Corbett Gardens, the centrepiece of the Festival is mass-planted with over 75,000 tulip bulbs and 15,000 annuals, while a further 40,000 tulips are planted across the district.

12. *Science*

The first pursuit of science in NSW is seen in the Indigenous understanding of and relationship with the environment, demonstrating a keen understanding of all elements: earth, sea, sky, weather, flora and fauna.

Possibly the earliest non-Indigenous scientist to try to comprehend the environment of the colony was Lieutenant William Dawes (1762–1836), an officer in the marines who volunteered to come to NSW. He was a distinguished astronomer selected to observe an anticipated sighting of a comet in the southern hemisphere. Although the anticipated sighting did not occur, Dawes's skills as a botanist, engineer, surveyor and mapmaker were useful to the colony's expansion.

In an area just north of The Rocks, Dawes built an observatory by paying those marines who laboured for him with rum and water. Here he searched the skies, but also befriended local Aboriginals, particularly a young *Eora* woman, recording some of their conversations in his notebooks.

Dawes departed the colony in December 1791 following a dispute with Governor Arthur Phillip. It was not until Sir Thomas Brisbane (1773–1860), a soldier scientist, arrived as colonial Governor that an observatory was built at Parramatta and systematic observations of weather were commenced. Although these were sporadic for some time, they did continue to maintain scientific observation. In 1859, the English economist and logician William Stanley Jevons (1835–1882) published a 52-page study on Australian climate generally, with specific reference to rainfall patterns.

Following the use of the telegraph for the collection of meteorological data, from the 1870s onwards both records and forecasting improved. NSW was advantaged by the appointment of the first locally born Government Meteorologist, Henry Chamberlain Russell (1836–1907). He established observation networks throughout the state, issued the first synoptic chart to be published in an Australian newspaper, and convened the first inter-colonial conference to coordinate data collection, held in Sydney in 1879.

The Royal Botanic Gardens are the oldest scientific establishment in NSW and Australia. They are a heritage-listed 30-hectare botanical garden, located at Farm Cove on the eastern fringe of the Sydney, specialising in botany and horticulture. Its first superintendent was the Colonial Botanist Charles Fraser (1786–1831) who collected Indigenous plant specimens. By 1825 the gardens also displayed exotic plants.

NSW has produced a number of eminent scientists. In the field of microbiology, scientists such as Sydney-born Frank Tidswell (1867–1941), had to fight against the idea that infections were caused by atmospheric poisons instead of the germ theory espoused by Louis Pasteur. Tidswell, a strong-minded person, was often at odds with his superiors and with the Board of Health. He was convinced, correctly, that bubonic plague was caused by fleas on rats and not, as then thought, by person-to-person contact. According to medical historian Peter Tyler, Tidswell was never given credit for this discovery, but Tidswell's 1906 publication on snake and spider bites, *Rare Bites: Researches on Australian Venoms*, did mark the beginning of a new area of biomedicine.

Born in Bathurst NSW in 1899, Sir William Ian Clunies Ross (1899–1959) was a veterinary scientist, described as the 'architect of Australia's scientific boom', for his stewardship of the Commonwealth Scientific and Industrial Research Organisation (CSIRO). John Cornforth (1917–2013), born in Sydney, won the 1975 Nobel Prize in Chemistry for his work on the stereochemistry of enzyme-catalysed reactions, becoming the only Nobel laureate born in NSW. David Karoly, also Sydney-born, is an internationally acclaimed Australian atmospheric scientist, who has greatly contributed to the field of atmospheric sciences. Another Sydneysider, Robert McCredie May (1936–2020), Baron May of Oxford, was

President of the Royal Society from 2000 to 2005, and a professor at the University of Sydney and Princeton University.

Another good example of scientific invention in NSW is the 'Mills cross', first demonstrated at the Fleurs field station around Badgerys Creek, about 40 kilometres west of Sydney, in 1954 by the Sydney-born Australian astronomer Bernard Yarnton Mills (1920–2011). This was a two-dimensional radio telescope based on the interferometer, an instrument that uses the interference patterns formed by waves. It consisted of two interferometers erected in two straight rows intersecting at right angles. Each arm of the cross was 450 metres long, running N-S and E-W, producing a fan beam in the sky.

Dame Bridget Ogilvie, born in Glenn Innes, NSW, in 1938, is a renowned parasitologist and immunologist. She has received many honours and awards for her contributions to science and medical research, including 24 honorary doctorates. Sydney-born Fiona Juliet Stanley is an Australian epidemiologist noted for her public health work, her research into child and maternal health, as well as birth disorders such as cerebral palsy.

In 1926, Prime Minister Stanley Bruce (1883–1967) revised the Science and Industry Research Act, and the Council for Scientific and Industrial Research (CSIR) emerged from these changes. The Science and Industry Research Act was changed again in 1949 to form the

CSIRO, an Australian federal government agency responsible for scientific research. Its purpose is to carry out scientific research for purposes including assisting Australian industry, furthering the interests of the Australian community, contributing to the achievement of Australian national objectives or the performance of the national and international responsibilities of the Commonwealth, and encouraging or facilitating the application or utilisation of the results of such research.

Among many other accomplishments, CSIRO's legacy includes fast Wi-Fi, the personal insect repellent 'Aerogard', and polymer banknotes. Today CSIRO's research involves assisting to find the first gravitational waves in space, growing gluten-free grains, 3D-printing of replacement body parts, and pioneering new renewable energy sources. It is reported that the present value of benefits from their work is around $4.5 billion annually, almost three times their total annual budget and more than four times the funding provided by the Australian Government.

The CSIRO has 14 locations across NSW, including Albury, Armidale, Boorowa, Coonabarabran, Narrabri, Newcastle, Myall Lakes and Parkes, while those in Sydney include Eveleigh, Lindfield, Marsfield, Kensington, Lucas Heights and North Ryde.

Australia has one operating nuclear reactor, the OPAL research reactor at Lucas Heights which supplies most of Australia's nuclear medicine. It replaced the High

Flux Australian Reactor which operated from 1958 to 2007 on the same site. It produces neutrons, subatomic particles found in the nucleus of all atoms, through the process of fission—the splitting of a large atom, such as uranium, into two smaller ones. Fission tales place when a heavy nucleus absorbs a neutron and splits. Neutrons are given off in the process of fission and, after slowing down (losing energy), are used to keep the fission chain-reaction going.

The original purpose of the Lucas Height reactor was to test materials for their suitability in use in future power reactors. However, the Commonwealth Environment Protection and Biodiversity Conservation Act 1999 prohibits certain nuclear actions (specified in s.22A) unless federal approval is obtained, and specifically prohibits nuclear power generation (in s.140A). The Act states that the Minister must not approve an action consisting of or involving the construction or operation of a nuclear fuel fabrication plant, or a nuclear power station, or an enrichment plant, or a reprocessing facility.

The decision not to pursue a power reactor program in Australia meant that there has been a change in how the reactor has been used over the years. With around 40% of the Earth's identified sources of uranium, Australia has one of the largest deposits in the world.

The reactor is one of only 70 worldwide that can produce essential in-demand medical radioisotopes.

In addition, it makes material or carries out analyses for the mining industry, for forensic purposes and research. The nuclear process produces dangerous waste that must be carefully stored because of the harm is can cause humans and the environment.

13. *Crime, Punishment and Law Enforcement*

New South Wales was a colony of convicts. It was based on crime, or at least punishment. Establishing law and order in the colony was not easy. Common early crimes were theft of food or planning to rob stores, an offence which had to be dealt with severely in a colony with limited supplies. The bushranger John 'Black' Caesar (1764–1796), of African descent, was the first recorded runaway, or 'bolter', being convicted many times for the theft of food. It was made a hanging offence, for both convicts and marines. One of the first acts of Governor Phillip was to establish a criminal court. In mid-1789, due to increased robberies of food, and with supplies shrinking, he formed the first night-watch, consisting of well-behaved convicts but soon including free settlers in its ranks. To deter smugglers and stowaways, in 1789 he formed a Night Watch and Rowboat Guard, also drawn from the ranks of the best-behaved convicts.

The Night Watch was replaced by the Sydney Foot Police in 1790 and continued as an organised force (later known as the Sydney Police) until the amalgamation of all NSW colonial police forces in 1862. By 1800, there were 36 constables, and ex-convict Henry Kable (1763–1846) was appointed as the colony's first chief constable. Although an independent Water Police and part of the Sydney Police, the Row Boat Guard was the forerunner of today's Marine Area Command.

EARLY CORPORAL AND OTHER PUNISHMENTS

Convicts who were sent to NSW had been sentenced for periods of seven or fourteen years, or for life. Transportation to Botany Bay was itself a punishment akin to being sent into outer space with little hope of return. For those for whom transportation did not have a reformatory effect, secondary punishment was provided on government chain gangs or offenders were transported to penal settlements such as Macquarie Harbour or Norfolk Island. Founded initially as a place of settlement, Norfolk Island became a place for those who had offended in the colony.

Incidentally, Norfolk Island later made a strong connection with one of the most famous British maritime crimes of the late 18th century. The mutiny on the Royal Navy vessel *HMS Bounty* took place in the south Pacific on 28th April 1789. Disaffected crewmen, led by Acting Lieutenant Fletcher Christian, seized control of the ship from their captain, Lieutenant William Bligh, and set him and 18 loyalists adrift in the ship's open launch (they completed a voyage of more than 6,500 kilometres in the launch to reach safety). The descendants of the mutineers, and the other inhabitants of Pitcairn Island, were relocated to Norfolk Island on 8th June 1856, after outgrowing their island home (some later returned). This date is celebrated every year on Norfolk Island as 'Bounty Day'.

Punishment in the early Port Jackson colony was both corporal and capital, and public floggings were common. The sentence was usually up to 100 lashes, but it was not uncommon to be sentenced to between 100 and 200 lashes. If an emancipated man or one free by servitude transgressed, he would appear before one of the Benches of Magistrates where the commonest punishment handed down was again flogging. Other punishments included solitary confinement—then considered a useful aid to reform—and imprisonment with hard labour. For women, at the Parramatta Female Factory from 1821 to 1848 there was a 'third classification' for troublesome women or those who were convicted of a colonial offence.

Incarceration continued as a common form of punishment. Changing concepts and ideas of the role of incarceration influenced the rationale and organisation of the various prisons. In 1841, a new prison was opened at Darlinghurst and prisoners were marched along George Street to their new home, situated on a hill, providing entertainment for a jeering crowd. Men and women prisoners were held there in different wings and they had different exercise yards in which they were supposed to walk in a silent circle for an hour's daily exercise. When reformer sisters Rosamund and Florence Hill visited the prison in 1875, they noted that, while the men were actively involved in the workshops attached to the gaol, women had little to do but the longstanding prison work of picking oakum (a loose fibre obtained by untwisting old rope)—a job which badly affected their hands and nails. There was no rehabilitation through training available to women, and most of their work was done in their cells.

A Women's Reformatory at Long Bay was opened in 1909, near the equivalent men's prison. Much like the Female Factory, it included workshops and a hospital with a visiting surgeon. However, the work of the women's rights activist Rose Scott, whose reports indicted the prison system as unchanged since 1840, had led to some improvements, particularly in the individual cells. New exercise regimens were introduced, new occupations were introduced, and the oakum picking was dropped. The difficulties that had arisen with using male warders in the women's gaols were addressed by the simple method of using only female warders. A Prisoners' Aid Association was also established to provide assistance to the women when they left the gaol.

The early magistrates were commonly local landholders or notable settlers who had little or no legal training and who were inclined to wield their power as it suited them, despite attempts by Governors such as Richard Bourke to limit them. In consequence, stipendiary (salaried) magistrates were appointed in major centres. The first to be appointed was D'Arcy Wentworth in 1810, an Irish surgeon and the first paying passenger to arrive in the colony. By 1827 there were 32 men of independent means who were magistrates. The need for more led to 21 military officers being appointed. But the need for stipendiary magistrates was increasing as there were only 20 magistrates who were civil officials. The system of employing stipendiary magistrates was formalised in the Metropolitan Magistrates Act of 1881.

DEVELOPMENT OF THE POLICE FORCE

Governor Lachlan Macquarie was particularly committed to creating a law-abiding society. An example of an early occasion of mass violence was the 1804 'Vinegar Hill' battle, fought at Rouse Hill, but named for an earlier uprising in Ireland. Troops and civilian volunteers overwhelmed about 300 rebels who supported Irish nationalism. This, among other incidents indicated the urgent need for a dedicated force to deal with crime. In 1810, Macquarie increased night patrols in Sydney and in 1811, reorganised the police, such as it was (many were ex-convicts). The first police superintendent, Captain Francis Nicholas Rossi (1776–1851), arrived in 1825 and in the same year, Governor Richard Bourke established a mounted force to protect the hinterland as more settlers pushed beyond the boundaries of settlement (the 'limits of location'). The NSW Mounted Police force, colloquially known as the 'traps', is older than the Canadian Mounties as it traces its roots to the squatters who had originally formed the Governor's bodyguard. This force dealt mainly with runaway convicts who became bushrangers, and with the increasing confrontations with Aboriginals. So concerning were the activities of bushrangers that, between 1830 and 1842, legislation was passed permitting any person to arrest anyone found on the road with a firearm looking likely to commit robbery.

In 1825, the Military Mounted Police were formed following clashes between Aboriginals and settlers in the central west but were disbanded in 1850 in favour of a civilian Mounted Police (also known as the Mounted Road Patrol). These were another link in the chain leading to today's NSW Mounted Police. As settlement expanded beyond the designated boundaries of location and as a direct result of the Myall Creek Massacre (the killing of at least 28 unarmed Indigenous Australians by 11 colonists on 10th June 1838), the Border Police was formed (1839–46) and later the Mounted Native Police (1848–1859).

Dispossessed and displaced Aboriginals often took from the flocks and herds of settlers, who in turn killed and massacred Aboriginals. The conflict led to growing guerrilla warfare on a moving frontier. Unfortunately, the Police Force was poorly manned and spent more of its time in matters such as executing warrants and serving notices than in patrolling the large areas for which it was responsible. It was also caught up in a dispute between the Governor and the Legislative Council, the latter representing the interests of squatters.

As settlement expanded further, the police used Aboriginal trackers while leading forays to drive Aboriginals from areas newly occupied by colonists. The early attempts were not successful, as Aboriginal trackers were more loyal to their clans than to the police. A native police force was formed as a move to stem the increasing incursions by Aboriginals in the state's north. Aboriginal troopers worked under the command of a white officer, and the Force eventually achieved the aim of driving out Aboriginals. Acting on a request from a local clan elder, the Native Police Corps was reformed so that its members served outside their own areas.

In the following years, a range of specialised policing units were established with different remits. The Water Police, for example, was formed to address smuggling and stowaways. It was based at Cockatoo Island, Watsons Bay and Goat Island on Sydney Harbour. In 1862, it was incorporated into the NSW Police Force. In the early 20th century, the rescue of ships became its primary role, and during the Second World War it was responsible for port security.

The discovery of gold at Ophir near Bathurst in 1851 created a new challenge for the forces of law and order as people rushed to the goldfields pursuing the dream of riches. Life on the diggings was harsh, and provisions were in short supply. Tensions, which increased when a miner's licence was introduced, overflowed into race riots at Lambing Flats, near the present town of Young, during 1860–1861. On one occasion, an intoxicated mob of 3,000 miners, accompanied by a brass band, marched from Tipperary Gully to the Chinese camp, destroyed the camp, cut off the pigtails of the Chinese men living there and overwhelmed 300 police.

During the 1860s, mobs of 'larrikins' increasingly disturbed the peace in Sydney, their disruptive behaviour leading to violence. This characterised the streets of Sydney for the next few decades. They formed gangs or 'pushes', dressed in 'sharp' clothes and were generally subversive of polite culture. At the same time, in the NSW countryside, bushrangers were holding up coaches, robbing settlers and cattle 'duffing' (stealing). For these crimes they could spend long periods imprisoned or could face death. In 1862, a gang including Ben Hall and Frank Gardiner held up a coach carrying 14,000 pounds sterling and gold bullion. Bushrangers often adopted romantic names and created similar personas. Frederick Ward was known as Captain Thunderbolt; Jack Donahue became known as 'Bold' Jack. He and his gang were known as 'Strippers' as they stripped their victims of literally everything.

There was a reluctance to condemn bushrangers in rural areas. This had a number of probable causes. Some bushrangers terrorised and blackmailed neighbourhoods: those who should have acted against them were unwilling to do so as they knew their property could well be attacked in reprisal. However, others actually bought support or acted in the settlers interests, and one of the major contributors to inaction against bushrangers was a sympathy that many in the bush felt for them—plus often an antipathy to police.

The first police detective in the colony was Israel Chapman (1794–1868), a Jewish convict given a life sentence for assault and robbery who, on arriving in the colony in 1818, industrially commenced gaining positions for himself, receiving a conditional pardon for good conduct. He was later granted an absolute pardon and in the mid-1820s, was appointed a police 'runner', a position which, like the Bow Street Runners in England, was predominantly that of detective.

In 1862, a twelve-man detective force was formed. These men assisted in locating the notorious bushrangers and outlaws Ben Hall, Frank Gardiner and Frederick Wordsworth Ward, the 'gentleman bushranger' know as Captain Thunderbolt. In 1879, a detective branch was formally established.

In the period following the ending of transportation, attacks on life and property actually *increased*. This was blamed on unemployment and lack of supervision of those convicts still serving their time. Added to this, excessive drinking and gambling in the colony attracted comment. The diversity and lack of unity of the various policing forces was a hindrance to efficient regulation and law enforcement. This was addressed in 1862 when the *Police Regulation Act* was passed by the colonial Parliament.

The forces amalgamated to become the NSW Police Force, under the command of Inspector General John McLerie (1809–1874), who was a former captain and commandant of the Yeomanry Cavalry, a mounted component of the British Volunteer Corps.

The NSW Police Force, probably because of the nature of the colony, has been described as an 'armed paramilitary organisation', based on the Royal Irish Constabulary. Its members were sent regularly to Ireland for training and this meant that it concentrated less on community policing and used a more military approach. Its structures and order of command remained relatively unchanged until 1985.

The force has frequently been called upon to deal with challenges to public order. The depression of the 1890s led to bank failures and industrial collapse. The police had to deal with the resulting strikes and attendant violence—like the many strikes in shearing sheds in western NSW. In 1916, during the First World War, members of the International Workers of the World, known as 'Wobblies', were arrested and convicted of sedition. The police were involved in their arrest and conviction and came under attack for 'framing' the 12 men involved.

In the period following the First World War, confidence tricksters, pickpockets and card sharps seem to have increased their activities. 'Con artists' used both simple and elaborate stories to gain money under false pretences, while card sharps favoured the three-card trick, using dexterous sleight of hand to confuse punters. They operated in a range of situations, such as at agricultural shows, on trains and at race meetings. Pickpockets favoured areas around Central Railway Station, noisy populated areas such as markets, department stores and hotels, and the shipping terminals of Sydney.

The period of the 1920s records a wide range of crimes from the simple 'snatch and run' to elaborate and planned strategies. Many of these exploits were reported in the sensationalist Sydney newspaper, the *Truth*. An extraordinarily athletic thief, Ethel 'Ettie' Benn, was a prime example of the former. She would grab what she could and, using uncanny skills at running and jumping, would attempt to evade pursuers. Although impressive, this relatively simple technique led to her frequent arrest.

During the Great Depression of the 1930s, there were clashes between the New Guard, nationalists and fascists on the one hand, and communists, socialists and the unemployed, on the other. With the state facing collapse, the police had to maintain law and order, sometimes violently. The Scottish-born police officer, William Mackay (1885–1948), trying to suppress the New Guard on one occasion, when its supporters were particularly difficult, allegedly told his men to 'go out there and belt their bloody heads off'. In 1931, there were battles between police and members of the

Unemployed Workers Union, particularly in the Sydney suburbs of Newtown and Bankstown. At this point in the Great Depression, many people were being evicted from houses, often that they were occupying illegally, and police with drawn revolvers confronted those who sought to protect them.

During the 1920s and 1930s, the Sydney underworld was led by a number of villains, but two particularly notorious figures were Tilly Devine (1900–1970) and Kate Leigh (1881–1964). Tilly's background in prostitution led her to the running her own brothels, while Kate ran a 'sly grog' operation. Both women vied for supremacy, and both were noted characters. The law banned men, but not women from living off the immoral earnings of prostitution, and both women exploited this. These were the days of the 'razor gangs', so-called for their choice of weapon. The members of the gangs were involved in a range of crimes, including drug running and gambling—all involving violence. John Henry 'Chow' Hayes (1911–1993), for example, was a thug whose crimes included the straightforward refusal to pay for drinks at a hotel to 'demanding money with menaces' and assault. He spent over 30 years in prison at different times.

The work of the police force continually expanded as a result of social change and legislative requirements. In 1894, the police were armed following an attack by a number of criminals on the Union Steamship Company's office and a consequent attack on police. Cars also made traffic control necessary. The amendments to the Vagrancy Act in 1905 meant police had to be more assertive in addressing drunkenness and obscene behaviour, while the Police Offences Act of 1908 gave police the power to be harsher in their dealing with brothels, pimps, prostitution and off-course betting. In 1915, the Liquor Amendment Act led to the 'six o'clock swill', where patrons were forced to finish their drink by 6.00pm, which created increasing challenges to public order.

Technology has also changed the nature of law enforcement. In 1903, a fingerprint section of the police force commenced operations. About 1910, Sydney police started taking 'mug shots' of offenders, possibly in an attempt to allow police to recognise professionals and recidivists. In 1913, the first motorcycle patrol was established to control traffic, and in the 1930s, ballistic and photographic analysis were used to assist investigations. In 1938, the scientific investigation bureau was formed. Following a growing number of suicides, the NSW police 'Cliff Rescue Squad' was formed in 1942; it's now called the Police Rescue Unit. Its activities were expanded to include cliff accidents, tracking murderers (as in the unsolved Wanda Beach murders in January 1965) and rescuing those trapped by natural disasters. The Police Dog Squad was formed after William Cyril Mosley/Moxley raped and killed a young woman and beat her boyfriend to death. The resulting drawn-out search for evidence indicated the need for a trained dog unit and this was formed in 1932. From 1954 to 1979 the squad was disbanded but later reconstituted.

NOTABLE CRIMES AND CRIMINALS

A number of crimes and their attendant issues of law enforcement have caught public attention, mainly because they were crimes of passion, sensationalised and sometimes unsolved.

The Pyjama Girl mystery

The case known as the 'Pyjama Girl' mystery arose when the body of a young woman who had been shot, burned and battered, was found near Albury in NSW in 1934. Police anticipated an early solution to the crime as she was wearing very distinctive pyjamas: striped green and cream, with a distinguishing dragon motif on the pyjama top. The fragments of the pyjamas took on a life of their own, but despite the body being displayed in a glass coffin in Sydney, and modified photographs circulated, over ten years passed before it was identified as that of Linda Agostini (née Platt). The same year, her husband, Antonio Agostini (1903–1969), admitted to her manslaughter, claiming that she had threatened him with a gun and, in the ensuing struggle, had allegedly been shot. Agostini had then doused the body with petrol or kerosene and burned it.

The case was supposedly solved by the NSW police commissioner, William Mackay, who interrogated Agostini, who had been a waiter in Romano's, a Sydney restaurant that Mackay had frequented. In recent years, some doubt has been cast on whether the body was really that of Linda as some elements of the case do not sit properly. The body had brown eyes while Linda's were blue, the victim had a different bust size to Linda and had a different shaped nose.

The story of the Pyjama Girl has given rise to several books purporting to tell the 'truth' of the event, with some obviously being much nearer to fiction. Antonio Agostini was eventually convicted of manslaughter and sentenced to six years' imprisonment with hard labour. Upon his release in August 1948 he was deported to Italy where he later married a widow, Giuseppina Gasoni, at Cagliari, Sardinia.

Darcy Dugan

As far as colourful criminals in NSW go, there was none better known than Darcy Ezekiel Dugan (1920–1991). Born in Newtown, Sydney, Dugan grew up in the nearby suburb of Annandale, later becoming a bank robber and New South Wales' most notorious prison escape artist. He escaped from 'escape-proof' circumstances six times, including going through a ceiling, the roof and sneaking over the outer wall at Sydney's Long Bay Jail in broad daylight. He was located 30 metres away from an armed guard and this was the second incident in the same day 25 minutes after being imprisoned.

During his criminal career, Dugan committed many armed holdups, including bank robberies and even a robbing a hospital. However, his fame grew more as a result of his daring escapes than for his actual crimes. On 4th March 1946, he escaped from a prison tram that was transporting him between Darlinghurst Courthouse and Long Bay jail. As the tram passed the Sydney Cricket Ground, Dugan escaped using a kitchen knife to saw a hole through the roof. The tram is still kept today at the Sydney Tramway Museum.

On 16th December 1949, Dugan and accomplice, William Cecil Mears (1920–2002), both escaped from Central Police Station, Sydney, during a court recess. Mears was in court after being charged with possession of an unlicensed pistol and Dugan was subpoenaed as a witness. During a break for lunch, the pair hacksawed through an iron bar in their cell and escaped from the police complex and headed to the surrounding streets packed with Christmas shoppers. Although police gave chase, the pair were last seen boarding a passing tram.

On 13th January 1950, Dugan and Mears robbed the Ultimo branch of the Commonwealth Bank of Australia in Sydney, with Mears shooting and seriously injuring the bank manager. Several months later, Detective Sergeant Ray Kelly and his colleagues arrested the pair at Collaroy, this being the first of four arrests by Kelly of Dugan. In court in May, Dugan made yet another attempt to escape, this time unsuccessful. In June 1950, Justice Leslie Herron sentenced Dugan and Mears to death for the Ultimo bank shooting. Although an appeal against sentence failed, the Labor government of 'Jim' McGirr, re-elected later that month, commuted their sentences to life imprisonment in Grafton gaol.

Dugan served a total 35 years in prison, with his final sentence being served at Long Bay Correctional Centre. After being released on parole in May 1980, in July he married Canberra businesswoman Jan Simmonds, whom he had met in prison while she was researching a book about her brother Kevin, also infamous for being an escapee and fugitive in the late 1950s. Dugan worked as a rehabilitation officer during his final years of freedom until his health declined. Although the couple separated not long after, they remained friends and Jan looked after Darcy when his health began to fail upon his final release from prison. Dugan passed away at age 70 in the Sydney suburb of Glebe from Parkinson's disease on 22nd August 1991.

Graeme Thorne kidnapping

The kidnapping of eight-year old Graeme Thorne shocked not only the people of NSW but the whole nation. In June 1960, Graeme's father Bazil had had a windfall. He won £100,000 (about $3 million in 2020) in the Sydney Opera House lottery. Stephen Bradley, an immigrant and also a father of three children, obtained the Thorne's phone number and convinced Graeme that he would drive him to school. But when he got into his car, Bradley bound him, wrapped him in a blanket and stowed him in the boot. Bradley phoned the family demanding a ransom or he would 'feed the boy to the sharks'. It was the first known kidnap/ransom case in the country.

It was shortly afterwards that Bradley discovered that Graeme was dead. He then disposed of Graeme's possessions along the area near the Wakehurst Parkway in northern Sydney and placed the body in a nearby crevice under a sandstone rock. In mid-August, Graeme's body was found by several children and the case launched a new age in which forensic science was used in a criminal investigation. Small samples of soil, leaves and vegetation from the location of Graeme's body and the blanket it was wrapped in allowed police to describe the possible place where his body had been stored at Grandview Grove in Seaforth, Sydney. By this time, Bradley and his family had fled to Colombo, but he was extradited to Sydney, tried and sentenced to life imprisonment. In December 1961, the NSW Parliament amended the Crimes Act to include kidnapping as a crime as previously there had been no statutory law for this crime. Bradley died in Goulburn prison on 6th October 1968 of a heart attack, aged 42.

The Bogle-Chandler mystery

There was much intrigue surrounding the deaths of Dr Gilbert Bogle (1924–1963), a physicist who worked at the CSIRO on the campus of the University of Sydney, and Margaret Chandler (1934–1963), married to Geoffrey

Chandler, who worked in the same CSIRO building as Dr Bogle. Married with several children, Bogle was considered to be a brilliant scientist and had been a Rhodes Scholar.

Dr Bogle, the Chandlers, and several others attended a New Year's Eve party in 1962 at Chatswood on Sydney's North Shore. A week or so earlier, just before Christmas, on the way home from a barbeque, Mrs Chandler told her husband Geoffrey that she was attracted to Dr Bogle and he later told police that he and his wife had 'an understanding', giving her the 'green light'. Dr Bogle and Mrs Chandler left the party soon after 4 a.m. and drove to the nearby Lane Cove River, a section known as a 'lover's lane'.

What happened next is a mystery, but, several hours later, Dr Bogle's body was discovered. When police arrived at the scene, they discovered that Bogle's body was half-undressed. However, person(s) unknown had placed his trousers over the back of his legs in such a way that he appeared to be dressed, although he was not.

Soon after, Mrs Chandler's body was discovered a short distance away, also in a state of undress, and her body had also been covered, this time with a broken-up cardboard beer box.

It seemed probable at the time that both had died from some sort of poisoning, as at the scene there were signs of vomit and excreta from both victims. Because New

Year's Day was a public holiday, forensic examination of the bodies was delayed for 36 hours. It found no traces of any known poison. At the subsequent inquest, medical evidence was also tendered that Mrs Chandler had not had recent sexual intercourse.

The case attracted widespread publicity and there was even speculation that Bogle was involved in scientific research important in the Cold War. The inquest in May 1963 could not shed any light on the mystery, with the coroner, Mr J J Loomes, concluding that Bogle and Chandler had died because of 'acute circulatory failure'. But 'as to the circumstances under which such circulatory failure was brought about, the evidence does not permit me to say'.

In September 2006, an ABC documentary by Peter Butt, *Who Killed Dr Bogle and Mrs Chandler?* suggested that the two deaths may have been caused by accidental hydrogen sulphide poisoning. However, to this day, no definitive answer has been found.

Wanda Beach murders

On 11th January 1965, best friends and neighbours, Marianne Schmidt and Christine Sharrock, disappeared at Wanda Beach, a small and isolated stretch in the Sydney suburb of Cronulla. They were both just 15 years old and four of Marianne's younger siblings had accompanied them. When they reached the beach, they found it was closed due to windy weather, so they all sheltered in the nearby rocks.

At some point during the picnic, Christine wandered off. No one knows where she went or what she was doing during that time, but after her death it was discovered she had consumed some alcohol and eaten some different foods from the rest of the group. During a later walk, Christine and Marianne told the younger children to wait while they headed back to the rocks to collect their bags and belongings. It is reported that the girls then headed further into the sand hills and laughed when the kids told them they were going the wrong way.

The next day, their battered bodies were found on the beach, partially covered by sand. More than 50 years later, no one has been charged with their murders, and their deaths still haunt the shire community.

Anita Cobby murder

Due to the shocking nature and randomness of the attack, the murder of the 26-year-old registered nurse and beauty pageant winner Anita Cobby (1959–1986), on 2nd February 1986, in Blacktown, Sydney, aroused considerable public anger and distress. A farmer found her naked body in a field two days after her murder. She had been sexually assaulted, abused, raped, beaten and her head was almost severed from her body. Subsequent interviews and evidence filled out the story.

After dining with friends, Anita was walking to her parents' home around 9.45 pm. Along the way five men dragged her into a stolen car. A witness related to the group's ringleader collected taped evidence of their guilt. All five men had histories of violence and each was convicted and sentenced to imprisonment 'for the terms of their natural lives'. The harshness of the sentence possibly reflected the horror felt at the callous nature of the crime and the need for retribution and vengeance.

Backpacker murders

The backpacker murders were a series of homicides committed by Ivan Milat (1944–2019) that took place in NSW between 1989 and 1993. The bodies of seven missing young people aged 19 to 22 were discovered partially buried in the Belanglo State Forest, 15 kilometres south-west of the NSW town of Berrima. Five of the victims were foreign backpackers (three German, two British), while two were Australian travellers from Melbourne.

On 27th July 1996, Milat was convicted of the murders and sentenced to seven consecutive life sentences, as well as 18 years without parole. He died in prison on 27th October 2019, never having confessed to any of the murders for which he was convicted.

14. *Finance*

The initial coinage of the colony was haphazard, with foreign currency frequently being used. When colonists sold produce to government stores, they were issued with receipts, which became a form of currency. Rum was an early currency of the colony until it was prohibited in 1806 by Governor William Bligh, whose actions made enemies of most of the Marine Corps and the leading citizens of the day. These included John Macarthur, a former member of the Corps who had significant land and commercial interests in the colony. He had secured the support of the so-called Rum Corps and on 26th January 1808, Major George Johnston led the Corps to Government House and arrested Bligh. Two years of military rule followed in what was known as the Rum Rebellion. When news of their actions reached England, both Johnson and Macarthur were arrested and sent to England for trial. The Marine Corps was recalled in 1810, the same year that Governor Lachlan Macquarie arrived.

Other products, such as tea, tobacco and sugar, had been used for barter and so the three forms of early currency were foreign coins, barter and government receipts. Frustrated with the proliferation of currencies, in 1812 Governor Lachlan Macquarie imported 40,000 Spanish dollars, *reales*, and had the convicted forger, William Henshall, cut the centre out to double the number of available coins. The outer ring was called a 'holey dollar' and the smaller piece, a 'dump'.

In the first few decades of the establishment of the colony of NSW, one of the potential and eventual sources of revenue—trade and duties raised—was not encouraged by the British government as it was considered a threat to British interests.

Different forms of financial transactions were prevalent, some of these fraudulent, and many promissory notes circulated as currency. Macquarie had long favoured the idea of a bank in the colony and, although at first frustrated by the Colonial Office in his attempts, in 1817 the Bank of New South Wales was established. This bank was set up by investors (mainly magistrates and merchants), each buying £100 shares. It was founded in the house of Mary Reibey (1777–1855) at 6 Macquarie Street, Sydney. Reibey, convicted of horse-stealing, was one of the colony's successful entrepreneurs. When her husband died leaving her with seven children to raise, she successfully took over his hotel, shipping and trading business concerns. The Bank of NSW prospered, particularly during the 1850s goldrush and from its ability to lend to a burgeoning wool industry. In 1982 it merged with the Commercial Bank of Australia, becoming the present Westpac Banking Corporation.

The opening of the bank exposed many of the social divisions within colonial society, as emancipists were involved in its founding. In 1826, the rival Bank of Australia was founded as an 'exclusives only' bank. However, it did not survive the 1840s Depression.

Another early bank was founded by Thomas Barker (1799–1875), an engineer, manufacturer and pastoralist. He arrived in the colony in 1813 as a free settler and quickly established interests in cloth making, milling and railways. In the 1830s, he established the Commercial Banking Company of Sydney and helped establish the Royal Exchange in Gresham Street, opposite Macquarie Place. The building was officially opened by the then Governor General, Sir William Denison, on 30th October 1857.

In 1849, five investors established the Australian Mutual Provident Society (AMP Society) in which the merchant David Jones (1793–1873) was a founding director. Other prominent figures included George King who was chairman for 15 years from the 1850s and Richard Teece, the general manager and actuary from 1890 and a director from 1917 to 1927. This was the first of the friendly societies in NSW—mutual *associations* formed for the purposes of insurance, pensions, savings or cooperative banking.

Inexpensive land and cheap convict labour encouraged men of capital to come to the colony of NSW in the early days, or at least to invest their money in the colony. Much of their profits came from trade rather than produce. In the 1860s and 1870s, such local capital was considerably supplemented by British investment, which also applied to the funding of public works.

Much of the development of NSW from 1788–1822 was financed by the British Government. Officer-farmers had been granted land and their convict labour force was provided by Britain. They then sold their crops to the government store, thereby having a guaranteed market for their produce. In return, officers were paid in the form of British Treasury Bills, which could be redeemed for gold if presented in London. These bills became a form of currency as they were so highly valued.

In 1828, government revenue in the colony had a number of sources: duties on imports, casual revenues (fines, land-sales), and duties levied under the Legislative Council's authority. Most money was raised from the first of these, but the efficiency of the collection and disbursement of revenue depended on the competence and character of the relevant official. One such example is that of the military officer, public servant and landowner Captain John Piper (1773–1851), after whom the affluent suburb of Point Piper in Sydney is named. Piper was a close friend of Governor Lachlan Macquarie, who in 1819 made him a magistrate. In 1825 he became chairman of directors of the Bank of New South Wales. After a varied career, he became Collector of Customs in Sydney, but was dismissed in 1827 because of 'great neglect' of his office.

New South Wales experienced an inflationary period during the 1870s, due to British capital investment and land sales. Building Societies and land banks developed as a result of this and because of lax banking laws. An investment boom in Australia in the 1880s heralded increased economic expansion, although investments were providing less of a return. This growth came about as more foreign funds became available to the country. This influx of capital led to Australians having the highest per capita incomes in the world during the late 19th century.

Although some of the early financial institutions were reasonably well-run, many of them closed during the collapse of the 1890s depression. People lost their savings, unemployment followed and soup kitchens were inundated. There were also banking scandals. Francis Abigail (1840–1921), an ex-bootmaker and Minister for Mines in the Henry Parkes government, had founded the Australian Banking Company of Sydney during Sydney's land boom. However, Abigail and a few of his fellow directors managed to exploit their positions, extracting most of the Bank's available cash. On 3rd November 1892 Abigail was sentenced to five years hard labour in Darlinghurst gaol.

In 1888 the Australian Mercantile Loan & Guarantee Company was established by an uncertificated insolvent, Alexander Hastings Malcolm. Two of its directors later defrauded the company of its ready cash, went to Melbourne, changed their names and appearances, and then headed to the South Seas. These events caused lack of faith in other banks, such as the Commercial Banking Company of Sydney (established in 1834) and the government Savings Bank that had been founded in Barrack Street in 1871.

During a series of financial crises, the NSW government intervened to prevent the collapse of the monetary system. In the 1840s depression, the NSW Bankruptcy Act of 1842 enabled insolvents to control their own resources, if this was likely to improve their ability to repay debts. In the 1890s depression, when depositors' accounts were frozen and employers could not pay workers, people were exchanging bank notes for gold coin. To offset the resulting run on the banks, the government of Premier George Dibbs (1834–1904) legislated to make banknotes legal tender for six months.

Like the other Australian colonies prior to Federation in 1901, NSW raised capital from customs and excise. This was despite the many advocates and practitioners of free trade such as the administrator and politician Edward Deas Thomson (1800–1879) and Henry Parkes (1815–1896). This also meant over-reliance on overseas borrowing balanced by good prices for land financed by escalating pastoralism. The 1880s fall in export income challenged this precarious balance in public financial wellbeing. Dibbs, who succeeded Parkes as Premier, introduced new tariffs to address this. Public income was also based on charges for government services, such as railways and postal services.

Following Federation, the Commonwealth controlled tariffs, giving back to the states varying amounts of the money so raised. In 1928, by a constitutional amendment, all states lost their role as independent borrowers. In 1936, these arrangements were voluntarily brought under the control of the Loan Council under a 'Gentlemen's Agreement' that remained in effect until 1984–85 when Global Borrowing Limits were introduced.

One of the biggest financial challenges to NSW came with the Great Depression that began in August 1929 and continued until the late 1930s. Since the early days of Federation, the Commonwealth government had encouraged the states to borrow. In consequence, all states were vulnerable when the Depression commenced. Jack Lang, NSW Premier from 1930–32 and a strong figure in the ALP generally, took a stance that earned him both denigration and adulation. Lang had consistently opposed the deflationary policies favoured by the federal Labor government of James Scullin (1876–1953) and instituted under the advice of the British banker and civil servant, Sir Otto Niemeyer.

In 1930, Lang unsuccessfully proposed the suspension of overseas interest payments and the reduction of Commonwealth borrowings. Given NSW's increasingly straitened circumstances, in 1931 Lang simply decided to refuse to pay interest on overseas loans. The federal government legislated for the repayment of loans to be the first call on any state's finances. Lang, while backing down on his stance, rejected a federal act obliging NSW revenues (and the revenues of other states) to be paid to the Commonwealth. The federal government prevailed, and Lang was dismissed by the NSW Governor, Sir Philip Game (1876–1961) on 13th May 1932.

The financial control of the Commonwealth over the states increased through the establishment of the Commonwealth Grants Commission in 1933. Its task was to advise the Commonwealth on the grants to be made to the states, recognising the loss of customs and excise from their revenues, and responding to fiscal differences between them, which had been exposed during the depression years. The formula and its rationale changed over time, but the principle remained. This, as the Australian historian and author Alan Shaw observed, was on the principle that 'he who pays the piper calls the tune'. And in 1942, during the Second World War, NSW along with all other states, lost the right to levy their own direct taxes.

GAMBLING

Like the rest of the country, the people of NSW have a demonstrated fondness for gambling, with a total state gambling turnover in 2016–17 of $82.3 billion. From this, the NSW government reaped $2.1 billion in taxes. The biggest contributor by far are gaming machines (mainly poker machines). In fact, since the First World War, the NSW government has raised significant and increasing revenue from gambling. While the amount raised has varied, it equates to about 10% of the state's tax revenue, with only payroll tax, stamp duty and licences bringing in higher income.

Gaming machines made their appearance in Sydney's hotels in 1921 but were quickly declared illegal. A legal loophole, however, permitted their use in clubs. While the availability of clubs has been an off-and-on affair, there are now in excess of 1100 clubs in NSW with more than 6.7 million members. In the six months ending 30th June 2019, these clubs made $1.945 billion profit from poker machines while public hotels ('pubs') made another $1.242 billion profit.

In 2016–17, the turnover and expenditure (and gamblers' losses in brackets) for various types of gambling in NSW included: gaming machines $80.3 billion ($6.2 billion), instant lotteries $118.2 million ($41 million), Keno $646.1 million ($160 million), other lotteries $117.5 million ($44 million) and Lotto $1.06 billion ($423.8 million).

Betting turnover on racing was $6.2 billion, from which the government received $96.3 million in taxes.

Lotteries were banned in NSW from 1852 to 1901, although they existed illegally in other forms, such as sweepstakes. In 1921 there was pressure within the ALP government to introduce a lottery to finance hospitals. When the ALP lost office, this did not proceed. However, with the onset of the Great Depression, the Jack Lang Labor Government successfully introduced the State Lotteries Act 1930. State run lotteries were to raise revenue for hospital funding. In August 1931, the first state lottery was held with a first prize of £5,000 pounds (worth about $468,000 in 2020) for the investment of a ticket at five shillings and threepence. It was won by a Manly housewife, Eileen Morton, in a ticket she shared with her grandmother. Eileen and her husband Jim used their winnings to build a waterfront house in Manly, in northern Sydney. After several changes of owners over the years, it sold for $5.7 million in October 2017.

PHILANTHROPY

Philanthropy has its historical roots in charitable work. In the 19th century, this was aimed at the poor population and focused on preventing starvation and homelessness. Much of this work was carried out by women, although men controlled the finances. Charitable activities were expected of privileged women, much of it being related to religious conviction or a sense of social requirement.

Dr Lucy Edith Gullett (1876–1949) is a prime example of a philanthropist. Educated at Sydney Girls' High School and the University of Sydney, she had both a private practice and worked in hospitals as a medical officer. She served in the French Red Cross during the First World War and, during the subsequent Spanish influenza epidemic, worked at the City Road emergency hospital in Sydney. She went on to establish the Rachel Foster Hospital for Women and Children in George Street, Redfern, Sydney, with another doctor, Dr Harriet Biffen (1866–1939).

An earlier example of female philanthropy is provided by the life of Lady Mary Windeyer (1836–1912) who organised the Exhibition of Women's Industries and Centenary Fair in 1888. From the sale of works so exhibited she financed the Temporary Aid Society, which lent money to women experiencing financial problems. She was an active promoter of economic independence for women and continued to support women's industries. She also helped establish the Crown Street Women's Hospital, Sydney, to assist poor women and to train nurses.

Early philanthropists, however, varied their chosen endowments. Dr William Bland (1789–1868), emancipist and first private medical practitioner in the colony, supported various educational institutions such as the Sydney School of the Arts and the Mechanics Institute. He also assisted literary workers.

The term 'philanthropy' also refers to giving will bequests for the broader good of the community. Funding scholarships, for example, has made an important philanthropic financial contribution to society. It has also come to refer to combined government and private contributions to social wellbeing and a newer term, 'social entrepreneurship' has been coined. Companies and entrepreneurs contribute to solutions to community-based problems. In NSW, for example, WH Paling (1825–1895), musician and businessman, endowed the Camden Home for Convalescents and Sir James Burns (1846–1923), shipping magnate, the Burnside Children's Home at North Parramatta.

In more recent times there have been quite a few generous philanthropists in NSW. Among these is the Sydney-born billionaire businessman and investor James Douglas Packer who in 2014 co-launched with Crown Resorts the $200 million a National Philanthropic Fund with the Packer Family Foundation. Based in Legion House, Sydney NSW, it is designed to benefit the Australian community.

Single with no children, the Bowral-born businessman Paul Ramsay (1936–2014) left most of his $3 billion fortune to charity in what is believed to be the largest donation in Australian history. He was the founder of Ramsay Health Care.

The Ian Potter Foundation, established by the Sydney-born stockbroker, businessman and philanthropist Sir Ian Potter (1902–1994) in 1964, has made grants to research institutes, charities, universities and arts organisations. It has distributed $325 million since its inception, including $25.8 million in 2018–19 alone.

15. *Community Organisations*

There are numerous and diverse community organisations in NSW. Many of them relate to the multicultural nature of the state, reflecting the waves of people who migrated here, particularly during the 20th century. These range from early established groups such as Greeks, Italians and Chinese, to more recent arrivals from such places as Macedonia, Bangladesh, Vietnam and Serbia. Community organisations assist in easing the movement from one culture to another, with one of the best known being the Italian CO.AS.IT. established in 1968 and based in Sydney's Leichhardt. It provides Italian language and community services, for example running out-of-school language courses, providing help for the aged and assisting in the establishment of businesses.

Other areas covered by community groups are diverse and numerous, such as mental health, social justice, disability, sport and recreation, animal welfare, conservation and heritage.

While community organisations employ some paid staff and are not-for-profit organisations, their staple support is from volunteers. The value of these groups to society cannot be assessed by traditional economic measurements. Research by Ernst & Young for the NSW Council of Social Services determined that, while these bodies did bring capital and employment to local neighbourhoods, their value went far beyond that. Through sharing, participating and joint collaboration, they contributed to the resilience and wellbeing of local communities.

NOTABLE COMMUNITY ORGANISATIONS IN NSW

The Benevolent Society of NSW

In 1813, under the patronage of Governor Lachlan Macquarie, the earliest charitable organisation in NSW was formed. In 1818, it adopted its present title of The Benevolent Society of NSW. The intention was to relieve the distress of the poor, the needy and the aged and to encourage industrious habits. On the location of Sydney's current Central Station, the Society erected an asylum in 1821 as a refuge for the homeless and destitute. Intended to house 60, by 1830 it was housing 144 people, predominantly men. The care of orphans and destitute women also became part of its remit.

By the early 1860s, reflecting the increasing economic problems of the colony, the demands for The Benevolent

Society's services were such that the government had to take over some of its responsibilities. Its initial role was largely the provision of outdoor relief: handouts of cash, clothing and provisions, but this later enlarged as it also provided hospital care and legal aid. As society has changed, so has the Society's role. It now runs, for example, a number of retirement villages and parenting services for single mothers. Initially founded to fulfil the obligations of Christian charity, it has become a completely secular organisation.

CanTeen

CanTeen is an Australian national support organisation for young people living with cancer—including cancer patients, their brothers and sisters and young people with parents or primary carers with cancer. It commenced operations in 1985 when a number of young people facing the challenges of cancer were brought together by a group of concerned and committed health professionals. From this meeting the Teenage Cancer Health Society was born and started providing camps for young people aged 12 to 24 who have cancer themselves or have a family member so affected. With its headquarters in Sydney, CanTeen provides individual counselling to assist those affected address problems, determine needs and set goals. It also helps them connect with other young people facing the same issues.

Country Women's Association of NSW (CWA)

Country life for women in the colony was often isolated and lonely, with many lacking support facilities. Medical services were particularly missed, especially when complications arose in childbirth. The situation was improved when Florence Laver (1874–1935) established the first branch of the Country Women's Association (CWA) in NSW at Crookwell in 1922, and it quickly grew. Its members have been responsible for the establishment of baby health centres and have raised funding for such matters as staffing schools and hospitals. At times assessed as being only about 'scones and tea', the women of the CWA have initiated and fought for programs that improve community life generally in rural areas.

It was particularly active after the Second World War and has since developed international links throughout rural women's organisations worldwide. The CWA is the largest women's organisation in Australia with a goal of improving conditions for both country women and children. They are involved in a number of activities, including lobbying for change, helping the local community, creating a network of support and meeting together in towns and cities.

Guide Dogs

The Guide Dogs Organisation of NSW has its roots in 1950, when Arnold Cook (1922–1981) returned to Australia with his UK-trained Guide Dog 'Dreena'.

First established in Perth, the Guide Dogs for the Blind Association commenced in NSW in 1957, becoming the Guide Dogs Association of New South Wales in 1979 at the request of the clients. Five years later, the Therapy Dogs Program was launched to provide companion dogs for people with a range of problems: ill-health, age, disability.

Courses have been developed for instructors and, in 2010, a puppy breeding program was established. Its continuing goal has been to boost the independence and mobility of its clients through the assistance of a guide dog. Members of the community can volunteer in a range of ways. One of the most popular ways is to become a puppy breeder, caring for and training potential guide dogs.

Legacy

In 1923, a group of veterans decided that there was a need to provide a 'family' for the widow(er)s and/or dependants of those who served in the First World War. As a result, the charity known as Legacy commenced in 1926 as a response to meet the needs of those who had not returned from war or who had returned, but with unresolved issues. The members of Legacy aim to provide basic needs, counselling and advocacy. Legacy NSW has its headquarters in Sydney, with branches in 19 other cities in the state, including Albury, Armidale, Orange, Newcastle and Tamworth.

Lifeline

Lifeline was founded in Sydney 1963 by the Reverend Dr Sir Alan Walker (1911–2003). After a man who had phoned him for help committed suicide, Walker decided that isolation should not lead to such a desperate outcome. He established a 24-hour crisis support line. The organisation's services are provided by many thousands of volunteers throughout Australia. Lifeline responds to around 1,800 calls each day, including about 50 calls from those at high risk of suicide. Its services are maintained by around 1,000 staff and 11,000 volunteers, operating from over 60 locations nationwide, including through phone, face-to-face, and online mediums.

Meals on Wheels NSW

'Meals on Wheels' has its origins in Britain where it assisted the frail and elderly to stay in their own homes. With this idea in mind, in 1957, the Sydney City Council established Meals on Wheels NSW. Meals were cooked in the Sydney Town Hall and the cost to recipients was two shillings. Today throughout the state, three-course meals are delivered by volunteers to people's homes at a cost of between $9 and $12. Volunteers provide more than a meal: for many people confined to their homes, they provide social contact and can assist in monitoring the general welfare of recipients.

Meals on Wheels has evolved to become a driving force of care in the community. In the course of a year, over 14.8 million meals are delivered by more than 78,700 volunteers to about 53,000 recipients Australia-wide in cities, regional and rural areas. Of these, about 4.5 million meals are delivered by 35,000 volunteers in NSW each year.

Police Citizens Youth Club (PCYC)

In 1929, NSW Police Commissioner, William Mackay visited America, England, and Europe, and returned to instigate many new initiatives that resulted in the total re-organisation of the Detective Branch, renamed as the Criminal Investigation Branch (CIB). He made a follow up trip in 1936 during which he became fascinated by the Police Boys Club in Norwich, England, and the Police Athletic League in the US. He was also impressed with the Hitler Youth, inasmuch as this organisation taught young men to respect their nation above themselves. Mackay had been brought up on the streets of Glasgow and understood the problems associated with a lack of occupation for young men.

When he returned to NSW from his 1936 trip, Mackay secured funding through the Rotary Club for an organisation for boys, aged generally from 10 to 16 (when formed in 1937). This organisation was originally called the Police Rotary Club. Against the background of the public disorder of the Great Depression of the

1930s, it was intended to provide sport and educational opportunities for young men and offered such varied activities as wrestling and debating. It also had a well-stocked library and the first club met in a disused police station in Woolloomooloo.

The movement spread, as more clubs opened through the state. Today it has increased its role to include young women, indicative of the changing attitude and values of society. It has also expanded its approach and now has youth case managers who work closely with other organisations and government departments.

The Smith Family

The Smith Family was founded in 1922 when five businessmen visited an orphanage in Sydney with gifts for the children. The children's circumstances inspired the men to address the issue of disadvantage as they saw it in that orphanage. The organisation's objective has broadened, but it is still focused on empowering young people in need, particularly through education. Those community members who volunteer emphasise the 'family' nature of the organisation, working in partnership with families, schools, governments, community organisations, business, philanthropy and universities to improve the educational outcomes of disadvantaged students. It is located in over 90 disadvantaged communities nationally, including 32 communities in NSW.

Stewart House

In 1929, Dr Harvey Vincent Sutton (1882–1963), the principal medical officer with the NSW Department of Education, distressed at the numbers of children suffering from malnutrition, approached Arthur McGuinness (1878–1970), President between 1929 and 1932 of the newly formed the Teachers' Federation. The resultant small group, the School Teacher's Hospital and Relief Society, offered respite care and nutrition for needy children, and the Teachers' Federation agreed to sponsor this organisation.

In 1931, the Governor of NSW, Sir Philip Game, opened 'Stewart House', so-called because Sir Frederick and Lady Stewart donated funds for the building. It was a difficult time to raise funds to run the organisation as the Great Depression of the 1930s had exhausted finances generally and Stewart House was often closed. In 1937, the Teacher's Federation took over the organisation and Stewart House was registered as a hospital. The role of Stewart House has since expanded and has come to deal with the mental and emotional health of children. It continues to provide short-term respite care for about 2,000 children annually.

St Vincent De Paul

The St Vincent de Paul Society was founded in 1833 in Scotland by a 20-year-old student named Frederic Ozanam (1813–1853). It was further established by those with similar views and who wished to put these into action. 'Vinnies', as it became familiarly known, is a faith-based Catholic charity, and was introduced to NSW by Adolphe Baudon (1819–1888) in July 1881, at the St Patrick's Church Hill Conference. It was at times hindered by anti-Irish/Catholic attitudes, but in 1895 it was consolidated in Sydney. It has since provided support for families in need and to address perceived social injustice, mainly through the activities of volunteer Catholic laity.

Surf Lifesaving

Increasing interest in swimming in the late 19th century and the attraction of the many beaches along the NSW coast, also led to an awareness of the dangers. Small groups of sea swimmers began to form themselves into clubs of 'lifesavers', to assist those unfamiliar with the perils of the surf. It was only in 1902 that it became permissible to swim at public beaches in NSW during daylight; it had been prohibited since 1838, due mainly to concerns about modesty as men swam naked in the latter part of the 19th century. Those who wanted to swim at beaches had to do so after dark and it was William Gocher who led a campaign to overturn these laws. Clad in a neck-to-knee costume, he swam at Manly beach at midday in October 1902 and was twice ignored by the authorities, though deliberately trying to attract their attention. After publicly criticising their lack of enthusiasm, on a third occasion he was escorted from the water and interviewed by the police but was not charged. In November 1903 Manly Council legalised all-day bathing, provided that a neck-to-knee costume was worn.

In 1905, Manly Council employed a lifeguard and two fishermen, the Sly brothers, who patrolled offshore. A formal organisation geared to local conditions commenced in 1907 at Sydney's Bondi beach and other areas quickly followed suit. In October 1907, the Surf Bathing Association of NSW was established to protect swimmers. It may well also have been considered necessary to preserve law and order, as the beaches of Sydney in the summer of 1907 began permitting the very controversial recreation of mixed bathing. But it also saved lives: the first rescue using a basic reel and line system saved a young Charles Kingsford Smith (1897–1935) who, in 1928, made the first transpacific flight from the United States to Australia. The first surf lifesaving reel in the world was demonstrated in 1906 at Bondi beach.

The value of surf lifesaving was emphatically demonstrated in 1938, when three huge waves at Bondi dragged people off the beach and into a channel out to sea. Fortuitously, 60 members of the Bondi Surf Club were present and about to commence their own races. Instead they raced into action. Approximately 300 bathers were rescued; many were injured but only five died.

For many decades it was a men's-only organisation. However, women formed their own Ladies' Life Saving Clubs until admitted as full members in 1980. As early as the 1920s, the organisation encouraged youngsters between the ages of seven and fourteen to train on the beaches. Both sexes were involved, although many clubs would accept boys only.

Surf lifesavers have assumed heroic status both in NSW and the rest of Australia, where beach culture—whether sunbathing, surfing or playing games on the sand—is important to the local way of life.

Surf Life Saving New South Wales now has over 75,000 members, making it one of the largest volunteer organisations of its kind in the nation. Their portfolio includes sport, partnerships, member services, lifesaving and education. The state's lifesavers are currently involved at 129 clubs, patrolling over 1,500 kilometres of coastline from Fingal Beach in the north to Pambula Beach in the south.

Tranby

The Reverend Alf Clint (1906–1980), an Anglican clergyman, had been active in establishing Indigenous co-operatives when working for the Australian Board of Missions in Australia and New Guinea. As a result of his success, the Reverend John Hope (1891–1971) of Christ Church St Laurence gave him the 'Tranby' building located in the Sydney suburb of Glebe. In 1962, on this base the

Co-operative for Aborigines Ltd was launched. Tranby is the nation's oldest independent Indigenous education provider. It has principally provided trade-based skills but also offers legal advice and advocacy for Indigenous people. The focus of the organisation was, and remains, to educate and empower Aboriginal and Torres Strait Islander people. Community volunteers can assist in the educational programs, IT support and application writing.

Volunteer Bushfire Organisations

Bushfires have been a challenge in NSW since the early days of colonisation. Inadequate understanding of bushfires and inappropriate land management have made such fires a frequent threat to expanding settlement, leading to loss of life and destruction of property.

From 1858, a series of laws allowed for local councils to take action to prevent and offset the effects of bushfires. In 1896, in the NSW town of Berrigan, the first volunteer bush fire fighting service was formed by local residents who were only too aware of the constant threat that bushfires presented. This organisation, the Rural Fire Service (RFS), was formally recognised at a meeting in November 1900 at the Royal Hotel on the Murray River.

The early part of the 20th century saw the consolidation of laws, culminating in the Bush Fires Act 1930, which gave local authorities greater powers in the prevention and alleviation of bushfires. The move towards organised local firefighting got a further advance with the Bush Fires Act 1949, which gave greater powers to councils to prevent, control and suppress bushfires.

Bushfires have continued, however, to pose a threat. In the early 1950s, fires devastated forest areas north of Newcastle and forests on the NSW south coast. In 1957, bushfires were exacerbated by gale-force winds; fires encircled Sydney, destroyed property and left hundreds of people homeless. Fires occurred in places as far flung as Armidale and Condobolin, and across the Blue Mountains west of Sydney. To address the widespread nature of such fires, a position was created to coordinate operations across local government margins.

The early 1980s saw eight people killed and half a million hectares scorched or destroyed and the latter part of the decade saw even more devastation and deaths from bushfires. A series of Acts followed the growing problem and led to better coordination of the volunteer community organisation. According to the RFS website, 'In the year ending June 2016 the Service had 73,162 volunteers in 2,029 brigades in 47 NSW RFS districts across 4 regions equipped with 3,783 tankers, 65 pumpers, 59 bulk water tankers, 40 communications vehicles, 81 catering vehicles and 30 marine craft attending a total of 23,520 incidents'.

The NSW statutory Bush Fire Danger Period usually commences on 1st October and continues until 31st March. However, with drought affecting 95% of the state in 2019–20, the fire season started early with persistent dry and warm conditions. This led to twelve local government areas starting the Bush Fire Danger Period two months early, on 1st August 2019; nine more fires started on 17th August 2019. On 12th November 2019, Sydney declared its first ever 'catastrophic' fire conditions. Other areas to suffer significant damage across the state included the mid-north coast, Blue Mountains, Hawkesbury, Southern Highlands, south coast and the Riverina. In all, there were 25 deaths and around 1,700 homes lost to out-of-control fires across the state. On 6th February 2020, a wide band of heavy rain swept through, extinguishing 20 of about 60 fires in the state.

16. *Organised Religion*

The First Fleet had both Christians and Jews on board. Religion was considered of immense importance in a colony consisting of convicts and emancipists whose debauchery was frequently commented on by official observers. Religious observance was made compulsory wherever possible. Governor Lachlan Macquarie ordered all convicts of whatever religious persuasion to attend Sunday services conducted according to the rites of the Church of England, and the different convict establishments had Anglican clerics appointed to them.

Settlers who were Catholic wanted their own priest and petitioned Governor Arthur Phillip for a chaplain. In 1803, the first public Mass was held under government supervision, conducted by Father James Dixon (1758–1840), a convict. But after a rebellion in 1804, led by Irish convicts attempting to overthrow British rule (the 'Castle Hill Rebellion'), Father Dixon was no longer permitted to conduct mass. In 1817, Father Jeremiah Flynn came to minister to convict Catholics, but without approval. After ignoring Governor Lachlan Macquarie's instructions not to perform as a priest, he was deported in 1818. However, in 1819, Father John Therry and Father Philip Conolly arrived in Sydney as the first official Catholic priests. In 1820 Father Therry opened the first Catholic school in the country, Parramatta Marist, in Hunter Street, Parramatta, and lobbied Governor Macquarie for land for the first Catholic church.

In the early days of the colony, although land was to be set aside for a church in all towns, this did not address the cost of building. When the Reverend Samuel Marsden (1765–1838) opened a church in Parramatta in 1796 at the now corner of George and Marsden Streets (the site of the present-day Woolpack Hotel), it was constructed using the materials gathered from two old huts. During the governorship of Lachlan Macquarie and with the valuable services of convict-architect Francis Greenway, this was rectified with the building of a number of stately churches in major centres of the growing colony. On 1st November 1798, the religious Governor John Hunter recorded that he had laid the foundation of a small church at Parramatta. It was later claimed that the foundation stone of St John's, the first brick church in Australia, was laid on 5th April 1797.

Built with convict labour and designed by Francis Greenway, St James' church in King Street in Sydney's CBD is the oldest church building in the city, opening in February 1824. It remains not only a centre for worship and a home of musical excellence and community activity, but also contains rare marble memorials and has a beautiful and unique Children's Chapel in a bay in the crypt.

Colonial chaplains were servants of the state, dependent upon it for finance and general support and official pronouncements were made from the pulpit. But clergymen from different faiths were often bitterly opposed to one another and jealous in the protection of their own denomination's position. The Reverend Samuel Marsden's fanaticism was matched by that of his successor, Bishop William Broughton, both of whom considered that the Church of England should be the pre-eminent church of the colony. Broughton (Anglican) and Bishop John Polding (Catholic) were known as excellent horsemen and travelled demanding distances throughout NSW to reach their parishioners. Travelling could be risky, with rivers sometimes swollen and the possible danger of confrontations with bushrangers. The firebrand Presbyterian, Reverend John Dunmore Lang (1799–1878), inspired by the strictures of Calvinism, declaimed particularly against the 'whore of Babylon' (Roman Catholicism) and the whole of evil humankind. Father John Therry (1790–1864), a zealous but unsophisticated man, was obsessively fearful that the adherents to his faith would be 'Protestantised'.

Roman Catholics were discriminated against in Britain until the 1829 Catholic Emancipation Act which removed the most substantial restrictions on them in the United Kingdom. The results of this change flowed onto the colony shortly thereafter and Catholics were subsequently allowed to hold government positions. This change in official policy, however, did not reduce the structural opposition to Catholics, most of whom were Irish. The resulting social antagonism led to Catholics being denigrated as inferior and dangerous, while Catholics, particularly under the guidance of Father Therry, felt persecuted and resentful.

Governor Richard Bourke's 1836 Church Act provided Government subsidies for clerical salaries and for new church construction for all religions until its repeal in 1862 when it was replaced by the Grants for Public Worship Prohibition Act. The aim was to promote the building of churches and chapels, and to provide for the Maintenance of Ministers of Religion in the state. Bourke's plan was to support churches by paying the salaries of their clergymen and match, pound for pound, monies raised to build churches. Like Governor Sir George Gipps who followed him, Bourke considered that all religions should be encouraged, in order to create a moral and happy society, supporting the idea of the plurality of Christian sects.

Religious sentiments were presented schismatically in early newspapers. From the *Sentinel* (1845–1848) to the *Protestant Standard* (1869–1895), sectarian Protestant opposition to 'papism' was promoted. The *Australian Chronicle* (1839–1848) championed the Catholic cause, but also espoused a more liberal ideology condemning the treatment of Aboriginals and supporting Governor George Gipps' attempt to introduce the Irish National System of education. The *Freeman's Journal* (1850–1932) also presented Catholic perspectives but was riven with the longstanding division between English and Irish Catholicism. The first Catholic Archbishop in the colony, John Bede Polding (1794–1877) may have built St Mary's Cathedral, laying the foundation stone in 1868, but he was treated warily by his Irish congregation. This was a problem not encountered initially by his successor, Cardinal Patrick Francis Moran (1830–1911), in 1885 becoming the first Cardinal appointed from Australia, whose devotion to the Irish religio-national cause was well known. Moran was, however, more broadminded in practice and valued both harmony and unity.

The Methodist Church was the first major denomination in the colony to become independent of British origins, while other Protestant religions depended on recruits from Britain for much longer.

The Anglican Church was slow to take to the outback but established missionary work through the 'bush brothers'. One such member of the Dubbo-based Brotherhood of the Good Shepherd, the Anglican clergyman Charles Henry Selfe Matthews (1873–1961), wrote of the rarity and the unfavourable image of clergymen in the bush. He claimed that the clerical life was one of hard work and commitment, often for little reward. Another bush brother, the rector J W Eisdell (1850–1900), sought to present muscular Christianity as the correct character of bush clergy. To address the stereotype of the 'foolish' Catholic cleric, it required another Catholic cleric, Narrandera-based Catholic priest Patrick Joseph (P.J.) Hartigan (1878–1952), writing as John O'Brien. His stories and poems, particularly 'Around the Boree Log' that were later made into a 1925 Australian silent film, tried to lift the reputation of rural churchmen.

The Congregationalists were the first denomination to consciously use the concept of 'the bush' to identify their missionary work in the colony. This was through support of the Home Missionary Society for NSW, founded in 1854, and the New South Wales Bush Missionary Society, established in 1856, to work in isolated parts of the developing settlement, running Sunday Schools, providing Bibles and religious tracts and preaching.

Protestant clergy were fearmongers, claiming for example that there was a Catholic plot to take over the colony. The fear of Irish Catholicism was fed by the attempted assassination of Prince Alfred, the Duke of Edinburgh, the second son of Queen Victoria, in 1868. It was discovered that the aggressor had not only trained for the priesthood but was a suspected Fenian (a member of an Irish nationalist secret society). The claim later proved false but increased religious divisions between Catholics and Protestants.

With the immigration of Greeks to Australia from the middle of the 19th century, their religious needs led to the establishment of a Greek Orthodox church. In May 1898, the foundations of the first Greek Orthodox Church, the Holy Trinity, were laid in Surry Hills, Sydney, funded by donations from Greek and Syrian Orthodox Christian businessmen. The first priest to serve the religious needs of the Greek Orthodox in Sydney and Melbourne was Archimandrite Dorotheos Bakaliaros from about 1896. The 'Metropolis of Australia and New Zealand' was established in March 1924 under the Ecumenical Patriarchate that promotes the expansion of the Christian faith and Orthodox doctrine. With increasing Greek immigration, new churches were built, and schools and community organisations, 'Philoptochos Societies', were established.

Most Jews in NSW prior to the end of the 19th century were either English-speaking convicts or migrants from Britain or their Australian-born descendants. In 1817, the Jewish Burial Society was formed, signalling the beginning of formal Jewish life in NSW. In 1821, the first Jewish free settlers arrived and the first regular Jewish services were held in a private home. Then, in 1837, the first synagogue was formally established. Most of the early settlers were Anglo-Jewish, middle class immigrants. The goldrush of the 1850s also attracted a large group of Jewish immigrants, which led to Jewish communities flourishing in provincial towns. In 1878 the Great Synagogue, Sydney, was consecrated with Rev.

Alexander Barnard Davis (1828–1913) as its first minister to the Sydney Jewish community. Its imposing structure remains an historic feature of the Sydney landscape, the building being substantially restored for the Bicentenary of British settlement in 1988.

During the 19th century Jews participated in every aspect of civic, economic and social life in NSW with prominent figures including Sir Saul Samuels, Sir Julian Salamons and later, Sir Daniel Levy and Justice Henry Emanuel Cohen. In 1917, the Legislative Assembly had to close on the Jewish holy day, Yom Kippur, because both the Speaker and Deputy Speaker were Jewish.

Jewish refugees who arrived from Central Europe in 1938–1939 to escape Nazism added to the Jewish community in NSW and led to the formation of community organisations, the Temple Emanuel (now the Emanuel Synagogue) and Moriah College in Sydney. With the further influx of Holocaust survivors after the war, the community grew, with a large number of suburban synagogues being constructed. Further waves of Jewish immigration from Hungary, South Africa, Russia and Israel have expanded the community. This has led to the establishment of Orthodox and Progressive synagogues, and schools.

The issue of funding of denominational schools proved a further spur to religious confrontation and antagonism. Sectarianism dominated the education debate. However, the division between religions was not as pronounced in the colony as in the United Kingdom. This can be seen in the absence of religious/ethnic enclaves and many community organisations having representatives of English, Scottish and Irish backgrounds on their governing boards. Nevertheless, by the early 20th century, Catholics and Protestants had become more antagonistic and separate in their organisations.

Universities in NSW have for much of their time been strongly secular, so isolating denominations from the general intellectual community. The halls of residence were, however, established by religious groups. The introduction of specifically religious institutions, such as the Australian Catholic University (1991), has been a more recent phenomenon.

The different religions and denominations have taken up a range of social issues, some of which have been divisive of the community and others which have resonated with sections of the general community. These include such matters as euthanasia, contraception and marriage reform.

For a number of sects, charity has been the centre point of their religious expression. The Salvation Army is a prime example. Although Adelaide was the first Australian 'home' of the Salvation Army, it has been very active in social work and advocacy in NSW, with centres such as Foster House in Surry Hills providing accommodation for homeless men since it opened in 1923. In 1963 the Reverend Alan Walker (1911–2003) of the Central Methodist Mission founded Lifeline, a non-profit organisation that provides free, 24-hour telephone crisis support service in Australia. An interesting figure in his own right, Walker was a theological conservative but was a pacifist and vocal opponent of government policy on several contentious issues.

Following the First World War, religious worship took on a patriotic tenor. Churches erected boards adorned with the names of those who had been killed and the national anthem was often sung at the beginning and end of religious services. One of the intriguing characters of Sydney's religious scene was the idiosyncratic Arthur Stace (1885–1967). Stace had been raised in poverty and on the fringe of the petty criminal world. Returning from the First World War, he continued his dissolute ways until inspired in 1942 by two evangelical preachers, one of whom, John Ridley, motivated him with the idea of shouting 'Eternity' to the world. Instead of shouting it, Stace set about writing it on pavements all over the city. With his piece of yellow waterproof chalk in hand, he inscribed footpaths 50 times a day with his copperplate handwritten one-word communication. After he died in 1967, a brass replica of his brief but direct message was unveiled near the Sydney Square waterfall.

As Australia has become a more multi-cultural society through patterns of migration, the nature of our religious affiliation has changed. This is reflected in census results which ask for religious adherence. From 1850–1947, major Protestant denominations—Anglicans, Methodists and Presbyterians—made up 60% of religious affinity, with Catholics representing 20%. From 1947–2001 religious diversity has included a wide range of other sects— Quakers, Mormons and Scientologists for example—and a greater number of non-Christian religions such as Jews, Muslims and Buddhists.

Those identifying actively as atheists has also increased. Such a change in religious affiliation also indicates the wider variety of countries from which people are migrating to Australia. But it is also indicative of globalisation, particularly the movement for charismatic religions such as Pentecostals. The practices of such religions, with their fervour and music have also affected the performance of more established religions. In addition, many Australians have changed their religious affinity, embracing, for example, Buddhism. This may well indicate that Australians have not become less spiritual but have widened the ways in which they express that spirituality. It may also simply reflect the growing numbers of passive adherents to the various religions and sects.

The 2016 Australian Census revealed the leading religions to be Western (Roman) Catholic (24.1%), Anglican (15.5%), Islam (3.6%), Uniting Church (2.9%), Buddhism (2.8%), Presbyterian and Reformed (2.5%), Hinduism (2.4%), Christian, no fixed denomination (2.2%), Greek Orthodox (1.7%) and Baptist (1.3%). There were 17.9% who stated they had no religion and 7.7% did not answer the question. Young people and males were more likely to be in the category of no religion, as were people with higher levels of formal education.

17. *Sport*

Sporting competitions were enjoyed by the Indigenous population, their contests including wrestling, spear-throwing, mock fights, various types of football using possum-skin balls, spinning discs and stick games. Those in coastal regions developed skills in swimming, canoeing and fishing.

With the arrival of the First Fleet in 1788, reportedly none of the convicts or officers demonstrated much interest in popular sporting contests of the time, but rather had their attention more firmly set on building a colony than recreational pursuits. However, there were a few who had a general affection for sport, including Lieutenant George Johnston, a racehorse breeder, who was the first European to set foot on land at Port Jackson in Sydney. Another in the same field was the military officer and landowner Captain John Piper, who arrived in Sydney in 1792.

It was not until 1810 that the first serious sporting event took place, in the shape of an athletics meet. Soon after, competitions in cricket, horse racing and sailing commenced, with Sydney being the centre of colonial sport. While the more disadvantaged played sport on public holidays, those well-off played on Saturdays. Indeed, sport was being used to enhance social integration across classes during the 1830s, 1840s and 1850s.

The 3rd British Empire Games, the modern-day equivalent of the Commonwealth Games, were held in Sydney from 5–12th February 1938. They were arranged to coincide with Sydney's sesqui-centenary, it being 150 years since the foundation of British settlement in Australia. The star athlete of the games was the Australian Decima Norman (1909–1983) who won five gold medals in track and field.

Today, Australia is known as a sporting nation that 'punches well above its weight' when it comes to many sports. For a country with a population well below that of the state of California in the USA, many champions from a range of fields have emerged. In particular, NSW has produced champions in many national and international sports, including in netball, cricket and various codes of football.

Sydney Olympics 2000

Sydney won the right to host the 2000 Summer Olympics Games, officially known as the Games of the XXVII Olympiad, in September 1993, after being selected over Beijing, Berlin, Istanbul and Manchester in four rounds of voting. The Sydney Olympics took place between 15th September and 1st October 2000. It was the second time the Summer Olympics were held in Australia, and also the Southern Hemisphere, the first being in Melbourne in 1956.

The opening ceremony commenced with a tribute to the Australian pastoral heritage of the Australian stockmen while the Australian National Anthem was sung, the first verse by Human Nature and the second by Julie Anthony. Nearly 11,000 athletes representing 199 IOC member countries (including three athletes from the United Nations dependency of East Timor) participated in the Games, there was a record 928 medals awarded in 300 events. Those events being contested at the Olympics for the first time in 2000 included men's and women's tae kwon do, trampoline, triathlon, and synchronized diving. Other inaugural women's events included weightlifting, modern pentathlon, and pole vault.

Australia finished fourth on the medal table, with the results for the top four nations being shown in Table 17.1.

Table 17.1 The medal tally for the top four nations at the Sydney 2000 Olympics

Rank	Nation	Gold	Silver	Bronze	Total
1	USA	37	24	32	93
2	Russia	32	28	29	89
3	China	28	16	15	59
4	Australia	16	25	17	58

There were high expectations for Indigenous athlete Cathy Freeman and she did not disappoint. After winning silver in the 400-metre track at the 1996 Olympic Games, she lit the Olympic flame at the Opening Ceremony and had the eyes of the nation, and the world, on her. With a time of 49.11 seconds, Freeman took out gold and ran a victory lap carrying two flags: the Australian and Aboriginal. At the Closing Ceremony, the then IOC President Juan Antonio Samaranch (1920–2010) called them 'the best Olympic Games ever'.

MAJOR SPORTS PLAYED IN NSW

Australian Rules Football

Australian Rules football had its origins in Victoria with the Victorian Football League (VFL) that commenced in 1897. It was renamed the Australian Football League (AFL) in 1990 to reflect its then national composition. Local competitions were established in Sydney 1880 and again in 1903, when it competed with rugby union and, later, rugby league. It had more success in the Riverina region, closer to the game's place of origin, Melbourne. AFL is now played in most of NSW with increasing popularity.

The AFL currently has two men's teams from Sydney, the Sydney 'Swans' and the Greater Western Sydney 'Giants' (GWS Giants). After experiencing financial difficulties in 1982, the South Melbourne club moved to Sydney and became the Swans. The Swans have won two premierships since moving to Sydney (in 2005 and 2012) and attendance at their matches has risen since their relocation. The Giants, now based in Western Sydney and in Canberra, joined the AFL in 2012 and finished last of the 18 teams in their first season. However, in 2018, they reached the semi-finals and made the 2019 Grand Final where they were beaten by Richmond before a crowd of over 100,000.

The AFL Women's (AFLW) is Australia's national Australian Rules football league for women. The inaugural season began in February 2017 with 8 teams, expanding to 10 teams in the 2019 season and to 14 teams in the 2020 season. The 2017 competition included a GWS Giants team that also finished in the last of eight teams in that season. In 2019 they finished 8th of the 10 teams with two wins and five losses.

Baseball

Baseball NSW is the governing body of baseball within the state and has the responsibility for selecting the NSW Sydney 'Blue Sox' team that competes in the Claxton Shield – an annual, national baseball competition currently contested between the five mainland states of Australia. It also oversees all levels of baseball in the state and manages the NSW Major League, the highest level of competition and the source of the majority of Australian-based players selected for the NSW Sydney Blue Sox.

The Sydney Blue Sox is a professional team, and one of eight foundation teams in the re-formed Australian Baseball League (ABL). It is the only team in the Australian Baseball League to introduce 'sabermetrics' to run their team with the assistance of volunteer statistician, Anthony Rescan. For the seasons 2010–11 to 2018–19, in all 336 matches, they achieved a 163–173 win-loss record (48.5% wins).

Basketball

Basketball NSW (BNSW) began in 1938 and today there are over 55,000 registered members across the state. The Sydney 'Kings' and Wollongong 'Hawks' are the NSW representatives in the National Basketball League (NBL). Both teams have taken part in the finals series since 2002–03, the Kings winning three consecutive premierships in 2002–03, 2003–04 and 2004–05. In the 2020 season, the

Kings finished on top of the competition ladder. In the best-of-five match finals series against the Perth 'Wildcats', they were down 2 matches to 1. Because of COVID-19 concerns, the Kings refused to play the remaining two matches of the series and so Perth was crowned the champions for 2020.

There are twelve teams in the NSW competition of the Australian Basketball Association, the Waratah League. The next level is the New South Wales State Basketball League. The Women's National Basketball League (WNBL) is the premier professional women's basketball league in the country and is currently composed of eight teams. New South Wales is represented by the Sydney Uni Flames, who won the competition in 2016-17.

The Spalding Waratah League is the senior basketball league in NSW, comprised of seven divisions. The season commences in March each year, the finals weekend being held in August, seeing the conclusion of the regular season. The semi-finals games played on the Saturday (14 games), with the Grand Finals games played on Sunday (7 games).

Sydney will host the Women's Basketball World Cup 2022.

Cricket

The Sydney Grade Cricket competition commenced in 1893, when several clubs that had been playing for many years on an ad hoc basis created a formal structure. Since that time there have been amalgamations, additions and deletions, but the competition has grown substantially so that by 1985, the competition comprised 20 clubs. From the beginning of the 2016–17 season, it was referred to as NSW Premier Cricket.

The junior competitions are known as the Poidevin-Gray Shield and A W Green Shield. Country Cricket NSW comprises teams that play for the McDonalds Country Championship, including the Northern Pool–Central Coast and Southern Pool–Goulburn teams.

In the Twenty20 Big Bash League and Women's Big Bash League, NSW is represented by the Sydney Sixers playing home matches at the Sydney Cricket Ground, along with the Sydney Thunder, whose home ground is the Sydney Showground.

The domestic first-class cricket competition of Australia is called the Sheffield Shield and consists of a tournament contested between teams from six states of Australia. The Shield, donated by Lord Sheffield, was first contested during the 1892–93 season, between New South Wales, South Australia and Victoria. Queensland was admitted for the 1926–27 season, Western Australia for the 1947–48 season and Tasmania for the 1977–78 season. New South Wales (known as the Blues) has won it the most times, 47 including the 2019/20 season.

The NSW Blues have played teams representing every Test-playing nation except Bangladesh. Their players have formed an important part of the Australian Test and One Day International teams, with some of the country's finest players, including, in the early years, Charles Bannerman, Charles Turner, Billy Murdoch, Fred Spofforth, M A Noble, Victor Trumper and Charlie McCartney.

Into the mid-20th century, the NSW Blues boasted Stan McCabe, Sir Donald Bradman, Bill Brown, Sid Barnes, Ray Lindwall, Keith Miller, Neil Harvey, Jeff Thomson, Alan Kippax, Bert Oldfield, Alan Davidson and Doug Walters. In more recent times, the team has produced Alan Border, Steve Smith, Mark Taylor, Steve Waugh, Mark Waugh, Brett Lee, Shane Watson, Michael Bevan, Pat Cummins, Glenn McGrath, Mitchell Starc, Josh Hazelwood, David Warner and Nathan Lyon, among many others.

Golf

There is firm evidence that Scotsman Alexander Brodie Spark and friends were playing golf at Grose Farm, on land now occupied by the University of Sydney and Royal Prince Alfred Hospital, by 1839. There are varying claims as to the oldest still existing course in the state, the strongest of which is probably that of the Australian Golf

Club in Rosebury, Sydney. With roots in 1882, the club had its formal beginning in 1884 and found a permanent home in 1895. The Royal Sydney Golf Club has been at Rose Bay since 1897.

Today nearly half a million Australians belong to a golf club and over a million play at least occasionally.

Netball

Originally called 'women's basketball', the first game of netball originated in England in 1892, when women used broomsticks for posts and the baskets were wet paper bags. Running was made extremely difficult due to their attire of long skirts, bustle backs, nipped waists and button-up shoes, while their 'leg-of-mutton' sleeves restricted arm movement. In 1897, the game was introduced to Australia and soon spread rapidly throughout the country—in 1924 interstate competitions began.

The name of the game was changed to 'netball' in 1970 and the word 'women's' was omitted, resulting in a change of name from the AAWBA to the All Australia Netball Association (AANA). The AANA was renamed as 'Netball Australia' in 1993.

The ANZ Championship commenced in 2007 as the new elite domestic netball competition in New Zealand and Australia, replacing the Commonwealth Bank Trophy in Australia. This trans-Tasman competition features five teams from each country, with those from Australia including one team from each of New South Wales, Victoria, South Australia, Queensland and Western Australia. These five franchises were formed from the merging of Commonwealth Bank Trophy teams, including the Sydney Swifts amalgamating with the 'Jaegars' from the Hunter region of NSW. They were still known as the 'Swifts' and their inaugural coach was Julie Fitzgerald, who had coached the Sydney Swifts.

On 28th July 2008, the Swifts defeated the Waikato/Bay of Plenty Magic 65–56 to win the inaugural season of the ANZ Championship. In 2010, the Swifts were officially the first ever team in the competition to go undefeated in the regular season. However, as they lost both their semi-final and preliminary final, they did not make the Grand Final. The Swifts have not yet won a Grand Final, although they have played in two more of them, losing to Queensland 56–57 in 2015 and 66–69 to the same team in 2016.

In 2017 and 2018, the Swifts played in the Suncorp Super Netball competition without a great deal of success. However, there was a second Sydney team admitted, the 'Giants', who reached the Grand Final in 2017, losing 48–65 to the Lightning. In 2019 they won the Grand Final with a 64–47 over the 'Lightning'. The Swifts currently play their home games at Australia's largest permanent indoor venue, Qudos Bank Arena in Sydney, as well as the State Sports Centre, both in Sydney's Olympic Precinct at Homebush Bay where the Sydney Olympics were held in 2000.

Netball NSW has grown to become one of the largest independent sporting organisations in the state, as well as maintaining its position as one of the most popular team sports for (mostly, but not exclusively) women and girls in the country.

Rugby League

The history of rugby league football dates to 1895 in Huddersfield, England, when the Northern Rugby Football Union separated from the country's established Rugby Football Union to launch its own separate competition. The game was formed as a rebel football code in a defiant gesture. However, by the turn of the century, players were becoming discontented and wanted to be compensated for lost payments when they took time off work and for when they took out sporting injury insurance. The rugby league was adamant that no compensation would be made and insisted that their amateur status remained.

It was a different outcome in NSW. On 8th August 1907, a group of leading rugby union players and supporters held a meeting at Bateman's Hotel in George Street, Sydney, to formulate a new type of game in which payment would be paid to the players. Among these rebels were key supporters including a businessman James Joseph Giltinan (1866–1950), a renowned cricketer, Victor Trumper (1877–1915) and a trade unionist and Labor politician, Henry Hoyle (1852–1926). Another key figure was the talented rugby player, Dally Messenger (1883–1959), 'the Master', who made the switch to the new game later that year, joining the Eastern Suburbs Rugby League Football Club.

The first full season of rugby league in Australia was played in 1908, with the initial match being played between Glebe and Newtown in Sydney. All the teams came from NSW, the others being Western Suburbs, South Sydney, North Sydney, Balmain, Eastern Suburbs, Newcastle and Cumberland. The following year, league football was played in Queensland. It took two years of competition for rugby league to get established, with growing attendances at club matches, as well as interstate games and a visit by a touring English side.

In 1911 there was a New Zealand rugby league tour of Australia in which the visitors won four of their eight matches. In 1911–12 there was a successful Australasian (Australia and New Zealand combined) 'Kangaroo' tour of Britain in which they won 35, drew 2 and lost 5 matches. These included winning two and drawing one match of the three Test (Ashes) series. This was the first time the Kangaroos won the Ashes (adapting the cricket concept) on British soil, a feat they did not repeat until the 1963–64 tour.

In 1947, Parramatta and Manly entered the Sydney competition and 1967 saw the addition of Cronulla and Penrith. Since then, there have been various amalgamations and deletions, with interstate teams now in Queensland, Melbourne, as well as one in New Zealand—the Warriors.

The headquarters of both the Australian Rugby League (ARL) and National Rugby League (NRL) are in Sydney, which is home to nine of the sixteen National Rugby League (NRL) football clubs. Those based in Sydney include the 'Eels', 'Roosters', 'Bulldogs', 'Rabbitohs', 'Sharks', 'Sea Eagles', 'Wests Tigers' and 'Panthers'. Another team, the Dragons, is half-based in Wollongong, while a tenth NSW team, the 'Knights', is located in Newcastle.

The winners of the Rugby League Grand Final for each of the 10 years 2010–2019 are shown in Table 17.2 with the final scores shown in parentheses.

Table 17.2 Winners of the Rugby League Grand Finals between 2010 and 2019

Year	Winner	Runner-up
2010	St George-Illawarra (32)	Sydney Roosters (8)
2011	Manly-Warringah (24)	Warriors (10)
2012	Melbourne (14)	Canterbury (4)
2013	Sydney Roosters (26)	Manly-Warringah (18)
2014	South Sydney (30)	Canterbury (6)
2015	North Queensland (17)	Brisbane (16)
2016	Cronulla (14)	Melbourne (12)
2017	Melbourne (34)	North Queensland (6)
2018	Sydney Roosters (21)	Melbourne (6)
2019	Sydney Roosters (14)	Canberra (8)

The premier state-level league is the New South Wales Cup, involving reserve teams from NSW and Canberra-based NRL clubs along with the first teams from other clubs. Country football is overseen by the New South Wales Country Rugby League.

The annual 'State of Origin' series between the New South Wales 'Blues' and the Queensland 'Maroons' is one of the highlights of the rugby league season, with the three-game series being held in Sydney and Brisbane, usually with the first and third games in one city, and the second in the other. The third game may be played in another city, such as Melbourne, but usually alternates between Sydney and Brisbane every year. Of the 38 full series played up to 2019, Queensland has won 21, New South Wales 15, with 2 series drawn. Queensland enjoyed a particularly remarkable run of success, winning eight successive series between 2006 and 2013.

The State of Origin results for the years 2017–19 are shown in Table 17.3.

Table 17.3 State of Origin results 2017–2019

Game	Winner	Score	Venue
2017 Game 1	NSW	28 – 4	Brisbane
2017 Game 2	Queensland	18 – 16	Sydney
2017 Game 3	Queensland	22 – 6 (Qld wins series 2–1)	Brisbane
2018 Game 1	NSW	22 – 12	Melbourne
2018 Game 2	NSW	18 – 14	Sydney
2018 Game 3	Queensland	18 – 12 (NSW wins series 2–1)	Brisbane
2019 Game 1	Queensland	18 – 4	Brisbane
2019 Game 2	NSW	38 – 6	Perth
2019 Game 3	NSW	28 – 20 (NSW wins series 2–1)	Sydney

Rugby Union

Rugby Union is possibly the oldest codified version of football in the world, but before it was codified, games involving two teams wrestling for and kicking around an inflated bladder have been played for centuries, and right around the world. It was reported that such a sport was played in NSW in the 1820s, when visiting ship crews would play army teams at Barrack Square in Sydney. The first Australian rugby union club was formed in 1863 at the University of Sydney. Today Australia holds Tier 1 status with World Rugby, with over 82,000 players nationwide.

During 1869, Newington College became the first Australian school to play rugby in a match against the University of Sydney. After 1872, rugby football clubs grew rapidly in number, with the first metropolitan competition in Australia being introduced two years later. The competition initially had six teams, with the first inter-colonial game taking place in 1882, when players from the four Queensland clubs travelled to NSW. With a crowd of 4,000 spectators, NSW won by 28 points to 4 at the Sydney Cricket Ground (SCG). In 1899, Australia's national team played their first match, in Sydney, winning against the visiting British Isles team.

The New South Wales Rugby Union (NSWRU) was founded in 1874 as the 'Southern Rugby Union', before changing to the current name in 1893. In 1939, with the start of the Second World War, the NSWRU decided to cancel representative games, although they continued with club competitions. The war took a heavy toll on the game, as many players and officials were killed or injured. As a result, in 1946, a restricted form of rugby was revived at the conclusion of the war.

During those post-war years suburban rugby expanded, and in 1963 the Sydney Rugby Union was founded with a view to expanding the game in the city area. In 1971, the Sydney Sub-Districts Rugby Union was established and the suburban ('Subbies') competition was rearranged into three divisions. In 1990, the Subbies were called the New South Wales Suburban Rugby Union, with the second division of the Sydney district competition merging with the Subbies in 1993, with 18 clubs contesting the Kentwell Cup competition in that year.

The New South Wales 'Waratahs' represent most of NSW in the Super Rugby competition. The team entered the Super 12 season in 1996, winning just under half of their games and finishing in the middle of the table. In 2005, they had their best regular season, finishing second in the table, before losing to the New Zealand 'Crusaders' in the Super 12 Final. Between 2006 and 2010, they contested the Super 14, finishing third on the table for the regular season in the first year.

Following the Super 14 competition, the Super Rugby competition commenced in 2011 and continues to the present day. The Waratah's best season took place in 2014, when they won the Australian conference with 13 more points than the second-placed team, the ACT Brumbies. They played the Crusaders in the final, narrowly winning the Super Rugby Championship by a score of 33–32.

In 2018, the NSW Waratahs entered a women's team into the newly formed 15-a-side Australian women's rugby competition. On 20th April that year, the team won the first season of competition, beating the Queensland Reds by 16–13 at Stadium Australia in Sydney. The Super Rugby women's teams completed their regular season in 2020 with the undefeated Waratahs sitting on top of the ladder after the four round robin rounds. With COVID-19 resulting in no further matches being planned in the season, they were declared champions for the third year in a row.

Soccer

Sydney also has a long tradition in Association Football, also known as soccer. Early soccer clubs in Sydney in the late 1800s were quite small and were largely English in appearance. Following the Second World War, many immigrants left Europe to settle in Sydney, and Australia generally. These migrants formed their own soccer clubs, based mainly on their ethnic origin. The three largest of these clubs were founded by the three largest post-war immigration groups—Marconi Stallions Football Club (Italian), Sydney Olympic Football Club (Greek), and Sydney United Football Club (Croatian). There were also smaller clubs formed by ethnic groups that dominated matches in Sydney, attracting large crowds. The late 1980s saw a shift in their fortunes with a rise in football hooligan violence, a lowering of the standard of play and subsequent falling attendances as they were not expanding their supporter bases.

Football Federation Australia (FFA) is the governing body of soccer, futsal (a five-a-side game that is a variant of soccer, played on a hard court, smaller than a football pitch, and mainly indoors), and beach soccer within the country. It embarked upon a strategy to eradicate ethnicity from the clubs and to attract a broader audience, resulting in new clubs such as Parramatta 'Power' and Northern

'Spirit' being founded, but without an ethnic fan base they failed to attract a following. During 2005, a review of the game was undertaken, and it was decided that further radical changes were necessary. A new club, 'Sydney FC', was founded, based in central Sydney. They were entered in a new competition known as the A-League (which had the aim of becoming the premier national football competition), along with similarly formed clubs from other large cities around Australia.

There is no type of relegation or promotion between the A-league and other football competitions. The previous national league reverted to its original form in state-based competitions. Sydney FC soon built up a solid support base of around 10,000 members, and sometimes attracting crowds of up to 40,000. They won the A-league final in 2005–6, 2009–10, 2016–17 and 2018–19.

In April 2012, the Western Sydney 'Wanderers' was established with a strong community focus. They currently play their home games at Bankwest Stadium at Parramatta. The club experienced a record-breaking inaugural season, winning the A-League premiership and reaching the 2013 A-league Grand Final. They also contested the 2014 A-League Grand Final, placing second in only their second season of the league. The Wanderers became Asian Champions in their debut Champions League season, becoming the first, and so far only, Australian side to win the tournament.

Outside of Sydney, soccer is played in the state's larger regional cities and clubs have been formed such as the Newcastle 'Jets' and Central Coast 'Mariners', which both play in the A-league. The Wollongong 'Wolves' FC plays in the New South Wales premier league as part of the 12-team competition that also includes ethnic clubs such as Apia Leichhardt FC and Marconi FC.

The top tier of the women's football competition in the state is the Football NSW Women's 1st National Premier League (NPL) comprising 12 teams. There are also other competitions, including the Under–14s, Under–15s, Under–17s and Reserves who each play a round-robin structure where each side plays one another twice. At the completion of all matches, a Premier is crowned.

Skiing

New South Wales enjoys Australia's highest snow country, oldest ski-fields and largest resorts. The country's recreational skiing has its origins around 1861 at Kiandra, NSW, when Norwegian gold miners introduced the sport to the hills around the town. The Kiandra Snow Shoe Club is thought to be the first and longest surviving ski club in the world, and was formed at Kiandra in that same year of 1861.

The gold discoveries in Australia in the mid-19th century invigorated the introduction of recreational alpine skiing, with Kiandra remaining a service centre for recreational and survival skiing for over 150 years. Australia's first 'T-Bar' ski lift was installed there in 1957, but in 1978, the ski facilities were relocated up the hill to Selwyn Snowfields, although steeper slopes and more reliable snowfalls lay further to the south. Eventually, the hub of recreational skiing in the state shifted to the Mount Kosciuszko region. The mountain was named by the Polish explorer Paweł Edmund Strzelecki (1797–1873) in 1840 in honour of Polish-Lithuanian freedom fighter General Tadeusz Kościuszko, as it supposedly resembled the Kościuszko Mound in Kraków, Poland.

The first Kosciuszko Chalet was built at Charlotte Pass in 1930, which at 1,760 metres has the highest village base elevation of any Australian ski resort and can only be accessed via over-snow transport in winter. Charlotte Pass took its name from Charlotte Adams who, in 1881, became the first European woman to climb Mount Kosciuszko. The increasing number of ski enthusiasts travelling there led, in 1939, to the establishment of a café at Smiggin Holes—a name of Scottish origin, for the depressions caused by cattle trampling to consume rock salt.

It was the construction of the vast Snowy Mountains Hydro-Electric Scheme from 1949 that opened up the Snowy Mountains for large-scale development of a ski industry, leading to the construction of Thredbo and Perisher as leading Australian resorts. Thredbo has the largest vertical drop of any Australian ski resort at 672 metres. The name 'Thredbo' is thought to derive from the language of the *Yaitmathang, Wolgalu, Wiradjuri* or *Ngarigo* people.

Perisher is a relatively more recent, being developed in March 1995. Its name supposedly refers to livestock trapped in the high country. The region combines the facilities and resources of Perisher Valley, Smiggin Holes, Guthega, Mount Blue Cow, The Station and the Skitube alpine railway. It is the largest snow resort operation in the Southern Hemisphere, having the highest terrain, the greatest number of lifts and the most reliable snow in Australia.

Tennis

Tennis NSW is the largest of the eight state and territory member tennis associations and, in 2020, supported 511 Clubs, Associations and Court Operators and over 100,000 registered participants. Their role is to coordinate, manage and promote the sport of tennis in NSW while supporting and servicing its members. Their charter is to help everyone in NSW to enjoy playing tennis for and they are governed by a Board of Directors.

In the Open Era (1969 onwards), winners from NSW of the Men's Australian Open title include Ken Rosewall (1971, 1972), John Newcombe (1973, 1975) and Mark Edmonson (1976). Winners from NSW of the Women's Australian Open title are Margaret Court (1969–71, 1973), Evonne Goolagong Cawley (1974–76, January 1977),

Kerry (Melville) Reid (December 1977) and Christine O'Neill (1978).

NSW has also produced an Open Era Wimbledon singles male champion in John Newcombe (1970 and 1971), and female champions in Margaret Court (1970) and Evonne Goolagong Cawley (1971 and 1980).

18. *Art, Literature, Music and Architecture*

Colonial art and literature have been undoubtedly influenced by British traditions and techniques. This is evidenced by the works themselves and by the various creators' visits to, and reliance on, mentors abroad. At the same time, artists and writers have also been shaped by local culture, history and landscape, which some consciously embraced in order to present a different world view.

VISUAL ART

Australian art was first expressed in the cave and rock depictions of life by Aboriginal people. These illustrations told stories of cultural significance, conveying events and beliefs. Body painting was also an important conveyor of culture with the materials and techniques used varying from area to area. Aboriginal art was mainly ignored until David Jones Art Gallery in Sydney organised a display in 1949, leading to the Art Gallery of NSW including Indigenous art in its exhibitions. Interestingly, it is Aboriginal art that has become the most sought after

Australian art by the international art market in the 20th and 21st centuries.

Once Australia was colonised by the British, European artistic concepts and techniques were employed. In NSW, Joseph Lycett (1774–1828), convicted of forgery, had patrons such as the first commandant of Newcastle, James Morrisset (1780–1852), and later Governor Lachlan Macquarie. Such patrons demanded accuracy, so that was what Lycett's paintings delivered. Lycett painted prolifically, many of his paintings depicting Aboriginal life. His painting of 'Aborigines hunting kangaroos', in around 1820 for example, shows thick forests with grassy lawns on which kangaroos grazed.

Many early artists were not painters but professionals who painted as part of their jobs. Surveyor Robert Hoddle (1794–1881) surveyed and planned NSW towns such as Berrima and Goulburn. As part of this project, he painted district scenes depicting hills, sparsely timbered, and open plains.

Eugene von Guerard (1811–1901) was a painter lured to Australia at the time of the goldrushes. His much lauded 'Sydney Heads', 1865, shows grassy inclines, ringed by trees and sloping down to the harbour.

Such early artists provide an important representation of NSW as it was before overgrazing and the introduction of cloven-hoofed animals, which badly affected native grasses and pastures. While artists like Conrad Martens (1801–1878) and Thomas Watling (1762–1814) may have exaggerated what many colonists perceived as boring terrain by painting portraits and landscapes that reflected favourably on their surroundings, the colonial world did not need over–embellishment to appear novel to those 'back home'.

In the second part of the 19th century, artists felt the need to spend time in the European art scene to gain the experience required of a professional. Landscape painter Arthur Streeton (1867–1943) spent twenty years in England. This constructed a twofold identity in Australian art as it bowed to the influence and origins of its heritage.

Streeton, along with Tom Roberts, Frederick McCubben and Charles Condor, were part of the legendary 'Heidelberg School' in Victoria. Their use of 'plein air' and insistence on creating a national imagery of warm, clear air was also used and expounded in Sydney by Alfred Daplyn (1844–1926) and Julian Ashton (1851–1942). These artists presented a pioneering and heroic Australia.

Australian artists in the 1910s, 1920s and 1930s became more international, as a widening world gave them the opportunity to incorporate, for example, oriental themes and techniques. Margaret Preston (1875–1963) was born in Adelaide and travelled widely abroad. She and her husband lived much of her productive life in Mosman and Berowra, two Sydney suburbs. She produced woodcuts in the Japanese style, while asserting an Australian influence in her choice of subjects. Sydney-based artists such as Grace Cossington Smith (1892–1984) and Roy de Maistre (1894–1968) were influenced by European modernist techniques. Others in the 1920s were influenced by cubism, an avant-garde art movement that revolutionised European painting and sculpture in the early 20th-century.

In the post-Second World War period, more international influences were evident in Australian art. With increasing multiculturalism, new influences were felt in music, literature and art. Located in NSW, the Archibald Prize was the first major Australian prize for portraiture. It was first awarded in 1921 after the receipt of a bequest from J. F. Archibald, the editor of *The Bulletin*, who passed away in 1919. Other prominent prizes for art include the Wynne Prize, the Sir John Sulman Prize and the Dobell prize, the latter named in honour of the renowned Australian portrait and landscape artist Ralph Dobell (1899–1970) who was born in Cooks Hill.

LITERATURE

Colonial writing was viewed variously in Britain and could be seen as presenting the 'exotic'. The 1830 novel, *Alfred Dudley or, the Australian Settlers*, published in London was based on the experience of the Dudley family making a comfortable living for themselves in NSW. Other stories told of the irredeemable disgrace of the most genteel of convicts. One of the earliest Australian novels was published in 1831, when the transported forger, Henry Savery (1791–1842), wrote *Quintus Servinton: A Tale Founded upon Incidents of Real Occurrence*.

The first official colonial poet was an educated convict, Michael Massey Robinson (1744–1826), who was the author of the first verse published in Australia, 'Ode on His majesty's Birthday', in 1810. His poetry was high-minded and used the literary conventions of English poetry. British poets, many of whom had never visited New South Wales, presented its oddity or its robustness as the colony's major characteristics.

Colonial writers, like colonial artists, looked to Britain as their foundation. The teacher, journalist, politician, leading suffragist and novelist Catherine Helen Spence (1825–1910), travelled to London in 1865 where she met such luminaries as John Stuart Mills and George Eliot (Mary Ann Evans). Born in Windsor, NSW, the poet Charles Harpur (1813–1868) was a man well-versed in British classical literature and had a deep love of colonial society and country. While being a European romantic, he came to terms with the environment of the colony. While non-Indigenous colonial literature sought to oppose itself to its British origins by claiming a larrikin or proletarian character, much of its nature lay in the dichotomy of being Australian and British. This can be seen in the currency lads (the first generations of native-born white Australians) of Rolf Boldrewood's 1888 novel, *Robbery Under Arms*, who adopt attitudes and language deemed to be local in a conventional novel of romance and adventure.

Other writers tried consciously to present a local world view. Henry Kendall (1839–1882) was a poet who deliberately represented the south coast of NSW with a strong emotional attachment to its landscape and flora and fauna. The poems of Orange-born Andrew Barton ('Banjo') Paterson (1864–1941) romanticised the colony's 'outback' in poems such as 'Clancy of the Overflow' and 'Waltzing Matilda' (now Australia's informal anthem). Born in Grenfell, NSW, the poems of Henry Lawson (1867–1922) celebrated both the bush ('Andy's gone with cattle') and the city ('Faces in the Street'), while his novels and short stories romanticised the drama and terror of bush life ('The Drover's Wife').

Barbara Baynton's short stories stressed the isolation of bush life. May Gibb (1912–1953), the much-loved children's author and illustrator, spent much of her life in Neutral Bay on Sydney Harbour. She had studied and worked in England in the early years of the twentieth century but, when she returned and lived in Sydney, she became fascinated in the local flora and fauna, writing her celebrated Gumnut Babies books.

The establishment of the magazine, *The Bulletin*, first published in Sydney in 1880, provided an outlet for Australian writing that was more locally situated in what has been termed 'bush nationalism'. During its lifetime, it employed such well-known writers as Mary Gilmore, Chris Brennan, Steele Rudd, Dorothea Mackellar, Henry Lawson, Vance Palmer and Ethel Turner.

While attempting to find a colonial voice, Australian writers of the 19th and 20th centuries were mindful of international currents and events. After the First World War, the move towards Europe increased, although most of these expatriates returned to Australia and many others never left. Fiction written in the period between the two World Wars was largely in the form of romantic sagas glorifying the spirit and characteristics that are now associated with the ANZAC ideal: endurance, courage and mateship. These stories were often set in Australia's colonial past. Eleanor Dark's *The Timeless Land* tells of early colonial settlement, while the work of Miles Franklin (1879–1954), *Up the Country*, tells the story of early squatters in the Monaro district of NSW.

In the post-Second World War period, publishing houses were being established in Australia, and British publishing companies were establishing branches in Australia. This assisted in the publication and dissemination of Australian literature and commenced the establishment of a localised literary system. Literary magazines, some short-lived but others with longevity, assisted in promoting Australian prose, poetry and literary criticism. They varied from the left-wing *Overland*, established in 1954, to the conservative magazine *Quadrant*, founded in Sydney in 1956.

New South Wales has produced a range of internationally recognised authors. Poets Henry Lawson, Banjo Peterson and Dorothea Mackellar have already been mentioned, but to this could be added Dame Mary Gilmore, Alec Derwent (A.D) Hope and Judith Wright. Acclaimed novelists include Miles Franklin, Christina Stead, Patrick White (born in London of a NSW family but returning to live in NSW), Thomas Keneally, Kevin John Gilbert, Ruby Langford Ginibi and Geraldine Brooks.

Prizes and awards currently given in the NSW Premier's Literary Awards include the Christina Stead Prize for Fiction, Douglas Stewart Prize for Non-Fiction, Kenneth Slessor Prize for Poetry, Ethel Turner Prize for Young People's Literature and Patricia Wrightson Prize for Children's Literature.

MUSIC

Singing and choirs were encouraged by churches in the early colony and four-part choral music was common in churches from the 1830s. These choirs included secular ones from the 1840s and the Sydney Philharmonic Society was formed in 1854, followed by a range of choral societies over the following decades. Religious music was still prevalent, however, with Handel's *Messiah* being a staple.

Domestically, the compact square piano was popular, the first piano coming with the First Fleet via surgeon

George Worgan (1757–1838). The first play, 'The Recruiting Officer', was staged in Sydney, possibly to the music of this piano. Other settlers who followed, such as Elizabeth Macquarie (1778–1835), the second wife of Governor Lachlan Macquarie, also brought their pianos with them. In 2011 at Rouse Hill House and Farm, the Sydney Living Museums project found a full song book of music used in the home of Lilias (1818–1869) and Willoughby Dowling (1812–1849). It had been bound in Sydney, probably in the early 1840s, by Sydney composer and music-seller Francis Ellard (1800–1854) and showed that in the far-flung colony of New South Wales, music from Europe was part of household entertainment and occupation.

Possibly the first opera in NSW was performed, apparently without accompanying music, in 1834. This was *Clari or The Maid of Milan*. Later operas were adapted for local conditions with music being used as conditions allowed and performers became available.

The goldrushes of the 1850s caused an increase in migration, leading to an upsurge in the music composed in Australia generally. While owing much to overseas influence, songs and melodies were often composed by ex-convicts and reflected a growth in local awareness and patriotic sentiment. In New South Wales, John Delany composed his cantata, 'Captain Cook', and musician Stephen Hale Marsh directed his composition, 'Advance Australia' in Sydney.

The music scene of NSW was greatly advantaged by the migration of Fortunato Amadio (1876–1953). The broad Amadio family, all musicians, were mainly born, lived and worked in Sydney with Fortunato's grandson, Clive Amadio, for example, being born in Sydney in 1903. Clive's facility on both clarinet and saxophone led to positions with the Sydney Symphony Orchestra and to a teaching position at the NSW (now Sydney) Conservatorium of Music, a heritage-listed music school in Macquarie Street, Sydney, that originally opened in 1916. It is known simply as 'the Con' and its tertiary studies are a part of the University of Sydney curricula.

NSW has produced a number of eminent composers. In the early part of the 20th century, most of these worked within the traditional British model of composition. John Antill (1904–1986) was born in Sydney. His best-known work, 'Corroboree', acknowledges the local setting, but he also composed opera, ballets and orchestral works. Later composers became more adventurous. Nigel Butterley, born in Sydney in 1935, was a pianist, composer and lecturer with an international reputation. Composer and lecturer Ann Carr-Boyd was born in Sydney in 1938 and later completed ground-breaking research into Australian music history.

Singers such as June Bronhill (1929–2005) and Dame Joan Sutherland (1926–2010), both born in NSW, became internationally acclaimed sopranos. Born in Nowra, NSW, Deborah Cheetham, a *Yorta Yorta* woman, has been recognised not only as an opera performer but as a composer and for her work in encouraging more Indigenous youth to be involved in singing and the arts. A soprano, Cheetham has performed in France, Germany, Switzerland, the United Kingdom and New Zealand, including singing at the opening ceremonies of the 2000 Summer Olympics and the 2003 Rugby World Cup.

In the area of popular music, NSW has contributed both composers and performers. Such music was encouraged by the 'hit parades' which radio promoted in the years following the Second World War. Jazz was encouraged by the Sydney Basement where Galapagos Duck first performed in 1973. Performers born in NSW include Don Burrows (Sydney), James Morrison (Boorowa), and Tommy Emmanuel (Muswellbrook), while popular singers include Lana Cantrell (Sydney), Col Joye (Sydney), Peter Allen (Tenterfield), Johnny O'Keefe (Sydney), Shannon Noll (Orange), Peter Garrett (Sydney) and Delta Goodrem (Sydney). There were many rock groups formed and based in NSW, including the Cockroaches, the Divinyls, the Easybeats, AC/DC, INXS and Men at Work. The Presets and Sick Puppies are more recent bands showing that the NSW music scene is still vibrant and innovative.

Country music found its high point in the Tamworth Music Festival held annually in this northern NSW town. It is one of the biggest country music festivals in the world, rivalling the the largest in the USA. In Parkes, NSW, the Parkes Elvis Festival is held every year in the second week in January, coinciding with Elvis Presley's birthday. The inaugural Parkes Elvis Revival started on Friday 8th January 1993 and continues to grow with more than 200 events held across five days.

What might be called 'folk' or 'bush' music was also active in NSW. It was celebrated in the 1953 musical, *Reedy River*, and saw a renewal in such events as the Newcastle Folk Festival and Sydney's Bush Music Club in the 1980s. Themes covered the hardships of transportation, the lives of bushrangers, and the lives of shearers and settlers. While celebrating colonial history in their lyrics, many of these songs used traditional tunes from Britain. One of the oldest of these songs, 'Bold Jack Donahue', tells the story of an Irish convict who, from 1826 to 1830, with his band of followers, survived by robbery. It is usually sung to an Irish tune, 'Brennan on the Moor'.

Warren Fahey founded both Larrikin Music Publishing in 1974, supporting folk music in NSW, and the Australian Music Centre located in Ultimo, Sydney, which provides access to recordings, scores, articles, analysis, digital samples, artist profiles, biographies, event listings and education. In 2014, Larrikin Music Publishing was renamed 'Happy as Larry Music Publishing'.

The classical music scene also blossomed again in the 1970s with the Renaissance Players, based at the University of Sydney under the artistic direction of Winsome Evans and other ensembles including the Brandenburg Orchestra, the Australian Chamber Orchestra and Pinchgut Opera.

Original Aboriginal music and dance has been recorded, most notably in northern NSW. The *Bundjalung* people have been anxious not to lose their traditional culture as told in their music and this is being recorded by Margaret Gummow. Many Aboriginal groups have embraced Western music styles. Coloured Stone, based in Sydney, toured widely in Australia and overseas, particularly in the 1980s, with their themes usually topical.

ARCHITECTURE

The colony's permanent architecture took off with Governor Lachlan Macquarie's appointment of the convict Francis Greenway as Colonial Architect. His design of Hyde Park Barracks, the 'Rum' Hospital and St James's Church in Sydney, and St Matthew's Church, Windsor, can be seen in the buildings today. They are of balanced design and restrained in decoration.

Early architectural style was clearly derivative as evidenced by the Georgian terraces in Sydney's Rocks area. The simplicity of this style made it suitable for the young colony. The settlement 'imported' romantic neo-Gothic, neo-Classical and Regency styles following their popularity in England. Good examples are the Darlinghurst Courthouse and the NSW Conservatorium of Music, originally the Government House Stables. Although the concepts were unoriginal, the local conditions started to have an impact on design, mainly because of cost.

Once gold was discovered in 1851, new wealth and increased migration led to a display of prosperity through domestic and commercial design and so decoration, such as the use of filigree and decorative cast iron were used. Italianate buildings were now favoured, along with Gothic and neo-Classical. Edmund Blacket (1817–1883), the Colonial Architect 1849–1854, found success in private practice and was responsible for the design of such buildings as St Andrew's Anglican Cathedral, the main buildings of the University of Sydney and numerous churches, shops, homes and public buildings. James Barnet (1827–1904), the colonial architect for NSW between 1862 and 1890, was influenced by the High Renaissance Italian style when he designed the Bathurst Gaol, and the Court House in Cooma shows the Palladian influence. A simple walk through the streets of the major towns in NSW exemplifies the variety of European styles adapted and favoured by the colony's architects and builders.

The last decades of the 19th century, with more of the population locally born, saw an increasing nationalism, exemplified by the International Exhibition, held in a glass and timber pavilion and occupying five acres of the Royal Botanic Gardens. Both the Art Gallery of NSW (1874) and the Queen Victoria Building (1888) in Sydney were built at this time in the Romanesque style, popular for its versatility. The 1890s Depression called a halt to most large-scale building, and even once the depression had eased, the style utilised in the expanding suburbs was the more restrained Queen Anne style. The Federation period also saw the influence of the Arts and Crafts movement in which domestic architecture in particular was informal, functional and homely. A good example of the Federation bungalow style can be seen in the uncomplicated and unpretentious Ranger's Cottage, built between 1898 and 1899 in Centennial Park, designed by Walter Vernon (1846–1914) during his term as the NSW Government Architect between 1890 and 1911.

After the First World War, American influence affected a range of aspects of NSW culture from music to fashion, and architecture was also influenced as is seen in the popularity of the Californian Bungalow. Local architects were also aware of other trends overseas, such as the Parisian Beaux-Arts School, Spanish Mission and Mediterranean styles. While many overseas styles were considered too extreme, Art Deco was favoured by milk bars and cinemas. Excellent examples can be found in the art deco style Anzac Memorial in Hyde Park, constructed in 1934, and the Orpheum and Ritz cinemas (1935, Cremorne and 1937, Randwick).

An understanding of working with the environment, typical of the 'Sydney School', is evident in the work of Walter Burley Griffin (1876–1937) and his wife, Marion Mahony (1871–1961), who had worked with the eminent architect Frank Lloyd Wright (1867–1959)—she was the first employee hired by him in 1895. Burley Griffin developed Sydney's Castlecrag peninsula ensuring its compatibility with the contours of the land. He also oversaw the design of North and South Canberra. But these pioneers were ahead of their time for many people of NSW.

After the Second World War, construction was affected by a shortage of materials. Soldiers returning from war and expecting some reward for their stoicism and courage, built fibro garages on blocks of land while awaiting bricks and tiles that did not turn up. By the 1950s, construction picked up, although modernists prevailed, and the design was functional.

During and after the 1960s, growth was the key word. Concrete was favoured and shopping centres and motels were built. During the 1950s, plans were being developed for a cultural centre on Bennelong Point in Sydney. The tram sheds which had existed there for 50 years were losing viability as other means of transport replaced trams. The design for the new 'Opera House' was put out to tender. The winning architect, Jørn Utzon, designed what has become Australia's single most iconic building (and one of the most famous in the world), but he conflicted strongly with the then Minister for Public Works, Davis Hughes (1910–2003), during construction (to be fair to Hughes, the building eventually cost nearly fifteen times over the original estimate). Utzon left the project and never saw the finished building, which was opened by Queen Elizabeth II in 1973.

Bibliography

'27 August 1902 – Women's Franchise Act (voting)', NSW Government, State Archives & Records, <www.records.nsw.gov.au/archives/ magazine/onthisday/27-august-1902>.

'A Century of Service', Australian Respiratory Council, <www.thearc.org. au/about-arc/century-of-service/ARC-Celebrating-100-Years.html>.

'A hundred years of science and service - Australian meteorology through the twentieth century', Australian Bureau of Statistics, <www.abs.gov.au/ AUSSTATS/abs@.nsf/7d12b0f6763c78caca257061001cc588/1d46b2e6 12b3af1eca2569de001f1082!OpenDocument>.

Adelaide, Debra, Ashton, Paul & Salt, Annette (2013), *Stories from the Tower: UTS 1988-2013, XOUM, NSW*.

'Agricultural sector', <https://www.agriculture.gov.au/abares/research-topics/aboutmyregion/nsw#agricultural-sector>.

Aitkin, Don & Jinks, Brian, (1981), *Australian Political Institutions*, Pitman Australia.

'Ambulance Service of NSW', NSW Government, Health, <www.ambulance.nsw.gov.au/about-us/History.html>.

Anderson, Jaynie [ed], (2011), *The Cambridge Companion to Australian Art*, Cambridge University Press, Melbourne.

Apperley, Richard, Irving, Robert & Reynolds, Peter, (1989), *Identifying Australian Architecture*, Angus & Robertson, Sydney.

Ashton, Paul, (2011), 'Constructed Landscapes: Centennial Park' in *Locality*, Autumn 2001 pp. 10-12.

Ashton, Paul, (2008), 'East Circular Quay' in *Dictionary of Sydney'*, <dictionaryofsydney.org/entry/east_circular_quay>.

Ashton, Paul, (2012), *Places of the Heart: Memorials in Australia*, Australian Scholarly Publishing, North Melbourne.

Ashton, Paul & Wilson, Jacqueline, (2014), *Silent System: Forgotten Australians and the institutionalisation of Women and Children*, Australian Scholarly Publishing, North Melbourne.

Ashton, Paul, Cornwall, Jennifer & Salt, Annette, (2006), *Sutherland Shire: A History*, UNSW Press, Sydney.

Attenbrow, Val, (2010), *Sydney's Aboriginal Past: Investigating the archaeological and historical records*, UNSW Press, Sydney.

Austin, A. G., (1961), *Australian Education 1788-1900*, Pitman.

'Australian Agricultural and Rural Life', State Library of NSW, <www.sl.nsw.gov.au/stories/australian-agricultural-and-rural-life>.

'Australia's Migration History', NSW Government Migration Heritage Centre, <www.migrationheritage.nsw.gov.au/belongings-home/about-belongings/australias-migration-history/index.html>.

'Australian Music History', <https://australianmusichistory.com/category/venues/>.

Aykut, Susan, (2007), 'A Lot of Hot Air; the Turkish Bath in Nineteenth Century Australia' in *Historical Papers, No. 6, Oct 2007*, Mt Wilson & Mt Irvine Historical Society, <www.mtwilson.com.au/documentation/historical-society/historical-society-papers/62-historical-paper-no-6-the-turkish-bath-in-19th-century-australia/file>.

Barcan, Alan, (1980), *A History of Australian Education*, Melbourne.

Bateson, Charles, (1974), *The Convict Ships 1787-1868*, AH & AW Reed, Sydney.

Bebbington, Warren (ed), (1998), *A Dictionary of Australian Music*, Oxford University Press, Melbourne.

Bebbington, Warren (ed), (1997), *The Oxford Companion to Australian Music*, Oxford University Press, Melbourne.

Behrendt, Larisssa, (2012), *Indigenous Australia for Dummies*, Wiley Publishing, Queensland.

'Birth of Surf Life Saving', National Museum of Australia, <www.nma.gov.au/exhibitions/between_the_flags/the_birth_of_surf_lifesaving>.

Blainey, Geoffrey (1966; 2001 edition), *The Tyranny of Distance: How Distance Shaped Australia's History*, Pan Macmillan Australia, Sydney.

Bouma, Gary, (2002), 'Globalization and Recent Changes in the Demography of Australian Religious Groups: 1947-2001' *in People and Place Volume 10, no. 4 2002*, pp. 17-23, Monash University, Clayton Victoria.

'Bridge types in NSW: Historical Overview', RTA, (2006), <www.rms.nsw.gov.au/documents/about/environment/bridge-types-historical-overviews-2006.pdf>.

Bugeja, Paul & Ferguson, Ian, (2010), *Crimes of passion that shocked Australia*, Brolga Publishing, Victoria.

Butlin, S.J., (1968), *Foundations of the Australian Monetary System 1788-1851*, Sydney University Press, Sydney.

Cannon, Michael, (1986 ed.), *The Land Boomers*, Lloyd O'Neill, Victoria.

Carey, Hilary M., *An Historical Outline of Religion in Australia*, <www.academia.edu/398970/An_Historical_Outline_of_Religion_in_Australia?auto=download>.

Chavura, Stephen A. & Tregenza, Ian, 'A Political History of the Secular in Australia, 1788-1945' in Stanley, Timothy (ed.), (2015), *Religion after Secularization in Australia*, Palgrave Macmillan, New York, USA.

Chavura, Stephen, (2014), "...but in its proper place..."- Religion, Enlightenment, and Australia's Secular Heritage: The Case of Robert Lowe in Colonial NSW 184201850' in *Journal of Religious History, Volume 38, No. 3*, Sept 2014.

'Chinese Migration Stories', NSW Government, State Archives and Records, <www.records.nsw.gov.au/archives/collections-and-research/guides-and-indexes/stories/chinese-migration-stories>.

Clark, Anna, (2001), 'Progress of the Past? History in New South Wales Secondary Schools' in *Public History Review, Volume 9*, Halstead Press, Leichhardt Sydney.

Clark, CMH, (1977), *A History of Australia Volume I*, Melbourne University Press, Melbourne.

Clark, CMH, (1975), *A History of Australia Volume II*, Melbourne University Press, Melbourne

Clark, CMH, (1973) *A history of Australia Volume III*, Melbourne University Press, Melbourne

Clark, CMH, (1980), *A History of Australia Volume IV*, Melbourne University Press, Melbourne

Clark, CMH, (1981) *A History of Australia Volume V*, Melbourne University Press, Melbourne

Clark, CMH, (1987) *A History of Australia Volume VI*, Melbourne University Press, Melbourne.

Clark, CMH, (1975), *Select Documents in Australian History 1788-1850*, Angus and Robertson, Sydney.

Clarke, Heather, 'The History of Music and Dance in Australia 1788-1840', <www.colonialdance.com.au/piano-of-the-first-fleet-29.html>.

Cleverley, John F., (1971), *The First Generation: School and Society in Early Australia*, Sydney University Press.

CO.AS.IT website, <www.coasit.org.au/CommunityServices.aspx>.

Cobley, John, (1970), *Crimes of the first Fleet Convicts*, Angus and Robertson, Sydney.

'Contribution of NSW Community Organisations', Council of Social Services New South Wales, 2015. <www.ncoss.org.au/sites/default/files/public/policy/EY_Final_Report.pdf.>.

'Contribution of NSW Community Services', (2015), NSW Council of Social Services, <www.ncoss.org.au/sites/default/files/public/policy/EY_Final_Report.pdf accessed 10/07/2019>.

Cornwall, Jennifer, (2001), 'The People's Park: Parramatta Park Oral History Project' in *Locality*, Autumn 2001, pp. 4-8.

Country Women's Association of NSW website, <www.cwaofnsw.org.au/page.php?id=49>.

Crowley, Frank, (1980), *A Documentary History of Australia, Volume 1: Colonial Australia, 1788-1840*, Nelson, Melbourne.

Crowley, Frank, (1980), *A Documentary History of Australia, Volume 2: Colonial Australia, 1841-1874*, Nelson, Melbourne.

Crowley, Frank, (1980), *A Documentary History of Australia, Volume 3: Colonial Australia, 1875-1900*, Nelson, Melbourne.

Crowley, Frank, (1973) *Modern Australia in Documents, Volume 1, 1901-1939*, Wren Publishing, Melbourne.

Crowley, Frank, (1973) *Modern Australia in Documents, Volume 2, 1939-1970*, Wren Publishing, Melbourne.

Crozier-de Rosa, Sharon, (2014), 'Perhaps tea and scones are OK: the CWA and feminism today' in *Conversation, April 15, 2014, <theconversation.com/perhaps-tea-and-scones-are-ok-the-cwa-and-feminism-today-25474>*.

Cummins, CJ, (2003), *A History of Medical Administration in NSW 1788-1973, NSW* Department of Health, *<www.health.nsw.gov.au/about/history/Publications/history-medical-admin.pdf>*.

'Defining Moments: Dunera Boys', National Museum of Australia, <www.nma.gov.au/defining-moments/resources/dunera-boys>.

Dow, Gwyneth M., (1974), *Samuel Terry: The Botany Bay Rothschild*, Sydney University Press, Sydney.

Doyle, Peter, (2009), *Crooks Like Us*, Historic Houses Trust of NSW.

Egan, Joanna, (Nov 7, 2013) 'On this day Sydney gets Electricity' in *Australian Geographic*, <www.australiangeographic.com.au/blogs/on-this-day/2013/11/on-this-day-sydney-gets-electricity/>.

'Eureka! The rush for gold', State Library of NSW, <www.sl.nsw.gov.au/stories/eureka-rush-gold>.

Evans, Richard, (2004), *The Pyjama Girl Mystery: a true story of murder, obsession and lies,* Scribe Publications, Melbourne.

Fahey, Warren, (2010), *Australian Folk Songs and Bush Ballads,* Harper Collins Publishers, Sydney.

Fletcher, Brian, (1976), *Landed Enterprise and Penal Society: A History of Farming and Grazing in New South Wales before 1821,* Sydney University Press, Sydney.

Fletcher, J & Burnswoods, J, (1983), *Government Schools of New South Wales 1848-1983,* Directorate of Planning Services, New South Wales Department of Education.

Fuller, Robert S., *et al,* (2014), 'Star Maps and Travelling to Ceremonies: The Euahlayi People and Their Use of the Night Sky' in *Journal of Astronomical History and Heritage, 17 (2),* pp. 149-160.

Fuller, Robert, Interview 13 May 2019.

Fuller, Robert S., (2004), 'The Astronomy of the Kamilaroi and Euahlayi Peoples and their Neighbours', MPhil thesis, Macquarie University, <www.aboriginalastronomy.com.au/wp-content/uploads/2018/05/Fuller-Thesis.pdf>.

Gammage, Bill, (2011), *The Biggest Estate on Earth: How Aborigines Made Australia,* Allen & Unwin, Sydney.

Gapps, Stephen, (2010), *Front Pages that Shaped Australia,* Pier 9 (Murdoch Books), Millers Point, NSW.

'German Migration Stories', NSW Government, State Archives and Records, <www.records.nsw.gov.au/archives/collections-and-research/guides-and-indexes/stories/german-migration-stories>.

Hamacher, Duane, Fuller, Robert & Norris, Ray, (2012), 'Orientations of Linear Stone Arrangements in New South Wales' in *Australian Archaeology,* Number 75, December 2012.

'History of Hyde Park', City of Sydney, (2016), <www.cityofsydney.nsw.gov.au/learn/sydneys-history/people-and-places/park-histories/hyde-park >.

'History of Innovation in Australia', Australian Government, <www.ipaustralia.gov.au/understanding-ip/getting-started-ip/educational-materials-and-resources/history-australian-innovation>.

'History of Manufacturing in Australia', Australian Made, <www.australianmade.com.au/media/1142330/ausmade-facts-history.pdf>.

'History of NSW Courts and Tribunals', NSW Government, Justice, <www.courts.justice.nsw.gov.au/Pages/cats/history/history.aspx>.

'History of NSW Government Schools', NSW Government, Department of Education, <education.nsw.gov.au/about-us/our-people-and-structure/history-of-government-schools/home>.

'History of Transport in NSW', NSW Government, <www.transport.nsw.gov.au/projects/community-engagement/sydney-trains-community/culture-and-heritage/history-of-nsw-railways>.

'History', UNSW, <www.unsw.edu.au/about-us/university/history>.

Hirst, John, (2014), *Australian History in 7 Questions*, Black Inc., Victoria.

Hooker, Claire, (2001), 'Diphtheria: Community and Disease in Australia', *Locality Summer 2001*, pp. 7-9.

Hosking, Bill & Linton, John Suter, (2017), *Justice Denied*, Harlequin Mira, Sydney Australia.

Hoskins, Ian, (2003), '"What's in Store?": Acquiring and interpreting the contents of the Wong family store' in *Locality Autumn 2003*, pp. 12-17.

Hunt, David, (2013), *Girt: the unauthorised history of Australia*, Black Inc, Carlton, Victoria.

'Hyde Park Barracks: What work did convicts do', (2017), Sydney Living Museums, <sydneylivingmuseums.com.au/convict-sydney/what-work-did-convicts-do>.

Irish, Paul, (2017), *Hidden in Plain View: the Aboriginal People of Coastal Sydney*, UNSW Press, Sydney.

'J.C. Williamson', National Library of Australia, <www.nla.gov.au/prompt/jc-williamson-theatres>.

Karskens, Grace, (2009), *The Colony: A History of Early Sydney*, Allen & Unwin, Sydney.

'Kelpie', ABC News 'Landline' 18 April 2016, <www.abc.net.au/news/2016-04-09/kelpie-the-mysterious-origins-of-the-australian-working-dog/7309992>.

Lake, Meredith, (2011), 'Provincialising God: Anglicanism, Place and the Colonisation of Australian Land' in *Journal of Religious History, Volu2011*. Volume 35, no. V1, orh_972 72.

Langton, Marcia, (2018), *Welcome to Country: A Travel Guide to Indigenous Australia,* Hardie Grant Publishing, Australia.

Levi, J.S. & Bergman, G.F.J., (1974), *Australian Genesis: Jewish Convicts and Settlers 1788-1850,* Rigby, Australia.

Lindsay, Patrick, (2012), *True Blue,* Harper Collins, Sydney.

'Living on Aboriginal reserves and stations', NSW Government Office of Environment and Heritage, <www.environment.nsw.gov.au/chresearch/ ReserveStation.htm>.

Maps, Guides and More, <www.mapsguidesandmore.com/Australia-New_ South_Wales>

McGillick, Paul & Bingham-Hall, Patrick, (2005), *Sydney Architecture*, Pesaro Publishing, Sydney.

McKenna, Mark, Research Paper 31, 1995-1996, 'The Traditions of Australian Republicanism', Parliament of Australia, <www.aph.gov.au/ About_Parliament/Parliamentary_Departments/Parliamentary_Library/ pubs/rp/RP9596/96rp31>.

McMartin, Arthur, (1983), *Public Servants and Patronage: the Foundation and Rise of the New South Wales Public Service, 1786-1859,* Sydney University Press, Sydney.

Martin, Ged [ed.], (1978), *The founding of Australia: the Argument about Australia's Origins,* Hale & Iremonger, Sydney.

Melbourne, A.C.V., (1963), *Early Constitutional Development in Australia,* Queensland University Press, Queensland.

'Mission and History of the PCYC', Police Citizens Youth Club NSW, <www.pcycnsw.org.au/mission-history/>.

'North Head Quarantine Station, Sydney', National Archives of Australia, (2019), <www.naa.gov.au>.

Norris, Ray, (2008), 'Emu Dreaming' in *Australian Science, 29/4,* May 2008.

Norris, Ray, (2016), 'Dawes Review 5: Australian Astronomy and Navigation' in *Astronomical Society of Australia Vol. 33.*

Norris, Ray *et al,* (2012), 'Wurdi Youang: an Australian Aboriginal stone arrangement with possible solar indications', Submitted to Rock Art Research 18 August 2011; this version 28 Sep 2012, <www.atnf.csiro.au/ people/Ray.Norris/papers/n258.pdf>.

'NSW Police Force, 1788-1888', NSW Government, <www.police.nsw.gov. au/about_us/history/history_pages/significant_dates>.

'NSW Road History', < www.ozroads.com.au/NSW/history.htm>.

'NSW Rural Fire Service history', NSW Government, <www.rfs.nsw.gov.au/about-us/history>.

O'Farrell, Patrick, (1977), *The Catholic Church and Community in Australia: A History*, Nelson, West Melbourne.

'Origin of the Kelpie', Working Kelpie Council of Australia, <www.wkc.org.au/About-Kelpies/Origin-of-the-Kelpie.php>.

'Our History', Benevolent Society of NSW, <www.benevolent.org.au/about-us/our-history>.

'Our History', Sydney Quarantine Station, <www.qstation.com.au>.

Pascoe, Bruce, (2019), *Dark Emu*, Magabala Books, Broome, Western Australia.

Perrott, Monica, (1983), *A Tolerable Good Success: Economic opportunities for women in New South Wales 1788-1830*, Hale & Iremonger, Sydney.

Petersen, Julie, (2001), 'Nielsen Park: The bush beach', *Locality, Autumn 2001*, pp. 13-16.

Pierce, Peter [ed.], (2009), *The Cambridge History of Australian Literature*, Cambridge University Press.

Pike, Douglas [ed.], (1983), *Australian Dictionary of Biography*, Melbourne University Press, Carlton, Victoria.

'Police Programs', Police Citizens Youth Club NSW, <www.pcycnsw.org.au/programs/police-programs/>.

'Queen Victoria Sanitorium', NSW Government Office of Environment and Heritage, <www.environment.nsw.gov.au/heritageapp/ViewHeritageItemDetails.aspx?ID=1170824>.

Robinson, Portia, (1988), *The Women of Botany Bay*, Macquarie University Library, Sydney.

Robson, L.L., (1976), *The Convict Settlers of Australia*, Melbourne University Press, Melbourne.

Rose, Deborah Bird, (1996), *Nourishing terrains: Australian Aboriginal views of landscape and wilderness*, Australian Heritage Commission, Canberra.

Salt, Annette, (2006), *The Fishermen of Iron Cove: In un mare diverso*, Leichhardt Council, Leichhardt.

Salt, Annette, (1984), *These Outcast Women: The Parramatta Female Factory 1821-1848*, Hale & Iremonger, Sydney.

Shaw, A.G.L., (1977), *Convicts & the Colonies*, Melbourne University Press, Melbourne.

Shaw, A.G.L., (1972), *The Story of Australia*, 5th edition, Faber & Faber, London.

Sherington, Geoffrey & Campbell, Craig, 'Education' in *Sydney Journal, 2 (1) June 2009,* <epress.lib.uts.edu.au/ojs/index.php/sydney_journal/index>.

Skinner, L.E., (1975), *Police of the Pastoral Frontier: Native Police 1849-59,* University of Queensland Press, St Lucia, Queensland.

Soil Quality, < http://www.soilquality.org.au/au/nsw>.

'Songs of Home: Exploring the Past through Music', Sydney Living Museums, <sydneylivingmuseums.com.au/exhibitions/songs-home>.

Spearritt, Peter, (2018), *Where History Happened: the Hidden Past of Australia's Towns and Places,* National Library of Australia, Canberra.

'Take a journey in time - water supply 1778 to now', Water NSW, <www.waternsw.com.au/supply/heritage/timeline>.

Taksa, Lucy, (1999), '"Between Medicine and Management": Considering Representations and Memories of Industrial Nursing' in *School of Industrial Relations and Organisational Behaviour,* UNSW, Working Paper Series 128, October 1999, <wwwdocs.fce.unsw.edu.au/orgmanagement/WorkingPapers/WP128.pdf>.

Tavan, Gwenda, (2005), *The Long Slow Death of White Australia,* Scribe Publications, Melbourne.

Tedeschi, Mark, (2015), *Kidnapped: the crime that shocked the nation,* Simon and Schuster (Australia).

Tench, Watkin, (1979 edition), *Sydney's First Four Years*, Library of Australian History, Sydney.

Tidswell, Dr Frank, (1906), *Researches on Australian Venoms*, University of Sydney, <usyd.libcal.com/event/3433119>.

'Tilly Devine and the Razor Gang Wars 1927-1931', NSW Government, State Archives & Records, <www.records.nsw.gov.au/archives/magazine/galleries/tilly-devine-and-the-razor-gang-wars>.

Tyler, Peter J., (2001), 'Our First Microbiologist' in *Locality, Summer 2001,* pp. 10-12.

Tyler, Peter J., (2011), *State Records NSW 1788-2011,* Desert Pea Press, Leichhardt, Sydney.

Tyquin, Michael, (2001), 'The NSW Railways Ambulance Corps' Heydey 1881-1960' in *Locality, Summer 2001,* pp. 4-7.

'Walk for Reconciliation', National Museum of Australia, <www.nma.gov.au/defining-moments/resources/walk-for-reconciliation>.

Walker, R.B., (1976), *The Newspaper Press in New South Wales, 1803-1920,* Sydney University Press, Sydney.

Walker, R.B., (1980), *Yesterday's News,* Sydney University Press, Sydney.

Wells, Andrew, (1989), *Constructing Capitalism; an Economic History of Eastern Australia 1788-1901,* Allen & Unwin, Sydney.

Wentworth, William Charles, (facsimile 1979 edition, first published 1819), *Statistical, Historical and Political Description of the Colony of New South Wales and its dependent Settlements in Van Diemen's Land,* Griffin Press, Adelaide.

Wilkinson, John, (2007) 'Manufacturing and Services in New South Wales', <www.parliament.nsw.gov.au/researchpapers/Documents/manufacturing-and-services-in-nsw/ManuFINALandINDEX.pdf>.

Willis, Ian,(2017), 'Sydney's Royal Botanic Gardens: an historical source' in *PHA NSW' 29 January 2017,* <www.phansw.org.au/sydneys-royal-botanic-gardens-an-historical-source/>.

'Women in Parliament', Parliament of NSW, <www.parliament.nsw.gov.au/about/Pages/Women-in-Parliament.aspx>.

Woollacott, Angela, (2015), *Settler Society in the Australian Colonies,* OUP, Oxford.

Wotherspoon, Gary (2010), 'The Domain', Dictionary of Sydney, <dictionaryofsydney.org/entry/the_domain>.

Willis, Ian, (2017), 'Sydney's Royal Botanic Gardens' in *Camden History Notes 26 January 2017, <camdenhistorynotes.wordpress.com/2017/01/26/sydneys-royal-botanic-gardens/>.*

Chapter Reference Notes

(full details are found in the Bibliography)

INDIGENOUS HISTORY

Attenbrow, Val, (2010), *Sydney's Aboriginal Past: Investigating the archaeological and historical records,* pp. xiii, 57-60, 83ff, 8-91, 107, 140, 148-149.

Australian Heritage Commission, *Dreaming Ecology*, p. 1.

Behrendt, Larisssa, (2012), *Indigenous Australia for Dummies,* pp. 8, 10, 11, 18-19, 28, 35-36, 39, 41, 52ff, 58, 60-61, 63-65, 94, 99-100, 109-110, 117, 120-121, 123-124, 127, 132, 172, 180, 194-5, 256-254,379, 399, 401-402.

Clark, CMH, *History of Australia, Volume I*, p. 277, 280.

Clark, CMH, *History of Australia, Volume V*, p. 218.

Cleverley, John F., (1971), *The First Generation: School and Society in Early Australia,* p. 116.

Fuller, Robert S., *et al,* (2014), *Star Maps and Travelling to Ceremonies: The Euahlayi People and Their Use of the Night Sky*, p. 152-158.

Fuller, Robert S., *The Astronomy of the Kamilaroi*, MPhil thesis, pp. 50-51.

Gammage, Bill, (2011), *The Biggest Estate on Earth: How Aborigines Made Australia,* p. 3, 15, 52ff, 123-124, 127, 129-132, 136, 151, 153, 157-158, 161, 175, 282.

Gapps, Stephen, (2010), *Front Pages that Shaped Australia,* p. 90.

Gory, Sarah, (2018), 'William Cooper, Kristallnacht, and a Radical Act of Empathy' in *Meanjin Quarterly*, 21 November.

Hamacher, Fuller & Norris, 'Orientations' in *Australian Archaeology,* pp. 52-53.

Interview with Bob Fuller, 13 May 2019.

Irish, Paul, (2017), *Hidden in Plain View: the Aboriginal People of Coastal Sydney*, pp. 12-15, 20-21, 23, 52-56, 58-60.

Karskens, Grace, (2009), *The Colony: A History of Early Sydney*, pp. 47-60, 350, 474-481, 533-537.

Langton, Marcia, (2018), *Welcome to Country: A Travel Guide to Indigenous Australia*, p. 3.

NMA, 'Walk for Reconciliation'.

Norris, Ray, (2008), *Emu Dreaming*, pp. 16-17.

Norris, Ray, quoting Fuller, 'Dawes Review' in *Astronomical Society of Australia*, p. 14.

Norris, Ray, 'Dawes Review' in *Astronomical Society of Australia*, p. 10.

Norris, Ray, *Wurdi Youang*, pp. 4, 10.

NSW Government office of Environment and Heritage, *Living on Aboriginal reserves and stations*.

Pascoe, Bruce, *Dark Emu*, pp. 14-21, 29-31, 36-37, 51-52, 70, 108-112, 137-140, 147, 149, 163, 164, 178, 186-187, 198, 205-206.

Rose, Deborah Bird, (1996*), Nourishing terrains: Australian Aboriginal views of landscape and wilderness*, p. 7, 8, 10, 23, 32, 36, 39, 72, 163ff.

Skinner, L.E., (1975), *Police of the Pastoral Frontier: Native Police 1849-59*, p. 2.

Spearritt, Peter, (2018), *Where History Happened: the Hidden Past of Australia's Towns and Places*, pp. 61-65.

State Heritage Commission, 'Brewarrina Fish Traps', <www.environment. nsw.gov.au/heritageapp/ViewHeritageItemDetails.aspx?ID=505 1305>.

Tench, Watkin, (1979 edition), *Sydney's First Four Years*, pp. 47-51.

Wells, Andrew, (1989), *Constructing Capitalism: an Economic History of Eastern Australia 1788-1901*, pp. 16-17.

Wentworth, William Charles, *Statistical, Historical etc*, p. 4.

Woollacott, Angela, (2015), *Settler Society in the Australian Colonies*, pp. 49, 75.

THE ARRIVAL OF BRITISH CONVICTS

Australian Dictionary of Biography 1788-1850, Volume 2, p. 31

Bateson, Charles, (1974), *The Convict Ships*, pp. 4-7, 9, 73, 89, 100, 229.

Blainey, Geoffrey, (1966; 2001 edition), *The Tyranny of Distance: How Distance Shaped Australia's History*, pp. 152-153.

Clark CMH, *History of Australia, Volume I*, p. 249.

Clark, CMH, *History of Australia, Volume II*, p. 322.

Crowley, Frank, *Colonial Australia, Volume 1, 1788-1840,* pp. 294-6

Dow, Gwyneth M., (1974), *Samuel Terry: The Botany Bay Rothschild,* pp. 101,105, 115.

Hirst, John, (2014), *Australian History in 7 Questions,* p. 30, 33, 42-43.

Martin, Ged [ed], (1978), *The Founding of Australia: The Argument about Australia's Origins,* (Hale & Iremonger), for a full discussion of the issues; Shaw, *Story of Australia,* pp. 36-37

Perrott, Monica, (1983), *A Tolerable Good Success: Economic opportunities for women in New South Wales 1788-1830,* pp. 14, 18-19, 35-38, 51-59.

Robinson, *Women of Botany Bay,* p. 14.

Robson, L.L., (1976), *The Convict Settlers of Australia,* pp. 4, 26, 14ff, 29ff, 40-43, 143, 164, 187-190.

Salt, Annette, (1984), *These Outcast Women: The Parramatta Female Factory 1821-1848,* p. 35-36, 44, 86-87.

Shaw, A.G.L., (1972), *The Story of Australia, 5ᵗʰ edition,* pp. 34-41, 46, 148-149, 151, 161, 164, 217.

Sydney Living Museums, 'Hyde Park Barracks: What work did convicts do', <sydneylivingmuseums.com.au/convict-sydney/what-work-did-convicts-do>.

FURTHER NON-INDIGENOUS COLONISATION AND SETTLEMENT

Ashton, Paul, *et al, Places of the Heart,* pp. 13-20.

Australian Dictionary of Biography, Volume 1, (1966).

Australian Dictionary of Biography, Volume 2, (1967).

Australian Dictionary of Biography, Volume 5, pp. 234-235.

Bateson, Charles, (1974), *The Convict Ships,* p. 93.

Clark, CMH, *History of Australia Volume I,* p. 124.

De Vries, Susanna, *Trailblazers,* pp. 4-5, 240-294.

'Eureka Gold Rush, 'State Library of NSW, <www.sl.nsw.gov.au/stories/eureka-rush-gold>.

Fletcher, Brian, (1976), *Landed Enterprise and Penal Society: A History of Farming and Grazing in New South Wales before 1821,* pp. 160, 181.

Gapps, Stephen, (2010), *Front Pages that Shaped Australia,* p. 55.

Hirst, John, (2014), *Australian History in 7 Questions,* pp. 81-83, 143.

Karskens, Grace, (2009), *The Colony: A History of Early Sydney,* pp. 227, 332.

Lake, *Provincialising God*, p. 73.

Levi, J.S. and Bergman, G.F.J, (1974), *Australian Genesis: Jewish Convicts and Settlers 1788-1850*, pp. 196-197.

National Museum of Australia, 'Defining Moments: Dunera Boys', <www.nma.gov.au/defining-moments/resources/dunera-boys>.

NSW Government Migration Heritage Centre website.

NSW Government, State Archives and Records, 'Chinese Migration stories'.

NSW Government, State Archives and Records, 'German Migration Stories'.

O'Farrell, Patrick, (1977), *The Catholic Church and Community in Australia: A History*, pp. 84-86.

Shaw, A.G.L., (1972), *The Story of Australia, 5ᵗʰ edition*, pp. 86. 94-95, 132-133.

Spearritt, Peter, (2018), *Where History Happened: the Hidden Past of Australia's Towns and Places*, p. 42.

'Squattocracy', State Library of NSW, <www.sl.nsw.gov.au/stories/australian-agricultural-and-rural-life/squattocracy>.

Tyquin, Michael, (2001), *The NSW Railways Ambulance Corps' Heydey, 1881-1960*, pp. 12-16.

Walsh, G., (1993), *Pioneering days: People and innovations in Australia's rural past*, p. 126.

Woollacott, Angela, (2015), *Settler Society in the Australian Colonies*, pp. 16, 22.

CITIES AND TOWNS

'About Margaret', Tweed Regional Gallery, <artgallery.tweed.nsw.gov.au/MargaretOlleyArtCentre/AboutMargaret>.

'Alex Buzo' in 'A Play for Every Stage', <australianplays.org/playwright/ASC-4163>.

Ashton, Paul and Freestone, Robert, (2008), 'Town Planning' in *Sydney Journal*, 1(2) 2008, pp. 11-12, 14, <epress.lib.uts.edu.au/ojs/index.php/sydney_journal/index>.

'Aussie Towns', www.aussietowns.com.au.

Australian Bureau of Statistics, <itt.abs.gov.au/itt/r.jsp?RegionSummary&region=114021284&dataset=ABS_REGIONAL_ASGS2016&geoconcept=ASGS_2016&measure=MEASURE&datasetASGS=ABS_REGIONAL_ASGS2016&datasetLGA=ABS_REGIONAL_LGA2018&regionLGA=LGA_2018&regionASGS=ASGS_2016>.

Australian Dictionary of Biography, Volume 6, (1976).

Australian Dictionary of Biography, Volume 8, (1981).

Australian Dictionary of Biography, Volume 14, (1996).

Australian Dictionary of Biography, Volume 16, (2002).

Barker, Geoff, (2013), 'Ben Hall, Australian Bushranger' at the Museum of Applied Arts and Sciences, < maas.museum/inside-the-collection/2013/02/20/ben-hall-australian-bushranger/>.

'Barnes: Here's proof I'm not the father', *Sydney Morning Herald*, 23 February 2003.

'Beach boy Simon Baker's biggest role yet', *Good Weekend, SMH*, 2 July 2015.

'Blue Mountains and Jenolan Caves Illustrated Tourist Guide: Health in Height', <www.infobluemountains.net.au/history/health.htm>.

'Blue Mountains, Australia', <www.bluemts.com.au/info/towns/katoomba>.

Blue Mountains Tours, 'Aboriginal History of the Blue Mountains', <bluemountainstoursydney.com.au/blog/aboriginal-history-in-the-blue-mountains/>.

'Bonegilla Migrant Experience', <bonegilla.org.au/about-us/about-bonegilla-migrant-experience.asp>.

'A Brief History' in 'Southern Cross University, <www.scu.edu.au/about/history/from-teachers-college-to-university/>.

Broome, Hamish, 'Famous People who call the Northern Rivers home' in *Northern Star*, 11 May 2016, <www.northernstar.com.au/news/famous-people-who-call-the-northern-rivers-home/3023440/>.

Bursill, L., Donaldson, M. & Jacobs, M., (2015), *A history of Aboriginal Illawarra Volume 1: Before Colonisation*, pp. 3-4.

Charles Sturt University, <about.csu.edu.au/our-university/history/timeline>.

City of Sydney, 'Archives and History', <www.cityofsydney.nsw.gov.au/learn/archives-history/sydneys-history>.

Clark, CMH, (1977), *A History of Australia, Volume I*, pp. 173, 236, 235, 277-278.

Clark, CMH, (1973) *A History of Australia, Volume III*, p. 255.

Clark, CMH, (1978), *A History of Australia, Volume IV*, pp. 378, 395.

Clark, CMH, *A History of Australia, Volume V*, pp. 64, 414-416.

'Community Profile', Wollongong City Council, <profile.id.com.au/wollongong/birthplace>.

Craig, Mitchell, 'Kerry Saxby-Junna walks into Hall of Fame', *Northern Star*, 10 April 2013, p. 1.

Crowley, Frank, (1980), *Colonial Australia, Volume 1*, p. 322.

Crowley, Frank, (1973), *Modern Australia, Volume 2*, pp. 423-444.

Crowley, Frank, (1980), *Colonial Australia, Volume 3*, pp. 120, 262-3.

'Discovery and Founding of Newcastle', City of Newcastle, <www.newcastle.nsw.gov.au/Explore/History-Heritage/Our-history-our-stories/Discovery-and-founding-of-Newcastle>.

'Early History of the Barkindji', <www.platform09.com/bbs_site5/pdf/early_history_barkindji.pdf>.

'Early History of the Murrumbidgee, Wagga Wagga' in 'Remembering the Past – Australia', <remembering-the-past-australia.blogspot.com/2017/05/early-history-murrumbidgee-wagga.html>.

'Engineering Masterpiece of the 19th Century: A short History', <www.zigzagrailway.com.au>.

Ellis, Greg, (2019), 'New Governor General a proud Wollongong boy', *Illawarra Mercury*, 3 July 2019, <www.illawarramercury.com.au/story/6249918/new-governor-general-a-proud-wollongong-boy/>.

Ellis, Greg, (2019) 'How Growing up in Wollongong....', *Illawarra Mercury*, 1 Sept 2019, <www.illawarramercury.com.au/story/6359848/national-treasure-anthony-warlow-reminisces-about-growing-up-in-wollongong/>.

'Famous People born in Newcastle', <www.thefamouspeople.com/newcastle-1635.php>.

Ferry, John, (1999), *Colonial Armidale*.

'Flooding in Maitland', Maitland City Council, <www.maitland.nsw.gov.au/play-explore/history-and-heritage/flooding-in-maitland>.

'Fossils in Lightning Ridge, NSW', Australian Museum, <australianmuseum.net.au/learn/australia-over-time/fossils/sites/lightning-ridge/>.

'Glenn Donald McGrath' in *Encyclopaedia Britannica*, <www.britannica.com/biography/Glenn-Donald-McGrath>.

'The Hills Look Down to the Sea'in Part 3 of *A Thematic History of Ballina Shire*, pp. 74-75, 78-79, 80-81, 83, 84, 87-77,118, 130-131, 147, 151, 154-155, 192, <www.ballina.nsw.gov.au/cp_themes/default/page.asp?p=DOC-ZAA-26-48-72>.

'History', Broken Hill City Council, <www.brokenhill.nsw.gov.au/Community/About-the-city/History>.

'History and Heritage', Wollongong City Council, <www.wollongong.nsw. gov.au/about/history-heritage>.

'A History of Lismore', Lismore city Council, <www.lismore.nsw.gov.au/ cp_themes/default/page.asp?p=DOC-GBX-81-65-46>.

'History in Detail' in 'About the Blue Mountains' <www.bluemts.com.au/ info/about/history/history-detail/>.

'History' in 'Welcome to Albury-Wodonga', <www.albury-wodonga.com/ docs/history.htm>.

'History and Culture, Lightning Ridge, Kamilaroi Highway', <kamilaroihighway.com/information/lightning-ridge-history-culture/>.

'History, City of Wagga Wagga', <wagga.nsw.gov.au/city-of-wagga-wagga/ wagga-wagga/history-2>.

'History', University of Wollongong, <www.uow.edu.au/about/history/>.

'Home' in 'Cadel Evans', <www.cadelevans.com.au>

'House History' in 'Our Story', <www.sydneyoperahouse.com/our-story/ sydney-opera-house-history/tubowgule.html>.

'Indigenous Heritage', <www.coffscoast.com.au/play/category/ indigenous-heritage/>.

International Movie Database, <www.imdb.com>.

'Japanese midget submarine attack on Sydney Harbour' in Royal Australian Navy, <www.navy.gov.au/history/feature-histories/japanese-midget-submarine-attack-sydney-harbour>.

'Judith Wright' in 'Judith Wright Estate', <www.judithwrightestate.com>.

Jupp, James, (2008), 'Immigration' in *Sydney Journal*, 1(2), June 2008, pp. 44-51. <epress.lib.uts.edu.au/ojs/index.php/sydney_journal/index>.

Karskens, Grace, (2009), *The Colony*, pp. 119, 307.

Lambert, Tim, 'A Brief History of Sydney, Australia', <www.localhistories. org/sydney.html>.

'The Last of the Gardiner Gang', *Dubbo Despatch*, 16 March 1937 <trove.nla.gov.au/newspaper/article/228640049>.

'Lex Marinos' in 'A Living Collection', State Library of NSW, <www2. sl.nsw.gov.au/archive/events/exhibitions/2010/onehundred/100-objects/ALC_Lex-Marinos.htm>.

'Lightning Ridge', Australian Government, <www.indigenous.gov.au/ community/lightning-ridge>.

'Lightning Ridge', Lightning Ridge Historical Society, <www.wj.com.au/ lrhistory/>.

'Lightning Ridge', Walgett Shire council, < www.walgett.nsw.gov.au/about-walgett/our-history/lightning-ridge/>.

'Lismore History' in 'Richmond River Historical Society', <www.richhistory.org.au/lismore-history/lismore-chronology/timeline/>.

'Local History', Maitland City Council, <www.maitland.nsw.gov.au/play-explore/history-and-heritage/local-history>.

'Local History', Newcastle Library, <www.newcastle.nsw.gov.au/Library/Heritage-History>.

Macken, Lucy, 'How the Southern Highlands is giving Palm Beach a run for its money' in 'Domain', *Sydney Morning Herald*, 22 September 2016.

'Maitland NSW' in 'Living Histories @ UON', University of Newcastle, <livinghistories.newcastle.edu.au/nodes/view/59742>.

'Margaret Court' in 'Who2 biographies', <www.who2.com/bio/margaret-smith-court>.

'Mark Taylor', Museum of the Riverina1, <museumriverina.com.au/exhibitions/sporting-hall-of-fame/taylor,-mark>.

McGhee, Karen, (2014), 'Broken Hill: a thriving outback town' in *Australian Geographic*, 21 July 2014.

Moorhouse, Geoffrey, (1999), *Sydney*, pp. 4-5, 24-28, 63, 101-105.

'Noeline Brown' in 'The Australian Women's Register', <www.womenaustralia.info/biogs/AWE1272b.htm>.

'Old Bells Line of Road', Office of the Environment, <www.environment.nsw.gov.au/heritageapp/ViewHeritageItemDetails.aspx?ID=1170630>.

'Opal Fields at Lightning Ridge', NSW Government, <www.resourcesandgeoscience.nsw.gov.au/miners-and-explorers/applications-and-approvals/opal-mining/about/opal-fields>.

'Our first Peoples' in 'History of Lismore', Lismore City Council, <www.lismore.nsw.gov.au/cp_themes/default/page.asp?p=DOC-GBX-81-65-46>.

'Past and Present: Bowral' in 'Bowral History', <www.highlandsnsw.com.au/past_present/bowral_history.html>.

'Paul Hogan', Famous People, <www.thefamouspeople.com/profiles/paul-hogan-2527.php>.

'Prison Officer Reflects on Life inside Maitland Gaol', *ABC News*, <www.abc.net.au/news/2018-01-29/prison-officer-reflects-on-life-inside-maitland-gaol-20-years-on/9370868>.

'Ruth Cracknell' in 'The Australian Live Performance Database', <www.ausstage.edu.au/pages/contributor/1514>.

Shaw, AGL, (1983), *Story of Australia*, pp. 558, 100-101.

'A Short History of Orange', New South Wales Government, <www.orange.nsw.gov.au/wp-content/uploads/2018/08/Short-History-of-Orange.pdf>.

'The Shire's European History', Ballina Shire Council, <www.ballina.nsw.gov.au/cp_themes/default/page.asp?p=DOC-ZAA-26-48-72>.

Spennemann, Dirk HR, (2015), *Nineteenth Century Indigenous Land use of Albury (NSW)*, pp. 4-7, <www.csu.edu.au/research/ilws/publications/ilws-eports/2015/ILWS_Report_83.pdf>.

Swinton, Sage, (2018), 'Maitland history over the past 200 years and earlier' in *Maitland Mercury*, September 14, <www.maitlandmercury.com.au/story/5643468/a-brief-history-of-maitland-in-200-years/>.

Taronga Conservation Society, 'Australia', <taronga.org.au/about/history-and-culture/sydney>.

'UNE Origins' in 'UNE, University of New England', <www.une.edu.au>.

'Wagga Wagga, New South Wales, Australia', Encyclopaedia Britannica, <www.britannica.com/place/Wagga-Wagga>.

'The Wreck of the Sydney Cove', Australian Maritime Museums, <maritimemuseumsaustralia.com/profiles/blogs/the-wreck-of-the-sydney-cove>.

'Wollongong, New South Wales, Australia', *Encyclopaedia Britannica*, <www.britannica.com/place/Wollongong>.

AGRICULTURAL AND PASTORAL INDUSTRY

'A Hundred Years', *Australian Bureau of Statistics*,

'Agricultural Produce', State Library of NSW, <www.sl.nsw.gov.au/stories/australian-agricultural-and-rural-life/agricultural-produce>.

'Australian Agricultural Company', State Library of NSW, <www.sl.nsw.gov.au/stories/australian-agricultural-and-rural-life/australian-agricultural-company>.

'Agricultural sector', <https://www.agriculture.gov.au/abares/research-topics/aboutmyregion/nsw#agricultural-sector>.

Australian Dictionary of Biography, *Volume 1*, p. 93, 115-116, 186.

Australian Dictionary of Biography, *Volume 2*, pp. 404-405.

Australian Dictionary of Biography, *Volume 6*, (1976).

Australian Dictionary of Biography, Volume 9, (1983).

'Australian Wool', State Library of NSW, <www.sl.nsw.gov.au/stories/australian-agricultural-and-rural-life/australian-wool>.

'Communities', <www.environment.gov.au/system/files/resources/7ba1c152-7eba-4dc0-a635-2a2c17bcd794/files/rabbit.pdf>

Blainey, Geoffrey, (1966; 2001 edition), *The Tyranny of Distance: How Distance Shaped Australia's History,* pp. 43-44, 155-156, 199, 276-279.

Clark, CMH, *History of Australia, Volume I*, pp. 113, 118, 204, 331.

Clark, CMH, *History of Australia, Volume II*, pp. 63-65.

Clark, CMH, *History of Australia, Volume VI*, pp. 179-180, 226.

Clark, CMH, *History of Australia, Volume IV*, pp. 140-143, 166-173.

Clark, Noreen R, (2003), *A Dog Called Blue: The Australian Cattle Dog and the Australian Stumpy Tail Cattle Dog, 1840–2000.*

Crowley, Frank, *Colonial Australia Volume 1*, pp. 291, 316, 553-554.

Crowley, Frank, *Modern Australia. Volume 1*, p. 575.

CWA NSW, <cwaofnsw.org.au>.

'Feral European Rabbit', Australian Government, Department of Sustainability, Environment, Water and Population.

'First Farms', <www.sl.nsw.gov.au/stories/australian-agricultural-and-rural-life/first-farms>.

Fletcher, Brian, (1976), *Landed Enterprise and Penal Society: A History of Farming and Grazing in New South Wales before 1821*, pp. 26-27, 29-36.

'Fruit Industry', State Library of NSW, <www.sl.nsw.gov.au/stories/australian-agricultural-and-rural-life/fruit-industry>.

Hirst, John, (2014), *Australian History in 7 Questions*, p. 62, 77.

'History of Australian Innovation', Australian Government.

Karskens, Grace, *The Colony*, (2009), pp. 64, 84, 101, 130-131, 140-141.

'Kelpie', *ABC News*, 18 April 2016, <www.abc.net.au/news/2016-04-09/kelpie-the-mysterious-origins-of-the-australian-working-dog/7309992>.

'Looking after the Land', State Library of NSW, <www.sl.nsw.gov.au/stories/australian-agricultural-and-rural-life/looking-after-land>.

'Macarthurs' State Library of NSW, <www.sl.nsw.gov.au/stories/australian-agricultural-and-rural-life/macarthurs>.

'Natural Disasters', State Library of NSW, <www.sl.nsw.gov.au/stories/australian-agricultural-and-rural-life/natural-disasters>.

'Origin of the Kelpie', Working Kelpie Council of Australia <www.wkc. org.au/About-Kelpies/Origin-of-the-Kelpie.php>.

Robertson, Bill, (2016), *Origins of the Australian Kelpie: Exposing the Myths and Fabrications from the past.*

'Royal Easter Show', State Library of NSW, < www.sl.nsw.gov.au/stories/ sydney-royal-easter-show>.

Shaw, A.G.L., (1972), *The Story of Australia, 5ᵗʰ edition,* pp. 38-40, 46-49, 51-51, 95, 207.

Soil Quality, < http://www.soilquality.org.au/au/nsw>.

Sydney Gazette, 6 August 1809, quoted in Crowley, *Colonial Australia Volume 1,* p. 168.

Tench, Watkin, (1979 edition), *Sydney's First Four Years,* p. 192.

Walsh, G., (1993) *Pioneering days: People and innovations in Australia's rural past,* pp. 1-8, 11-14, 68, 80-81, 123, 133-148, 150-152, 171, 207, 212, 226-227.

Wells, Andrew, (1989), *Constructing Capitalism; an Economic History of Eastern Australia 1788-1901,* pp. 1-2, 17-19, 23, 34-35, 37-39.

POLITICS

'27 August 1902 – Women's Franchise Act (voting)', NSW Government, State Archives & Records,

Aitkin, Don, and Jinks, Brian, (1981), *Australian Political Institutions,* p. 4, 21, 123-125.

Australian Dictionary of Biography, Volume 9. See Chapter on Finance.

Clark, CMH, 'The Australian Colonies' Government Act 1850'in *Select Documents in Australian History 1788-1850,* p. 379.

Clark, CMH, *History of Australia, Volume I,* pp. 218–219.

Clark, CMH, *History of Australia, Volume V,* pp. 53-54, 59-62, 115-116, 122-123, 152, 328-29.

Clark, CMH, *History of Australia, Volume VI,* p. 387.

Crowley, Frank, *Modern Australia, Volume 1,* pp. 13-18, 406.

Drabsch, *Women in Politics,* pp. 6, 8, 9, 12, 14.

Fletcher, Brian, (1976), *Landed Enterprise and Penal Society: A History of Farming and Grazing in New South Wales before 1821,* p. 142.

Gapps, Stephen, (2010), *Front Pages that Shaped Australia,* pp. 173, 182-184.

Governors of NSW, <www.governor.nsw.gov.au/governor/role-of-the-governor>

Hirst, John, (2014), *Australian History in 7 Questions*, pp. 49-51, 89-91, 106-107, 112-121, 131-132, 149, 172-173, 191-192, 406.

Luck, Peter, (2016), *Australian Icons*, p. 57.

McKenna, Mark, 'The Traditions of Australian Republicanism' in Research Paper 31, 1995-1996, Parliament of Australia

Melbourne, *Early Constitutional Development*, pp. 202-209, 427-432.

'Political Parties', Parliament@Work.

'Pre-History of Federation', Australian Bureau of Statistics, *Year Book 1989*, pp. 16-19.

'Premiers of NSW', Parliament of NSW, *Australian Dictionary of Biography, Volumes 8 & 10* (these Premiers were William McKell, James McGirr, Joe Cahill, Robert Heffron, John Renshaw).

Shaw A.G.L., (1972), *The Story of Australia, 5th edition*, pp. 92-93, 244-245.

Walker, RB, (1976), *The Newspaper Press in New South Wales, 1803-1920*, pp. 96ff.

Wells, Andrew, (1989), *Constructing Capitalism; an Economic History of Eastern Australia 1788-1901*, pp. 13, 14, 16.

'Women in Parliament', Parliament of NSW.

EDUCATION

Adelaide, Debra, Ashton, Paul & Salt, Annette, (2013), *Stories from the Tower*, p. 18.

Australasian Chronicle, 3 January 1840, 1d & 4 a-b.

Barcan, Alan, (1980), *A History of Australian Education*, pp. 35-37, 41-44.

Bateson, Charles, (1974), *The Convict Ships 1787-1868*, p. 76.

Bourke to Stanley, 30 Sept. 1833, *HRA, I, XVII*, pp. 224ff.

Chavura, Stephen, (2014), '...but in its proper place...', pp. 362-364, 373.

Chavura, Stephen & Tregenza, Ian, (2014), 'A Political History', in Stanley, *Religion after Secularization*, pp. 10-12.

Clark, CMH, *History of Australia, Volume I*, pp. 204, 258.

Clark, CMH, *History of Australia, Volume II*, pp. 201-202, 239-242.

Clark, CMH, *History of Australia, Volume IV*, pp. 284-287.

Clark, CMH, *History of Australia, Volume VI*, p. 410-411, 433.

Clark, CMH, 'Progress of the Past', p. 108.

Cleverley, John F., (1971), *The First Generation: School and Society in Early Australia*, pp. 3, 23-43, 73-86, 93, 116, 117-120.

Colonial Secretary's Statements on Population, June 1843, *1843 Vs & Ps NSW L.C.* p. 448; *1846 Vs & Ps NSW L.C.* Session I, p. 202.

Fletcher, J. & Burnswoods, J., (1983), *Government Schools of New South Wales 1848-1983,* pp. 7-9, 12-13.

'History of NSW Government Schools', NSW Government, Dept of Education.

How Universities are funded, <www.universitiesaustralia.edu.au/policy-submissions/teaching-learning-funding/how-universities-are-funded/>.

Hunt, David, (2013), *Girt: the unauthorised history of Australia,* p. 237.

O'Farrell, Patrick, (1977), *The Catholic Church and Community in Australia: A History,* pp. 138-139.

Shaw, A.G.L., (1977), *Convicts & the Colonies,* p. 77.

Shaw, A.G.L., (1972), *The Story of Australia, 5th edition,* pp. 98-100, 147, 296-297.

Sherington, Geoffrey & Campbell, Craig, 'Education' in *Sydney Journal, 2 (1) June 2009,* pp. 2-6, 8, 10, 14, 16, 17.

UNSW website, <www.unse.edu.au.>.

Wilkinson, John, (2007), *Manufacturing and Services in New South Wales,* pp. 45-48.

INFRASTRUCTURE AND TRANSPORT

'A Brief History', Tramscrolls.

'Australia's first traffic lights', NSW Government, State Archives.

Australian Dictionary of Biography, Volume 1, p. 471.

Barangaroo development, <www.barangaroo.com/the-project/progress/barangaroo-development/>

Blainey, Geoffrey, (1966; 2001 edition), *The Tyranny of Distance: How Distance Shaped Australia's History,* pp. 131-133,146-150, 233, 236-240.

'Bridge Types', RTA, pp. 1-13, 21-23.

'Cities Worldwide: Sydney', <www.caingram.com/Worldwide/Pic_htm/sydney.htm>.

Clark, CMH, *History of Australia, Volume I,* pp. 113, 269-271, 280, 303.

Crowley, Frank, *Colonial Australia Volume 2,* pp. 168, 550.

Crowley, Frank, *Colonial Australia Volume 3,* p. 13.

GPSMYCITY, <www.gpsmycity.com/tours/walking-tour-pyrmont-area-3053.html>.

Gunter, John, (1978). *Across the harbour: the story of Sydney's ferries*.

'History of Roads in Australia', ABS.

'History of the NSW Railways', NSW Government.

Karskens, Grace, (2009), 'Harbour Life' in *The Colony*.

Kass, Terry, (2006), *Roads and Traffic Authority Heritage and Conservation Register: Thematic History, 2nd edition*.

Knezevic, E., National Broadband Network, <aph.gov.au/About_Parliament/Parliamentary_Departments/Parliamentary_Library/pubs/BriefingBook45p/NBN>.

McGillick, Paul & Bingham-Hall, Patrick, (2005), *Sydney Architecture*, pp. 32-33.

Newton, Laura Brierly, (2018), 'Sydney once had the biggest tram system in the southern hemisphere' in *Curious Sydney*, 12 April 2018.

Shaw, A.G.L., (1972), *Story of Australia*, p. 182.

SMH, 27 Sept 1855, quoted in Crowley, *Colonial Australia Volume 2*, p. 317.

'Solar and battery Power', <energysaver.nsw.gov.au/households/solar-and-battery-power>.

Spearritt, Peter, (2018), *Where History Happened: the Hidden Past of Australia's Towns and Places*, pp. 70-75.

'Sydney Light Rail', NSW Government Dept. of Transport.

'Sydney Metro', <www.transport.nsw.gov.au/sydney-metro>.

'Traffic Signal Photos and Information', Expressway.

Waterways Authority, <researchdata.ands.org.au/waterways-authority-1995-authority-2004/164626>.

Wells, Andrew, (1989), *Constructing Capitalism; an Economic History of Eastern Australia 1788-1901*, p. 24.

Wotherspoon, Gary (2010), 'The Domain', *Dictionary of Sydney*: 'Buses'.

Wotherspoon, Gary (2010), 'The Domain', *Dictionary of Sydney*: 'Ferries'.

MANUFACTURING AND INDUSTRIAL DEVELOPMENT

Australian Dictionary of Biography, Volume 2: 1788-1850, pp. 25-26, 128-129, 566.

Blainey, Geoffrey, (1966; 2001 edition), *The Tyranny of Distance: How Distance Shaped Australia's History,* pp 109-112, 309.

Clark, CMH, *History of Australia, Volume I,* pp. 204, 240, 249.

Crowley, Frank, *Colonial Australia, Volume 2,* pp. 15-154, 163-164, 426, 616-617.

Crowley, Frank, *Colonial Australia, Volume 3,* pp. 10-11, 416.

Hirst, John, (2014), *Australian History in 7 Questions,* pp. 66-67, 87.

'History of Australian Innovation', Australian Government.

'History of Manufacturing in Australia', Australian Made, p. 2.

Karskens, Grace, (2009), *The Colony: A History of Early Sydney,* p. 175.

Mann, D., *The Present Picture of New South Wales,* in Crowley, *Colonial Australia Volume 1,* pp. 165-167.

Safework NSW <www.safework.nsw.gov.au/__data/assets/pdf_file/0008/344870/Manufacturing-Sector-Plan-SW08928.pdf>.

Shaw, A.G.L., *Story of Australia,* pp. 59, 134-135, 209-212, 260, 280.

Spearritt, Peter, (2018), *Where History Happened: the Hidden Past of Australia's Towns and Places,* p. 48.

Wells, Andrew (1989), *Constructing Capitalism; an Economic History of Eastern Australia 1788-1901,* p. 24.

Wilkinson, John, (2007), *Manufacturing and Services in New South Wales,* pp. 2, 5-10, 51-54.

HEALTH

'A Century of Service', Australian Respiratory Council, pp. 2-11.

'Ambulance Service of NSW', NSW Government Health.

Aykut, Susan, (2007), *A Lot of Hot Air; the Turkish Bath in Nineteenth Century Australia.*

Cummins, *History of Medical Administration,* pp. 1, 8, 24, 37-38, 40-43, 58, 65-69, 78.

Health Direct, <healthdirect.gov.au/severe-acute-respiratory-syndrome-sars>.

'History of Australian Innovation', Australian Government.

'North Head Quarantine Station, Sydney', National Archives of Australia, (2019).

'Our History', Sydney Quarantine Station.

'Queen Victoria Sanatorium', NSW Government Office of Environment and Heritage.

Taksa, Lucy, *Between Medicine and Management*, pp. 1-5.

'The Evolution and Devolution of Mental Health Services In Australia' in *Inquiries Journal, Volume 9, No.10*, <www.inquiriesjournal.com/articles/1654/the-evolution/and-devolution-of-mental-health-serviced-in-Australia>.

Tyquin, Michael, (2001), *The NSW Railways Ambulance Corps' Heydey, 1881-1960*, pp. 4-8.

Wilkinson, John, (2007), *Manufacturing and Services in New South Wales*, pp. 3-36.

ENTERTAINMENT

Ashton, Paul et al, *Sutherland Shire,* pp. 48-51.

Ashton, Paul, *Centennial Park*, pp. 10-12.

'Australian Music History', <https://australianmusichistory.com/category/venues/>.

Bateson, Charles, (1974), *The Convict Ships 1787-1868*, (quote), p. 3.

Clark, CMH, *History of Australia, Volume I*, p. 153.

Clark, CMH, *History of Australia, Volume II*, p. 167

Clark, CMH, *History of Australia, Volume IV*, pp. 91-2.

Cornwall, Jennifer, (2001), 'The People's Park: Parramatta Park Oral History Project' in *Locality*, p. 4-8.

Crowley, Frank, *Colonial Australia, Volume 1*, p. 438.

Crowley, Frank, *Modern History of Australia, Volume 1*, p. 186.

Fahey, Warren, (2010), *Australian Folk Songs and Bush Ballads*, p. 7.

'History of Hyde Park', City of Sydney, <www.cityofsydney.nsw.gov.au/learn/sydneys-history/people-and-places/park-histories/hyde-park>.

'History of the Australian Museum', <australianmuseum.net.au/about/history/>.

'J.C. Williamson', National Library of Australia.

Petersen, Julie, (2001), 'Nielsen Park: The bush beach' in *Locality, Autumn 2001*, pp. 13-16.

'Rural Communities', State Library of NSW, <www.sl.nsw.gov.au/stories/australian-agricultural-and-rural-life/rural-communities>.

Sea Museum, <www.sea.museum/about/about-the-museum/what-we-do>.

Shaw, A.G.L., (1972), *Story of Australia*, pp. 100-101.

Tyler, Peter J. (2011), *State Records of NSW 1788-2011*, pp. 10-11.

'International Exhibition Supplement', 17 Sept 1879, in *Sydney Morning Herald*, in Crowley, *Colonial Australia, Volume 3*, pp. 64-66.

Willis, Ian, 'Sydney's Botanic Gardens' in *Camden History Notes*, <camdenhistorynotes.wordpress.com/2017/01/26/sydneys-royal-botanic-gardens/>

Wotherspoon, Gary, 'The Domain', in *Dictionary of Sydney*, <dictionaryofsydney.org/entry/the_domain>.

SCIENCE

'A Hundred Years', Australian Bureau of Statistics.

'Australia's First Nuclear Reactor', <dl.nfsa.gov.au/module/56/>.

Australian Dictionary of Biography, Volume 1, 1788-1850, pp. 297-298.

Clark, CMH, *History of Australia, Volume I*, pp. 75-76.

Clark, CMH, *History of Australia, Volume VI*, p. 251.

CSIRO, <www.csiro.au/>.

Karskens, Grace, (2009), *The Colony: A History of Early Sydney*, pp. 71-72 (area now called Dawes Point.)

'Mills Cross', <www.britannica.com/science/Mills-cross>.

'Researches on Australian Venoms', University of Sydney.

Science and Industry Research Act 1949, <www.legislation.gov.au/Details/C2012C00352>.

Tyler, Peter J, (2001), 'Our First Microbiologist' in *Locality, Summer 2001*, pp. 10-12.

Willis, Ian, 'Sydney's Royal Botanic Gardens: an historical source' in *PHA NSW*, 29 Jan 2017.

CRIME, PUNISHMENT AND LAW ENFORCEMENT

Australian Dictionary of Biography, *Volume 1*, p. 217.

'Australian Police', <www.australianpolice.com.au/>.

Bateson, Charles, (1974), *The Convict Ships 1787-1868,* pp. 80, 90, 198, 200.

Bugeja & Ferguson, *Crimes of Passion,* pp. 12-15, 218-221.

Clark, CMH, *History of Australia, Volume I*, pp. 115, 121,

Clark, CMH, *History of Australia, Volume IV*, p. 201-203, 228.

Crowley, Frank, *Colonial Australia, Volume 1*, pp. 5-6, 12-13.

Crowley, Frank, *Colonial Australia, Volume 2*, pp. 69-70, 411-413.

'Darcy Dugan', <peoplepill.com/people/darcy-dugan/>.

'Darcy Dugan biography', <adb.anu.edu.au/biography/dugan-darcy-ezekiel-25998>.

Doyle, Peter, (2009), *Crooks Like Us,* pp. 17, 21, 34, 37, 77, 79, 102-103, 233-234.

Evans, *Pyjama Girl,* pp. 11-12, 16, 28, 44ff, 84, 102-104, 197-201.

Gapps, Stephen, (2010), *Front Pages that Shaped Australia,* pp. 57, 148-149.

Hirst, John, (2014), *Australian History in 7 Questions,* p. 30.

Hosking, B. & Linton, J, *Justice Denied*, p. 259.

'Ivan Milat', <edition.cnn.com/2019/10/28/australia/ivan-milat-serial-killer-dead-intl-hnk/index.htm>.

'Justice', NSW Government, <www.courts.justice.nsw.gov.au/Pages/cats/history/history.aspx>.

Levi, John S. & Bergman, George F, (2002), *Australian genesis, Jewish convicts and settlers, 1788-1860,* pp. 62-63.

Lindsay, Patrick, (2012), *True Blue,* pp. 20-21, 25-27, 38-42, 43, 45-56, 58-59, 63, 66-67, 80-81, 84, 86-87, 90, 91, 94, 96, 100-102, 106-109, 138, 141, 143, 150, 154, 160-161, 223.

'Police Force, 1788-1888', NSW Government, <www.police.nsw.gov.au/about_us/history/history_pages/significant_dates>.

Ramsland, John, 'Punish or Discipline' in Ashton, *Silent System*, pp. 29-39, 39-41.

Salt, Annette, (1984), *These Outcast Women: The Parramatta Female Factory 1821-1848,* pp. 85-98.

Shaw, A.G.L., (1977), *Convicts & the Colonies,* pp. 80-81, 196-197, 206-207, 225-226.

Skinner, L.E., (1975), *Police of the Pastoral Frontier: Native Police 1849-59*, pp. 17-22.

Tedeschi, Mark, (2015), *Kidnapped: the crime that shocked the nation*, pp. 1, 13, 41-42, 45-46, 52, 64, 99-100, 124 ff, 131, 138-141, 159-161, 256, 274.

'Tilly Devine', <www.records.nsw.gov.au/archives/magazine/galleries/tilly-devine-and-the-razor-gang-wars>.

Walker, R.B., (1980), *Yesterday's News*, pp. 6-7.

'Wanda beach murders', <www.mamamia.com.au/wanda-beach-murders>.

'Wanda beach murders', <startsat60.com/discover/news/wanda-beach-murders-sydney-cold-case-unsolved>.

'Wanda Beach Murders', Case File, <casefilepodcast.com/case-1-the-wanda-beach-murders/>.

Woollacott, Angela, (2015), *Settler Society in the Australian Colonies*, pp. 10, 71.

FINANCE

Australian Dictionary of Biography, Volume 1.

Australian Dictionary of Biography, Volume 2, p. 374.

Australian Dictionary of Biography, Volume 9.

Australian Dictionary of Biography, Volume 12.

BK de Garis, '1890-1900' in Crowley, *A New History*, pp. 222-223.

Butlin, S.J., (1968), *Foundations of the Australian Monetary System 1788-1851*, pp. 4-5, 18-19, pp. 79-84, 110ff.

Cannon, Michael, (1986 ed.), *The Land Boomers*, pp. 119-128.

Clark, CMH, *History of Australia, Volume I*, pp. 149-150, 332.

Crowley, Frank, *Colonial Australia, Volume 1,* p. 203.

Dow, Gwyneth M., (1974), *Samuel Terry: The Botany Bay Rothschild*, pp. 150, 152, 158.

Hirst, John, (2014), *Australian History in 7 Questions*, pp. 62-64.

Irving, T. '1850-1870', in Crowley, *A New History*, p. 125-126.

Karskens, Grace, (2009), *The Colony*, p. 148.

Lemon, *In Her Gift: Women Philanthropists in Australian History.*

McMartin, Arthur, (1983), *Public Servants and Patronage: the Foundation and Rise of the New South Wales Public Service, 1786-1859*, pp. 185-186.

O'Brien, Anne, (2008) 'Charity and Philanthropy' in *Dictionary of Sydney.*

Radi, Heather, '1920-1929' in Crowley, *A New History*, p 382.

Roe, Michael, '1830-1850' in Crowley, *A New History*, p. 108.

Shaw, A.G.L., '1788-1810' in Crowley, *A New History*, p. 27.

Shaw, A.G.L., *Story of Australia*, pp. 240-244, 262-264.

Wells, Andrew, (1989), *Constructing Capitalism; an Economic History of Eastern Australia 1788-1901*, pp. 8-9, 98-103.

Wilkinson, John, (2007), *Manufacturing and Services in New South Wales*, p. 24.

COMMUNITY ORGANISATIONS

Ashton Paul et al, *Sutherland Shire*, pp. 112-113.

'Birth of Surf Lifesaving', NMA website.

CO.AS.IT, <www.coasit.org.au/CommunityServices.aspx>.

Council of Social Services, p. 5, <www.ncoss.org.au/sites/default/files/public/policy/EY_Final_Report.pdf>.

Country Women's Association, <www.cwaofnsw.org.au/>.

Clark, CMH, *History of Australia, Volume I*, p. 325.

Clark, CMH, *History of Australia, Volume III*, p. 378.

Clark, CMH, *History of Australia, Volume V*, p. 279

Cummins, *History of Medical Administration*, pp. 51-53.

Crowley, Frank, *Colonial Australia, Volume 1*, p. 186-188, 272.

Gapps, Stephen, (2010), *Front Pages that Shaped Australia*, pp. 232-234.

'History of Australian Innovation', Australian Government.

'History of the RFS', NSW Government, <www.rfs.nsw.gov.au/about-us/history>.

Crozier-de Rosa, 'Perhaps tea and scones' in *Conversations*, <theconversation.com/perhaps-tea-and-scones-are-ok-the-cwa-and-feminism-today-25474>.

'History of the Benevolent Society of NSW', <www.benevolent.org.au/about-us/our-history>.

Issuu, New England Focus i103 <issuu.com/focus.mag/docs/nei103/33>.

Lindsay, Patrick, (2012), *True Blue*, pp. 142-143.

Police Citizens Youth Club, <www.pcycnsw.org.au/programs/police-programs/>.

Surf Lifesaving, <www.surflifesaving.com.au/>.

ORGANISED RELIGION

Australian Dictionary of Biography, Volume 12.

Austin, A. G., (1961), *Australian Education 1788-1900.*, pp. 36-8, 44,

Bateson, Charles, (1974), *The Convict Ships 1787-1868,* p. 76.

Bouma, Gary, (2002), *Globalization and Recent Changes in the Demography of Australian Religious Groups: 1947-2001,* pp. 17, 19, 22.

Carey, Hilary M. (2010), *Bushmen and Bush Parsons,* pp. 1-8, 12, 16-18, 22.

Clark, CMH, *History of Australia Volume I,* pp. 138, 152, 269, 270, 303, 321

Clark, CMH, *History of Australia Volume II,* pp. 30-31, 172, 191-192, 237.

Clark, CMH, *History of Australia Volume VI,* p. 155.

Franklin, James, *Sydney Intellectual/religious Scene,* pp. 20, 27.

Gapps, Stephen, (2010), *Front Pages that Shaped Australia,* pp. 131-133.

Gladwin, M., (2010), 'The Journalist in the Rectory: Anglican clergyman and Australian intellectual life, 1788-1850' in *History Australia, Vol. 7, No. 10,* p. 19.

Hirst, John, (2014), *Australian History in 7 Questions,* pp. 48-49, 144-145, 147-148.

'History of the Greek Orthodox Church in Australia', <www.greekorthodox.org.au/?page_id=3670>.

'Losing my Religion', Australian Bureau of Statistics.

Mayne, P.A., (2016), *A History of Tamar (1996-2008),* pp. 8-9.

NSW Jewish Board of Deputies, *History of NSW Jewry,* <www.nswjbd.org/history-of-nsw-jewry>.

O'Farrell, Patrick, (1977), *The Catholic Church and Community in Australia: A History,* pp. 30, 38-39, 54-56, 69, 140-142, 194-199.

'Our History', Salvation Army.

'Plunkett Centre for Ethics', ACU.

'Religion in Australia', Australian Bureau of Statistics.

Shaw, AGL, *Story of Australia,* pp. 98, 146, 310.

'St James Church', NSW Government, Office of Environment & Heritage.

Stephen A. Chavura and Ian Tregenza, 'A Political History of the Secular in Australia' in Stanley, Timothy (ed.), (2015), *Religion after Secularization in Australia,* pp. 5-7.

Walker, R.B., (1976), *The Newspaper Press in New South Wales, 1803-1920,* pp. 148-151.

Walsh, G., (1993), *Pioneering days: People and Innovations in Australia's Rural Past*, pp. 265-271.

SPORT

2000 Summer Olympics, <web.archive.org/web/20130115080441/ databaseolympics.com/games/gamesyear.htm?g=25>.

'AFL: 130 years of history', <aflnswact.com.au/130-years-of-history/>.

Baseball news, <www.baseballprospectus.com/news/article/26787/bp-daily-podcast-effectively-wild-episode-700-sabermetrics-australia-style/>.

Baseball NSW, <susfc.com.au/fixture-results>.

Basketball NSW, <www.bnsw.com.au/>.

Cricket Australia, <www.cricket.com.au/>.

Cricket NSW, <www.cricketnsw.com.au/>.

'History of Australian Football', <www.afl.com.au/about-afl/history>.

'History of the Modern Summer Games', *Encyclopedia Britannica*, <www.britannica.com/sports/Olympic-Games/History-of-the-modern-Summer-Games>.

'Milestones in Australia's soccer history', <www.ak-tsc.de/hp/History/ aushistory.htm>.

National Rugby League, <www.nrl.com.au>.

Netball NSW, <nsw.netball.com.au/>.

NSW Australian Football History Society, <www.nswfootballhistory.com.au/>.

NSW Football, <footballnsw.com.au/>.

NSW Premier League Netball, <www.nnswpremierleague.com.au/home>.

NSW Rugby History, <saintsandheathens.wordpress.com/states/nsw-waratahs>.

NSW Rugby League, <(susfc.com.au/fixture-results>.

NSW Rugby Union, <nsw.rugby>.

NSW Tennis, < www.tennis.com.au/nsw/about>.

'Perisher History', <www.perisher.com.au/resort-info/know-perisher/our-history>.

Sydney 2000 Olympic Games, <www.britannica.com/event/Sydney-2000-Olympic-Games>.

Sydney Blue Sox, <sydneybluesox.com.au>.

Tennis NSW, <www.tennis.com.au/nsw/>.

'Timeline of Australian Football', <web.archive.org/ web/20141217101940/www.migrationheritage.nsw.gov.au/exhibitions/ worldcup/timeline.shtml>.

'What's the score? A survey of cultural diversity and racism in Australian sport', <www.humanrights.gov.au/sites/default/files/content/racial_ discrimination/whats_the_score/pdf/whats_the_score_report.pdf>.

Woman's Soccer, <susfc.com.au/fixture-results>.

ART, LITERATURE, MUSIC AND ARCHITECTURE

Apperly et al, *Identifying Australian Architecture*, pp. 32-36, 60-62, 100, 144-147, 149, 162, 188, 211, 227.

Australian Dictionary of Biography, Volume I, pp. 547-548.

Australian Music Centre, < www.australianmusiccentre.com.au>.

Bebbington, *Oxford Companion Dictionary*, pp. 7-8, 10-11, 26, 34, 47, 50-51, 62-64, 71, 118-119, 124, 176, 362, 430ff.

Butler, Roger, 'Printmaking' in Anderson, *Cambridge Companion to Australian Art*, pp. 100-101.

Carter, David 'Publishing, Patronage and Cultural Politics' in Pierce, *Cambridge History of Australian Literature*, pp. 360-361, 366, 369.

Caruana, Wally & Clark, Jane, 'Buying and selling Australian Art' in Anderson, *Cambridge Companion to Australian Art*, p. 300.

Clarke, Heather, 'The History of Music and Dance in Australia 1788-1840', <www.colonialdance.com.au/piano-of-the-first-fleet-29.html>.

Clark, John, 'Asian Art and Australia', in Anderson, *Cambridge Companion to Australian Art*, p. 227.

Clark, CMH, *History of Australia, Volume II*, pp. 167-8.

Clark, CMH, *History of Australia, Volume VI*, pp. 499-450.

Crowley, Frank, *Colonial Australia, Volume 3*, pp. 192-3.

Eagle, Mary 'Social identity 1780s-1860s' in Anderson, *Cambridge Companion to Australian Art*, pp. 46-47.

Galbally, Ann, 'Heidelberg School', in Anderson, *Cambridge Companion to Australian Art*, pp. 72-75, 82-83.

Gammage, Bill, (2011), *The Biggest Estate on Earth: How Aborigines Made Australia*, pp. 18-19, 43-44, 62-63, 92-94.

Gapps, Stephen, (2010), *Front Pages that Shaped Australia*, pp. 278-280.

Inglis, Alison, 'Imperial Perspectives' in Anderson, *Cambridge Companion to Australian Art*, pp. 58-59.

Jones, Philip, 'Aboriginal Art, 18th-20th Centuries' in Anderson, *Cambridge Companion to Australian Art*, pp. 36-37.

McGillick, Paul & Bingham-Hall, Patrick, (2005), *Sydney Architecture*, pp. 4-5, 14-15, 38-40, 60.

Morphy, Howard, in Anderson, *Cambridge Companion to Australian Art*, pp. 157-160.

Nile & Ensor, 'The novel, the implicated reader and Australian Literary Cultures 1950-2008' in Pierce, *Cambridge History of Australian Literature*, p. 517.

Pierce, Peter, 'Australia's Australia', in Pierce, *Cambridge History of Australian Literature*, p. 141.

Smith, Vivian, 'Australian Colonial Poetry' in Pierce, *Cambridge History of Australian Literature*, pp. 74, 77-79, 81.

'Songs of Home: Exploring the Past Through Music', Sydney Living Museums, <sydneylivingmuseums.com.au/exhibitions/songs-home>.

Spearritt, Peter, (2018), *Where History Happened: the Hidden Past of Australia's Towns and Places*, pp. 67-68.

Stewart, Ken, (2009), 'Britain's Australia' in *Cambridge History of Australian Literature*, pp. 7, 15.

Walker, R.B., (1980), *Yesterday's News*, pp. 90-98.

White, Anthony, 'Australian Modernism' in Anderson, *Cambridge Companion to Australian Art*, pp. 110ff.

Index

Abigail, Francis, 259
Aboriginal schools, 144
Aboriginal stonehenge, 14
Aboriginal Welfare Board, 21
Aborigines Protection Act, 21
Absalom, Jack, 76-77
Adams, Charlotte, 318
adult education, 149
Afghan migrants, 41
AFL (Australian Football League), 300-301
Agostini, Linda and Antonio, 246-247
Agricultural Society of NSW, 110
agriculture, colonial, 105-120
agriculture, Indigenous, 3-6
Ah Sat, Wong, 42-43
Albury, 57-61
A-League, 316
Alfred Dudley, 324
Alienation of Crown Lands Bill, 110
Amadio family, 330
ambulance service, 191
AMP Society, 257
Anaiwan people, 61

Anglican Church, 285, 286-287, 289-290
Antill, John, 330
ANZ Championship, 306-307
ANZAC Bridge, 160
Archer, William, 19
Archibald Prize, 324
Archibald, J. F. , 214, 324
architecture, 333-336
Arena, Franca, 125
ARL (Australian Rugby League), 310
Armidale, 61-64
Art Deco, 335
art, Indigenous, 10, 321-322
artesian water, 119
arts, the, 321-336
Ashton, Julian, 323
Assange, Julian, 86
astronomy, Indigenous, 14-16
asylums, 185-186
Australian Agricultural Company, 92, 111
Australian Medical Association, 185
Australian Museum, 210

Australian Open, 319-320
Australian Rules Football, 300-301
Awabakal people, 90
Back to Town, 222
backpacker murders, 254
Baiame, 13
Baker, Simon, 67
Ballina, 64-67
Bank of NSW, 53, 256-257
Banks, Joseph, 3
Barangaroo, 20
Barangaroo (development), 153
Barker, Thomas, 257
Barkindji people, 74
Barnes, Jimmy, 73
Barnet, James, 64, 66, 334
Barney, George, 152, 154
Barrington, George, 199
Barton, Edmund, 127
baseball, 302
Bashir, Dame Marie, 125
basketball, 302-303
Bass, George, 100
bathhouses, 188
Baudon, Adolphe, 278
Bell, Archibald, 69
Bell, John, 89
Belvoir Theatre, 202
Benevolent Society of NSW, 270-271
Benn, Ethel, 243
Bennelong, 20
Berejiklian, Gladys, 125, 129
Bernhardt, Sarah, 201
Berry, Alexander, 108
BHP, 74, 76, 92, 102, 178
Bicentennial Park, 218
Biffen, Dr Harriet, 265

Big Prawn, 67
Bigge, John, 53
Biggs, Fred, 5-6
Bird Rose, Deborah, 3
Blackett, Edmund, 334
Blackman, John, 94
Blainey, Geoffrey, 34
Blamey, Sir Thomas, 98-99
Bland, Dr William, 185, 265
Blaxcell, Garnham, 184
Blaxland, Gregory, 17, 68, 109
Blaxland, John, 109
Bligh, William, 106, 122, 134, 234-235, 255
Blue Heeler, 114
Blue Hills, 204
Blue Mountains, 67-71
Blue, Billy, 167
Board of Health, 187
Board of National Education, 137
Board, Peter, 141-142
Bogle-Chandler Mystery, 250-252
Boldrewood, Rolf, 79, 325
Bondi Lifesaver, 202
Bondi Surf Club, 279
Booth, Edgar, 190-191
bounty system, 38
Bounty, HMS, 234-235
Bourke, Richard, 38, 122, 135, 288
Bowral, 71-74
Bradfield, Dr John, 164
Bradley, Stephen, 249-250
Bradman, Sir Donald, 72, 305
Brereton, Dr John, 188
Brewarrina fish pens, 3
bridges, 158-160
Brisbane, Thomas, 19, 226
British convicts, 25-34

British Empire Games, 298
Broken Hill, 74-77
Bronhill, June, 77, 330
Broughton, William, 287
Brown, Noelene, 73
Brown, Robert, 58
Browne, Thomas, 79
Brushmen of the Bush, 76-77
Bryant, William and Mary, 90
buildings in NSW, 151-153
Bulletin, The, 326-327
Bundjalung people/nation, 64, 83, 333
Burke, Henry, 117
Burley Griffin, Walter, 335-336
Burney, Linda, 125
Burns, Sir James, 266
Burra Burra people, 68
Busby, James, 113, 173
Busby's Bore, 173
buses, 165-166
Bush Nursing Association, 114
bushfires, 281-283
Butterley, Nigel, 330
Buttrose, Ita, 73
Buzo, Alex, 63
Caesar, John, 233
Caldwell, Arthur, 45
canoes, Indigenous, 168
CanTeen, 270
Captain Thunderbolt, 63, 240
car manufacturing, 179
Carr-Boyd, Ann, 330
Carrington, Lord, 23
Castro, Tom, 97
cedar cutting, 64-65, 100-101
Centennial Park, 216-217
Central Coast Mariners, 317

Chapman, Israel, 241
Charlotte Pass, 318
Charlton, Andrew, 220
Chauvel, Charles, 207, 208
Cheetham, Deborah, 330-331
Chickiba wetland, 67
Chinese migration, 40, 42-43
Chisholm, Caroline, 39-40, 89
Christian Missions, 21
Christian, Fletcher, 234-235
cinema, 205-209
Clarke, Marion, 141
Clay, Sonny, 45
Clint, Alf, 280
Clunies, Sir William, 227
coal mining, 87-88, 92, 101
Cobb & Co., 61, 95, 154, 156
Cobby, Anite, 253-254
Cockatoo Island, 57
Colleges of Advanced Education, 147-148
Coloured Stone, 333
Commonwealth Grants Commission, 262
Commonwealth of Australia, 45, 125-127
communications networks, 170-172
community organisations, 269-283
Conolly, Philip, 286
Conservatorium of Music, 330, 333
Constitution of NSW, 123
consumption, 189-190
Cook, Arnold, 272
Cook, James, 3, 26, 100
Cooper, William, 23
Cossington Smith, Grace, 324
Country Women's Association, 114, 272

Covid-19, 148, 194
Cowper, Charles, 128
Cox, William, 68, 155-156
Cracknell, Ruth, 89
cricket, 304-305
crime and punishment, 233-254
criminals and crimes, 246-254
Crocodile Dundee, 83
CSIRO, 229
culture, Indigenous, 6-11
Cunningham, Peter, 4
customs and excise, 260-261
dams, 173-174
Daplyn, Alfred, 323
Darcy, Les, 89
Dark, Eleanor, 327
Darkinjung people, 8
Darling, Ralph, 37, 84, 109
Darug people, 68
Darwin, Charles, 70
David, Sir Edgeworth, 87-88
Davis, Alexander, 292-292
Dawes, William, 225
de Bouillon Serisier, Jean Emile, 78
de Maistre, Roy, 324
Delany, John, 329
Department of Education, 139-140
Department of Main Roads, 157
Devine, Tilly, 244
Dharawal (Tharawal) people/nation, 71, 99-100
dinosaur fossils, 82
diseases, 192-194
Dixon, James, 285
Dobell, Ralph, 324
Domain, the, 56, 214-216
Donahue, Jack, 240

Donaldson, Stuart, 127
Dora Dora Massacre, 58
Doyle, Stuart, 201
Dreaming stories, Indigenous, 7-8
Dubbo, 78-80
Dudley, Lady Rachel, 114
Dugan, Darcy, 247-249
Dulhunty, Robert, 78
Dumaresq brothers, 38
Dunn, Johnny, 78
Dyer, Bob and Dolly, 205
dysentry, 192
education, 133-149
eight-hour day, 40
Eisdell, J. W., 290
electricity supplies, 169-170
Emu in the Sky, 15
entertainment, 199-223
Eora nation, 51-52
epidemics, 192-194
Euahlayi people, 16
Evans, Winsome, 332
Experiment Farm, 107
Fahey, Warren, 332
Family Colonisation Loan Society, 39
Farrer, William, 98
Federation, 125-127
Federation Drought, 112
Federation Pavilion, 217
female convicts, 32-33
Female Immigrants' Home, 39
Fennell, Willie, 205
ferry services, 166-168
finance, 255-267
fire, Indigenous use of, 4
First Fleet, 26
First World War, 43, 75

fish pens at Brewarrina, 3
fishing, Indigenous, 12-13
Fitzroy Falls, 73
Flinders, Matthew, 100
floggings, 235
Flowers, Frederick, 191
Flynn, Errol, 207-208
Flynn, Jeremiah, 285-286
Flynn, John, 115
Football Federation Australia, 315-316
Fort Denison, 57, 152
Franklin, Miles, 327
Fraser Government, 47
Fraser, Charles, 226
Fraser, Dawn, 219-220
Freedom Ride, the, 22
Freeman, Cathy, 300
Fuller, Bob, 15
Gadigal people, 51-52, 153
gambling, 263-264
Gamilaraay (Kamilaroi) people/nation, 20, 80
Garden Palace, 215
Gardiner, Frank, 78, 97, 240
Gardner, Andrew, 70
German migrants, 41
Giants, 301
Gibb, May, 326
Gilbert & Sullivan, 201
Gilbert, John, 78
Gilchrist, Adam, 86
Giltinan, James, 308
Gipps, Sir George, 39, 122, 136, 154
Gocher, William, 278-279
goldrush of 1850s, 40-41, 62, 65, 68, 94-95, 177, 239-240

golf, 305-306
Gordon, Lee, 203
Gough, June Mary, 77
Government House, 56
Governors of NSW, 130-131
Grassby, Al, 46
Great Depression, 82, 85, 129, 261-262
Great Synagogue, 291-292
Greater Western Sydney Giants, 301
Greek Othodox Church, 291
Greenway, Francis, 27, 151-152, 286, 333
Gregg, Dr Norman, 190
Guide Dogs Organisation of NSW, 272-273
Gullett, Dr Lucy, 265
Gummow, Margaret, 333
Gumnut Babies, 326
Gundungurra people, 68
Guring-gai people, 15
Hackney, Amelia, 42
Hall, Ben, 78, 89, 240
Hanson, Frederick, 96
Hargreaves, Edward, 40
Harpur, Charles, 325
Hart, Pro, 76-77
Hartigan, J. P. , 290
Hawkins, Jennifer, 93
Hayes, John, 244
health, 183-197
Heidelberg School, 323
Hill, Rosamund and Florence, 236
Hills Hoist, 181
Hillsborough, 28
Hirst, Johm, 31
Hoddle, Robert, 322

Hogan, Paul, 83
Holman, William, 128
Holmes, Susannah, 31-32
Hope, John, 280
Hoskins Steelworks, 178
Hoskins, Cecil, 102
Hovel, William, 58
Hoyle, Henry, 308
Hume Dam, 59
Hume, Hamilton, 58
Hunter Jaegers, 307
Hunter, John, 134, 286
Hurley, David, 103
Hyde Park, 213-214
Hyde Park Barracks, 29, 333
Immigration Restriction Act, 45
Indigenous art, 10, 321-322
Indigenous peoples,
   agriculture, 3-6
   Country, 3-6
   culture, 6-11
   fire, use of, 4
   science, 13-17
   social organisations, 6-11
   technology, 11-13
industrial development, 175-182
industrial health, 187-188, 196-197
infrastructure, 151-174
International Exhibition, 200, 334
internet network, 171-172
internment, 43, 44
Irish National System, 135, 137
Irish, Paul, 22-23
Jevons, William, 226
Jewish faith, 291-292
Jewish migrants, 40-41, 44, 292
Johns, Daniel, 93
Johnson, George, 255

Johnson, Richard, 134
Jones, David, 257
Jones, Riley & Walker, 176
Kable, Henry, 31-32, 175-176, 234
Kamilaroi people, 16, 61
Kangaroos, 309
Karoly, David, 227
Karskens, Grace, 105, 168
Katoomba, 70
Kelpie, 114
Kendall, Henry, 326
Keneally, Kristina, 129
Kiandra Snow Shoe Club, 317
King, George, 257
King, Philip Gidley, 31, 91, 134
Kingsford Smith, Charles, 279
kinship, Indigenous, 6-7
Koerstz, Christian, 115-116
Kosciuszko, 318
Kossoff, George, 191
Kristallnacht protest, 23
Kuttabul, HMS, 57
Labor Party, 132
Lane Cove Tunnel, 160
Lang, Jack, 128-129, 261-262
Lang, John, 287
Lansdowne Bridge, 158
Larrikin Music, 332
Laver, Florence, 272
law enforcement, 233-254
law, Indigenous, 11
Lawson, Henry, 326
Lawson, Louisa, 124
Lawson, William, 68
Legacy, 273
Leigh, Kate, 244
Lennis, John, 217
Lennox, David, 158

Levey, Barnett, 200
Levi, Walter, 41
Liberal Party, 132
Lidwell, Dr Mark, 190-191
Life with Dexter, 205
Lifeline, 274, 294
Lightning Ridge, 80-83
limits of location, 37-38, 84, 109
Lions, Mary, 196-197
Lismore, 83-86
literature, 324-328
live music, 202-204
Lord, Simon, 175-176
LoSurdo family, 44
lotteries, 264
Lowe Robert, 137-138
Lucas Heights nuclear centre, 181, 229-230
Luna Park, 220-222
Lycett, Joseph, 322
Lyric Theatre, 202
Macarthur, Elizabeth, 3-4, 47-48, 108
Macarthur, Hannibal, 108
Macarthur, John, 108, 255
Mack, Marie Louise, 48-49
Mackay, William, 243, 246-247, 275
Mackellar, Dorothea, 106
Mackie, Alexander, 143
Macquarie University, 146-147
Macquarie, Elizabeth, 329
Macquarie, Lachlan, 18, 32, 56, 135, 151, 155, 183-184, 237, 256, 270, 285
Mad Max II, 77
Madgwick, Dr Robert, 62
magistrates, 236-237
Mahony, Marion, 335-336

Maitland, 86-90
Malcolm, Alexander, 260
Maltese migration, 42
mammal fossils, 82
manufacturing, 175-182
Marinos, Lex, 99
maritime services, 166-168
Marsden, Samuel, 107-108, 286
Marsh, Stephen, 329
Martens, Conrad, 323
Mason, Frederick, 115-116
Matthews, Charles, 289
May (Baron), Robert, 227-228
McAdam, John, 156
McBride, William, 191
McGowen, James, 128
McGrath, Glenn, 79
McMahon brothers, 206
Meals on Wheels, 274-275
measles, 193
Medical Board, 185, 188-189
Medical Practitioners Act, 189
medicine, Indigenous, 13-14
Melba, Dame Nellie, 201
Meredith, Gwen, 204
Messenger, Dally, 308-309
meteorology, 226
Milat, Ivan, 254
Mills, Bernard, 228
Minchin, Eric, 76
Mindaribba people, 90
Mitchell, Thomas, 5, 9, 17-18, 74, 94
Moore, Charles, 217
Moore, Neil, 191
Morgan, Molly, 86-87
Morriset, James, 322
Mort, Thomas, 110-111

Mortimer, Steve, 99
Morton, Eileen, 264
Mounted Police, 237-238
Mungo Man and Lady, 2
Mungo National Park, 2
Murray, Jack, 81
museums, 210-213
music, 328-333
music, Indigenous, 333
My Country, 106
Myall Creek Massacre, 20, 238
National Broadband Network, 171-172
National Maritime Museum, 212-213
National Party, 132
National Premier League, 317
Native Institution, 135
Native Police Corps, 239
netball, 306-308
Netball Australia, 306
Netball NSW, 308
Nettleton Charles, 81
Newcastle, 90-93
Newcastle Jets, 317
New South Wales – *see NSW*
Ngarrindjeri people, 59
Nguril, 7-8
Nicolle, Eugene, 110-111
Nielsen Park, 217-218
Night Watch, 233
Norfolk Island, 234-235
Norman, Decima, 298
Norris, Ray, 14-15
North Connex, 160
NRL (National Rugby League), 310
NSW Blues, 305
NSW Constitution, 123

NSW Corps, 122
NSW Cup, 311
NSW Governors, 130-131
NSW Legislative Assembly, 125
NSW Legislative Council, 123, 125
NSW Mounted Police, 237-238
NSW Police Force, 242-245
NSW Premier Cricket, 304-305
NSW Premier League, 317
NSW Premiers, 127-130
NSW Rugby Union, 313
NSW Swifts, 307
NSW Waratahs, 314
nursing, 195-197
Ogilvie, Dame Bridget, 228
Olley, Margaret, 86
Olympics in Sydney, 299-300
opal mining, 81-82
Ophir, gold at , 40, 54
Orange, 93-96
organised religion, 285-296
Osburn, Lucy, 195
Overland, 327
Oxley, John, 71
Ozanam, Frederick, 278
Pacific Highway, 157
Packer, James, 266
Paling, W. H. , 266
Parkes Elvis Revival, 332
Parkes, Sir Henry, 126, 138-139, 195, 217, 260
parks, 213-218
Parramatta, 107
Parramatta Female Factory, 32-33, 151
Parramatta Native Institution, 18
Parramatta Park, 213
Pascoe, Bruce, 10-11

Paterson, 'Banjo', 96, 326
Paterson, William, 86
Pemulwuy, 19
Peppercorne, Frederick, 83-84
Perisher, 319
Perkins, Charles, 22
philanthropy, 264-267
Phillip, Arthur, 20, 26, 56, 105, 112, 133, 172
Pick-a-box, 205
Pickup, John, 76
pinball machines, 222
Piper, John, 258-259
Polding, John, 287
Police Citizens Youth Club, 275-276
Police Dog Squad, 245
Police Force, NSW, 242-245
Police Regulation Act, 241-242
Police Rescue Unit, 245
police, development of the, 237-245
political parties, 132
politics, 121-132
postal system, 170
Potter, Sir Ian, 266
pound-for-pound church subsidy, 288
pound-for-pound school subsidy, 135, 136
power supplies, 169-170
Powerhouse Museum, 210-212
Premiers of NSW, 127-130
Preston Stanley, Millicent, 125
Preston, Margaret, 323-324
Priscilla, Queen of the Desert, 77
prisons, 235-236
Public Instruction Act, 139

Public Schools Act, 138
Pyjama Girl , 246-247
QANTAS, 179-180
Quadrant, 327
quarantine station, 186
Quintus Servinton, 325
Quong Tart, Mei, 42-43
rabbits, 118-119
radio, 204-205
Rafferty, Chips, 77, 208
railways, 162-166
Ralph Rashleigh, 91
Ramsay, Paul, 266
Ranger's Cottage, 335
Rasp, Charles, 74
Raymond, James, 170
Reedy River, 332
refrigeration, 110-111
Reibey, Mary, 37, 256
Reid, George, 112
religion, organised, 285-296
remittance men, 36, 109
Rennaissance Players, 332
Richardson, Mervyn, 181
Richardson, William, 133
Riley, Alexander, 184
roads, 155-158
Robbery Under Arms, 325-326
Robinson, David, 191
Robinson, Michael, 325
Rocks, the, 53
Roman Catholics, 285, 287-289, 290
Rossi, Francis, 237
Rosson, Isabella, 133
Rous, John, 83
Royal Botanic Gardens, 56, 214-215, 226

Royal Easter Show, 113, 223
Royal Exchange, 257
Royal Flying Doctor Service, 115
Royal National Park, 218
rugby league, 308-312
Rugby League Grand Finals, 310
rugby union, 312-315
Rum Corps, 255
Rum Hospital, 184, 195, 333
Rum Rebellion, 122, 255
Rural Fire Service, 281-282
rural workers, 116-118
Ruse, James, 107
Russell, Henry, 119, 226
Salvation Army, 293-294
sand mining, 179
SARS, 194
Savery, Henry, 325
Saxby-Junna, Kerry, 67
scarlet fever, 193
Schmidt, Marianne, 252-253
School of the Air, 76
schools, 133-145
Schulz, Hugh, 76
science, 225-231
science, Indigenous, 13-17
sealing, 175-176
Second World War, 43-44, 45, 57, 76, 180
secret ballot, introduction, 124
See, John, 128
Shakespeare performances, 201
Sharrock, Christine, 252-253
Shaw, Alan, 262
shearing by machine, 116
sheep dogs, 113-114
Sheffield Shield, 304-305
shepherds, 116-117

shipping, 166-168
Shortland, John, 90
Simpson, Percy, 94
skiing, 317-319
Slater, Michael, 99
Slessor, Kenneth, 76, 96, 168
smallpox epidemic, 18, 186-187, 193
Smith Court, Margaret, 60
Smith Family, 276
Snowy Mountains Scheme, 46, 170, 318
soccer, 315-317
social organisations, Indigenous, 6-11
solar power, 170
soldier settlement scheme, 115
songlines, Indigenous, 6-7
Spanish Flu, 193-194
Spark, Alexander, 306
Speaker's Corner, 216
Spence, Catherine, 325
Splendour in the Grass, 203
sport, 297-320
sport, Indigenous, 297
squatters, 38, 109
Squire, Raimond, 115
St James' church, 286-287, 333
St Vincent de Paul, 278
Stace, Arthur, 294
Stanley, Fiona, 228
State of Origin, 311-312
State Theatre, 201
steel working, 92, 101-102, 178
Stewart House, 277
Stolen Generation, 21
Streeton, Arthur, 323
Strzelecki, Pawel, 318

Sturt, Charles, 5, 9, 58, 74, 96-97
sugar cane, 84
Super Rugby, 314
Surf Live Saving Clubs, 278-280
Sutherland, Dame Joan, 330
Sutton, Dr Harvey, 277
Swans, 301
swimming baths and pools, 219-220
Sydney, 51-57
Sydney Basement, 331
Sydney Blue Sox, 302
Sydney Corporation Act, 53-54
Sydney Cove, 100
Sydney FC, 316
Sydney GPO, 152
Sydney Harbour Bridge, 56, 159
Sydney Harbour Tunnel, 162
Sydney Hospital, 184, 195
Sydney Kings, 302-303
Sydney Mechanics Institute, 149
Sydney Metro, 161
Sydney Morning Herald, 53
Sydney Olympics, 299-300
Sydney Opera House, 56, 153, 204, 336
Sydney Philharmonic Orchestra, 328
Sydney Police, 233-234
Sydney Sixers, 304
Sydney Stadium, 203
Sydney Swans, 301
Sydney Swifts, 307
Sydney Symphony Orchestra, 330
Sydney Theatre Company, 202
Sydney Thunder, 304
Sydney Uni Flames, 303
TAFEs, 149

Tamworth Country Music Festival, 203, 222, 331-332
Tank Stream, 172-173
Taronga Western Plains Zoo, 79
Taronga Zoo, 56
Taylor, Mark, 99
technology, Indigenous, 11-13
Tedbury, 19
Teece, Richard, 257
telegraph system, 171
telephone network, 171
television, 209
Tench, Watkin, 17, 106
tennis, 319-320
Tennis NSW, 319
terra nullius, 16-17, 18-19
Terry, Samuel, 30
thalidomide, 191
theatre, 199-202
Theatre Royal, 200
Therry, John, 286, 287
Thompson, Andrew, 176
Thomson, Edward, 260
Thorne, Graeme, 249-250
Thredbo, 318-319
Three Sisters, 70
Throsby, Charles, 71, 101
Tichbourne fraud, 97
Tidswell, Frank, 227
Timeless Land, The, 327
Tom Thumb, 100
totems, Indigenous, 6-7
traffic lights, 155
trams, 154, 165
Tranby, 280-281
transport, 151-174
Trumper, Victor, 308
tuberculosis (TB), 189-190

Tucker, James, 91
Tulip Festival, 73, 223
tunnels, 160-162
Turner, Jane, 93
Twain, Mark, 97
Twenty20 Big Bash, 304
Underwood, James, 175-176
universities, 145-148, 293
University of New England, 62
University of Sydney, 146
Up the Country, 327
utilities, 169-174
Utzon, Jørn, 336
Vere Evatt, Herbert, 89
Vernon, Walter, 64, 66, 335
Victa lawnmower, 181
Victoria (colony), 123
video arcades, 222
Vietnamese migrants, 47
Villawood, 46
Vinegar Hill battle, 237
visual art, 321-324
Volunteer Bushfire organisations,
    281-283
von Guerard, Eugene, 322
Wagga Wagga, 96-99
Wake in Fright, 77
Walker, Dr Sir Alan, 274, 294
Wallis, James, 91
Wanda Beach murders, 252-253
Waratah League, 303
Waratahs, 314
Ward, Frederick, 63, 240
Warlow, Anthony, 103
Warragamba Dam, 174
Warrumbungle National Park, 80
Water Police, 239
water supply, 172-174

water transport, 166-168
Wathaurong people, 14
Watling, Thomas, 27, 323
Watson, Edna, 52
Webster, John, 216
Weir, Peter, 208-209
Wellington Caves, 80
Wentworth, D'Arcy, 36-37, 184,
    237
Wentworth, William, 4, 70, 123,
    145-146
West Connex, 162
Western Sydney Wanderers, 316
whaling, 175-176
wheat production, 112
White Australia policy, 45, 46, 55
White, John, 183
Whitlam Government, 46
Whitton, John, 163
Widjabul people, 83
Wilkins, William, 137
Williamson, J. C., 201
Wilson, William and Jane, 83
Windeyer, Lady Mary, 265
Windradyne, 30
Wiradjuri people, 19-20, 57-58, 78,
    93, 96
Wirrayaraay people, 20
Wodi Wodi people, 99-100, 101
Wollongong, 99-103
Wollongong Hawks, 302
Wolseley, Frederick, 116
Wombeyan Caves, 70
women in politics, 124-125
Women's Big Bash, 304
women's suffrage, 124-125
Wonnarua nation, 86
Worimi people, 90

Woy Woy Tunnel, 161
Wran, Neville, 157
Wright, Judith, 63
Wupa@Wanaruah, 223
Wyndham, Harold, 144
Wynyard Walk, 160-161
Yorta Yorta people, 59
Yuin people, 6, 8, 13
Yuwaalaraay people, 80
zig-zag railway, 68-69, 163

Notes

Notes

OTHER BOOKS AVAILABLE FROM WOODSLANE PRESS

Arthur Phillip
Australia's First Governor
$29.99   9781921683480

Governor Macquarie
His life, times and revolutionary vision for Australia
$29.99   9781921606915

Bligh in Australia
A New Appraisal of William Bligh and the Rum Rebellion
$29.99   9781921683503

Pandemic
The Spanish Flu in Australia 1918-20
$34.99   9781925868449

Outback
The Discovery of Australia's Interior
$24.99   9781921203923

The Other Side of the Mountain
How a tycoon, a pastoralist and a convict helped shape the exploration of colonial Australia
$29.99   9781925868210

To order please call 02 8445 2300 or go to
www.woodslane.com.au